Sailing in Grandfather's Wake

Reed's Maritime Library

Sailing in Grandfather's Wake

Captain Ian Tew

SHERIDAN HOUSE

This edition published 2001 by
Sheridan House Inc.
145 Palisade Street
Dobbs Ferry, New York 10522
www.sheridanhouse.com

First published in Great Britain 2001
by Thomas Reed Publications

Edited by Alex Milne
Series Consultant Tony Brunton-Reed
Design & Layout by C E Marketing
Produced by Omega Profiles Ltd.
Printed and bound in Great Britain

ISBN 1-57409-141-7

ACKNOWLEDGMENTS

I AM GREATLY INDEBTED to my aunt, Mrs Marguerite Roberts, mate of *Caplin*, for her enormous contribution to this book and, indeed, my own circumnavigation. Hers are the written accounts of the first part of *Caplin*'s voyage, from Bridgwater to Bermuda. It is thanks to her, too, that my grandfather's account of the Pacific leg of the voyage has survived. The photographs of *Caplin* are from her collection but, no less importantly, her own formidable memory supplied many details to fill in the gaps in the written records. Without her help, both as *Caplin*'s mate and as recorder of so much of *Caplin*'s voyage, this book could not have been written.

Thanks are also due to *Independent Freedom*'s mate, for sticking with the voyage through thick and thin and for fixing so many problems which were well beyond my technical capabilities.

I also wish to express my thanks to my brother and sister-in-law, Edward and Philippa Tew. Edward, as my 'mission control', has sorted out many a problem for me in the course of my voyage. Without his backup, the whole venture might well have come to grief on more than one occasion. Philippa has been most kindly and efficiently running my business in my absence and I couldn't have sailed off without her support.

Finally, I am grateful to my grandfather, Commander R. D. Graham, the central figure and driving force behind both voyages.

THE BOATS

CAPLIN

CAPLIN IS AN Eleven-ton gaff yawl, thirty feet long, built by Anderson in 1938. The working sails consist of a mainsail with roller reefing, a roller jib on a traveller so the sail can be hauled out to the end of the bowsprit, a staysail which can be reefed and a Bermudan mizzen. In fine weather a topsail can be set on top of the mainsail, and large and small spinnakers were carried for down-wind sailing. Her wardrobe also included two smaller jibs, another staysail and a trysail.

From the cockpit, the small well at the stern in which the helmsman sits to steer with the tiller, steps lead below to a sort of lobby which contains the galley consisting of two primus stoves, allowed to swing so it is possible to cook at sea. Forward of this lobby is the main cabin, a small room eight feet by eight feet with standing headroom made possible by the main deck being raised. In the middle is a fixed table, and on each side a settee. Forward of the main cabin is the 'Ladies cabin', rather like a rabbit hutch.

A small petrol engine was fitted, mainly for getting in and out of port, and only a small amount of fuel was carried, just sufficient to give a range of about 60 miles. A wooden dinghy was carried on deck at sea, propulsion being by oars and manpower. A main anchor and chain cable were used for anchoring, together with a kedge and line in bad weather. A third small anchor was also carried.

There was a meat safe on deck for fresh food, lockers under the settees and elsewhere for tins and other nonperishables, and 100 gallons of drinking water were carried.

The navigational instruments consisted of a compass, sextant and two watches. The radio which was on board to obtain time signals did not work at all after crossing the

Atlantic. It required real skill as a navigator to safely navigate across the trackless oceans, especially in a small sailing yacht with a low height of eye and a most unstable platform. The advent of modern electronic instruments, especially GPS, has relegated the sextant to the history books (until someone turns off the satellites!) A hand–held lead line was used for soundings.

The skipper was my grandfather, Commander R. D. Graham, and the mate was his daughter Marguerite, then in her twenties.

INDEPENDENT FREEDOM

INDEPENDENT FREEDOM IS A thirteen-ton Bermudan schooner, thirty-nine feet long, built by Freedom Yachts in 1991. The working sails consist of a fully battened mainsail and a foresail, both boomed and fitted with three reefs each, all controlled from the cockpit. Her wardrobe includes a trysail, reaching staysail and a light-weather spinnaker. The masts are unstayed and made from carbon fibre. The keel is a Collins wing keel.

The cockpit is big, and steering is by a large stainless-steel wheel. Steps on the starboard side lead down into the wide pilot house, where the navigation table and instruments are situated on the starboard side. On the port side is the folding table underneath which is the 49-horse-power diesel engine. A step down leads to the galley on the port side with a gas cooker, grill and oven, and on the starboard side are the heads and shower. Forward is a double-berth cabin. Aft on the starboard side, underneath the cockpit, is a double berth and on the opposite side is the workshop.

The fuel tank takes 120 gallons, giving a range of about 900 miles at the most economical speed in fine weather. There are two rubber dinghies, each with small outboard motors. A main anchor and chain are used for anchoring, and a new high-speed electric windlass for lifting them. There is also a kedge anchor with a chain and warp on board. A fridge keeps soft drinks cold along with fresh food. There is ample locker space under the bunks and settees, and room for 137 gallons of water.

The navigational instruments include two GPS, an echo sounder, radar, a fixed steering compass, weather fax, VHF, SSB radio, an electric log and speedo, anemometer and wind direction recorder, auto helm and wind-vane steering. A sextant together with the current Nautical Almanac are on board as backup. She sails like a witch!

The skipper is the author, Captain Ian Tew, and the mate a sailing friend, Michel.

The Quest

Independent Freedom, Pacific Ocean

001°N 85°W, Monday 6 April 1998.

I T WAS HOT, sultry and sticky, and everything was damp. The sea was glassy calm and the only wind was that made by *Independent Freedom* driven forward by the engine at a fuel-conserving 4 knots. Half our water had been lost through a broken pipe. *Independent Freedom* rose and fell, as though in a lift, in the long moderate southerly swell, oily under the blazing sun.

A visit to *Caplin's* mate

This was all a far cry from the cold, damp, foggy November morning when I had driven through the winding Shropshire country lanes to have lunch with my Aunt Marguerite. No one was with me because I wanted her to myself. I was not sure of the reception I was going to get when we discussed the purpose of my visit.

Visibility was down to less than fifty yards but, after a couple of wrong turnings, I finally arrived in good time. Her friendly greeting and chatter while she completed preparations for the meal allayed some of my fears, but how much would she remember? It was a long time ago, and she was now in her 83rd year. The hustle and bustle in the kitchen belied her years despite a damaged leg.

"I was checking on intruders in the orchard one night" she told me "and fell over a ladder", as though this was a normal activity for someone of her advanced years! She brought me up to date on the family news as she served up lunch.

It was difficult to believe – this lady had sailed across not only the Atlantic but the Pacific, too, some 58 years ago, with her father. Over coffee in the sitting room she told me about the Atlantic side, not so much the sailing but more about the parties in Bermuda and Trinidad!

"The Bermuda race had just finished and we were invited to the party" she explained. "Don't forget, your grandfather was quite a famous man; his single-handed Atlantic crossing attracted much attention. What is more, the Cruising Club of America had awarded him their Blue Water Medal." She showed me the bronze medallion on the mantelpiece.

"The Bermuda Yacht Club did not allow women into the bar, but as a special honour I was allowed in. It was such fun with all those men!" She laughed with a far-away look in her eyes, remembering events that took place before the Second World War.

"After we left Bermuda" she continued "we hit a storm and I can still hear the waves hissing at me when I looked out of the cabin. They were huge – great mountains of water which I was sure would overwhelm us, but *Caplin* rode them safely. In Trinidad we had a lovely time; cousin Mervyn was in the oil business, and stationed there. We used to reciprocate the hospitality by having tea parties on board."

Of the Pacific, which was my main interest, she was rather vague and my heart sank. Perhaps my journey had been in vain – and it was a long way from Miami in the States. She remembered some of the places – Lionel the sea-sick crew and giving tea to the Queen of Tonga's Consort onboard *Caplin*.

They arrived at one island where the resident Commissioner had the shakes. "Drink, you know" she said, looking at me. "He told us the War had started. He did not know what to do with us, so told us to go to New Zealand. For, of course, Father was a retired naval officer. In New Zealand we had to sell *Caplin* and Dad went home in a merchant ship. It was difficult for me to get a passage; I stayed there for three years but eventually got home to help Mummy on the farm. We were six women on a troopship all the way from New Zealand – what fun we had!"

"Any logs?" I asked.

"No, they were lost in a fire, but rummaging around I found this. I had forgotten he wrote it up and I typed it.

Perhaps you would like to read it."

She handed me a large brown envelope with fifty-odd pages of typed manuscript covering their Pacific sailing, some press cuttings and a photograph of *Caplin*. In addition there was her own diary of the beginning of the voyage, from Bridgwater to Bermuda.

I had struck gold! This was why *Independent Freedom* was now on her way to the Galapagos Islands. I was following in my grandfather's footsteps – or rather sailing in his wake.

.... Route of Independent Freedom

_____ Route of Caplin

SHAKE-DOWN CRUISE

CAPLIN: BRIDGWATER TO BANTRY BAY

*C*aplin WAS NOT WITHOUT PROBLEMS during her shake-down cruise. She had been launched in Bridgwater on Monday 17 January 1938. By Friday 28 February the Mate, grandfather's younger daughter and my Aunt Marguerite, had joined *Caplin* in Penarth, just across the Bristol Channel from Bridgwater Bay, to sail back to Bridgwater and final fitting out for their round-the-world cruise. The following account is from my aunt's diary.

ENGINE, BILGES AND PROP SHAFT

Penarth, Thursday 3 February 1938. Reporters from Daily Mirror and Western Mail, the latter being the dumbest creatures ever seen; they knew nothing and asked if we were doing our trip for pleasure or going to carry cargo! Launched dinghy. Very steady and easy to pull and scull – she looks funny painted white in this country.

Monday 7 February. Up at 06.00, ready for sea by 09.00. Anderson (the builder) and his son Johnnie joined the ship. Moved from dock into basin but had to wait till 10.00 before getting out. People on quay wished us luck; also passing ships outside. Rather foggy outside; we thought of waiting till next day but decided to go on. Picked up the buoys at the bar but stuck – had to wait for tide; had top sail and mizzen. Very light wind so we used the engine: not too satisfactory, stopped for no apparent reason but we cleaned the plugs and got her going again. Thought we had a lot of water in the bilge from a slight leak below. Pump wouldn't work; seemed to be sucking but no water came up. Skipper took it to pieces three times last night but still it wouldn't work. Johnnie got to work on it this morning, took up all the floorboards, awful business, unscrewing table and getting water tank out to look at sump. Reason no water coming out, no water in bilge, pump working perfectly! Anchored off Burnham pier.

Burnham, Tuesday 8 February. Went ashore after breakfast, telephoned mum and arranged to meet at Bridgwater docks about 13.00. No wind so we used the engine but it gave trouble; got within a mile of Dunball and it packed up altogether. Johnnie was in the dinghy keeping Caplin in middle of river – tide turned sooner than expected (almanac nearly two hours out). Light wind not enough to sail against tide so we headed down river and got into Combwich Creek. Tied up by a plank slanting up river bed to road. Tide falling rapidly, terrific list to starboard, beetroot in cup of vinegar fell on floor, bloody-looking stains all over the panelling and floor and cabin top! Had lunch, Johnnie and I on floor, legs propped against starboard bunks.

Went ashore to telephone home and get someone to come in to take the propeller shaft to Bridgwater Motor Co. John and Robin, my brother and sister-in-law, came in about three-quarters of an hour; it was a terrific business getting up and down the landing stage; angle of about 45 degrees, bottom half slippery with thick slimy black mud. With a rope made fast ashore we tried to haul ourselves up but our hands would keep slipping; after several futile attempts I wrapped swabs around rope – better but still very tricky. Jolly funny for onlookers, humans sprawling about plank, at any moment about to slip off into the mud below.

Smith at Motor Co. said the silt in the river was liable to make the shaft tight. Dad and I were covered from head to foot in mud. I had on slacks and had to run the gauntlet of horrified stares; Bridgwater not used to yachting people in trouble! Smith and another man, Bill, took us back to the yacht but found the plank for getting on board a bit disconcerting. They wouldn't believe me when I said the rope was too muddy to get a grip; they soon changed their minds when they started slithering down: so like men to think they know best and that a mere girl couldn't be right. They got the engine fixed and we all went ashore for supper at the local pub, the Anchor Inn. They had no food so we bought bacon and eggs which they cooked for us. I had a pint of beer and felt distinctly better. We wanted to go down to Burnham on the next tide but skipper didn't like it much in the dark; tricky windy river, no lights. The landlord got hold of a pilot, six foot three and looked a real villain, Cornish – he offered to take us down and arranged to be on board at 23.00. We all went back to the yacht. Anderson and I turned in at 21.00. I slept like a log; didn't hear the engine either start or stop nor the cable when the anchor was let go, though it was just forward of me. Was it the sea air or the beer?!

Cushions, lino and a date in Bermuda

Wednesday 9 February 1938. Woke up to find we had anchored two miles off Burnham up river. Horrid swell getting worse. By lunchtime I beginning to feel uncomfortable. After lunch skipper took Anderson and Johnnie ashore to catch the 13.51 train home. Read in my bunk for an hour or two. Skipper was busy screwing down floorboards which had been irritating us with their squeaking, then went ashore again at 16.00 to fetch mum who was coming by car. I prepared tea. Horrid wind and terrific tide running; Skipper had difficulty getting back to the yacht. He had one bosh shot and took half an hour altogether. Mum was glad to get on board in the warm.

Saturday 12 February. Went to Biddicks (furnishing people) in the morning and ordered stuff for the cabin floor, galley, cushions etc. Took their man down to the docks in the car to measure up everything; it was the first time he had furnished a yacht.

Friday 18 February. Got the linoleum put down on the cabin floor, forecabin and engine room – it looks very nice; I'm also working very hard to get covers for seats done. Miles of machining.

Sunday 6 March. Kenneth Pattison, whom Skipper and I met during Summer Ocean Racing, came down for the weekend to look at the yacht. We made a date to meet him in Bermuda in July. He is sailing in Bermuda Race.

Sunday 20 March. Going down river early; breakfast 07.00. Had to wait for two ships to go out before us; we used the engine to get out of the docks then set jib and foresail; after Dunball we stopped the engine and hoisted the mainsail and mizzen in a fresh breeze. *Caplin* sailing very well, relief to have engine off.

THE VOYAGE BEGINS

Bridgwater, Wednesday 20 April 1938. The crowd began to collect about 09.30 and all our friends in the neighbourhood came to wish us 'bon voyage'. The Mayor of Bridgwater, Mr Chard, came and made a speech on behalf of the town, and we had our photographs taken for the Press with him. Skipper replied briefly and I merely grinned! Several thousand people surrounded the docks, standing three or four deep. We left about 10.30 and there were people all the way down the river as far as Combwich. The Peacocks (my sister-in-law's family) were at Dunball. At Combwich someone played the Admiral's Salute; Mr Cornish the pilot, I think. We had one anxious moment near Dunball; the engine started to peter out, dirty plug I think, but she cleared herself. We took a pilot down the river, Mr Bell. First time Skipper has ever taken a Trinity House pilot but it was low tide and we were desperately anxious not to stick going down; it would have been such a dreadful anti-climax after our farewells. We had a pleasant sail over to Penarth, put the patent log out and did seven knots for a short period.

Saturday 23 April. Dick has joined and is sailing with us as far as Southern Ireland. (Dick Washbourne was a New Zealander, making his career in the Royal Navy; he was a keen sailor and had turned up with an introduction to my father. We got on well and he would love to have joined us for the whole trip but of course he couldn't get the leave. He went on to see active service during the War, notably on HMS *Achilles* in the Battle of the River Plate, and ended his career a Vice-Admiral.) Left Penarth docks 11.35. A little way out a pilot ship circled us to wish us luck and blew her siren. No wind so we used our engine, but set sail about 13.00. A fishing ship, *Oyama*, rapidly overhauled us and came very close – she hailed us and said "Best wishes from Mr Howard Neil". Jolly nice of him. Got to Ilfracombe about 19.00.

Sunday 24 April. Took helm at 06.30. Breakfast about 08.00. Lundy Island quickly left behind and soon no land was left in sight: a new experience for me but the sea is not as large as I thought it would be. Topsail and balloon staysail, light fair wind, *Caplin* sailing beautifully. I believe she is going to enjoy the adventure as much as I am. Skipper climbed up the shrouds like a two-year-old to set the topsail, jolly good as I said when he came down – pretty good for a grandfather.

South coast of Ireland

Tuesday 26 April 1938. Perfect sunny day and fair wind. We slipped away quietly under sail and forgot we had an engine. Dick sailed along the coast and sighted the Fastnet. Two trawlers passed us and waved. Dick and Skipper went below for sleep and I took the afternoon watch – decided to anchor at a creek, Castletown near Beerehaven, instead of being late and going on to Bantry. Dropped anchor about 19.00. Most alarming thing happened… Skipper and Dick got into dinghy to go ashore; the water is very clear and they had a look at the propeller. With horror we discovered that the shaft is practically out, hanging by a thread. I dashed below to see if water is pouring into the ship but the little bit of shaft left in the stern tube keeps it out. We put running bowlines round the blade and hauled taut. The men go ashore; not too sure I feel safe, but we have a cork that fits the hole if necessary! At 03.00 we turn out, Dick tows the ship ashore from the dinghy and we lie alongside a jetty. We ship the port leg to let her take the ground.

Wednesday 27 April. Early breakfast then to work to get our new folding propeller in. Skipper tried to connect up inside, Dick stood in the water to push the shaft through.

Fixed it up after a terrific struggle, had to file the key down to
fit the new shaft. After lunch we went on to Bantry with the
wind right ahead. Skipper went below and I tacked by myself.
We got to Bantry in the evening and Paddy O'Keefe, whom
Skipper had met four years ago on *Emanuel*, rowed out and
came on board; awfully nice man. He asked us up to supper
but like a true gentleman didn't press us when he saw we were
not too keen; also he did not stay too long which to my mind
is high praise. The Customs also came on board and after
bacon and eggs we turned in.

'A RIOT FROM START TO FINISH'

Thursday 28 April. Paddy O'Keefe hailed us and lent us a
large-scale chart of the district. He then had to go off to Cork.
We set sail for Glengarriff, at the head of Bantry Bay; quite a
decent breeze with a clear sky and lovely and sunny. We got
to Glengarriff about midday and went ashore to lunch at
Roches Hotel. It is a famous place; the landlady is Mrs
O'Flynn and she is a real character. I think she must know
more people in the Navy than anyone else in the world. She
remembered Skipper from when he was here four years ago
in *Emanuel* and welcomed us with open arms, made us have a
drink with her and insisted on us dining with her in the
evening. Dinner at the hotel was a riot from start to finish; our
hostess, 'Auntie May', gave us a drink and we sat in the bar
talking. Auntie held the floor! Three young men came in,
Naval subs – Dick knew them . . . we sat at the same table for
dinner. I can't get used to being the only girl when we go
about! I had a Guinness for dinner. I liked it but prefer lager.
After dinner we had coffee and liqueurs. I had a Benedictine.
I seem to have been imbibing all day – I hope someone will
see straight enough to get back to the yacht. Auntie May put
the gramophone on and insisted on us dancing; I danced with
Maxwell, and Auntie May's sons and daughters also danced
with us. Skipper says "Above all we won't tire ourselves out
with too much self-control".

INDEPENDENT FREEDOM

NEW YORK TO CHESAPEAKE

A few years ago I had inspected my dream boat at the Southampton Boat Show, but her price was miles beyond my means. However, it's amazing how life's fortunes change and in September 1996 I saw her sister ship in Lymington and thought 'she's for me'.

My Freedom 30, *Freedom Freyja*, was sold in August 1997 and I'd been looking, together with a sailing friend, Michel, who was to become my ship's mate, for a suitable Freedom 35, but none fitted the bill. The only Freedom 39 Pilot House Schooner, the boat I really wanted, was in the States, so I bought her and flew to Boston for the survey at Quincy, Massachusetts. A few things were wrong, but there was no time to fiddle around if I was to get south before winter set in, so I flew home on September 23 to sell the house and car.

Friday 10 October 1997. The owner had agreed to deliver her to Annapolis in Chesapeake Bay, but plans went awry, as is usual when one is in a hurry, and I agreed to take over *Independent Freedom* at Sandy Hook, 20 or so miles south of New York. So, on October 10, Michel and I flew to Baltimore and drove the 200 miles to Sandy Hook, where we took over the boat and her previous owner took over the car.

I was keen to get south as soon as possible and enter the intracoastal waterway. My idea of fun does not extend to winter in the North Atlantic. My grandfather, Commander R. D. Graham, had a bad time with a hurricane in his yacht *Emanuel* (which he owned prior to *Caplin*) on his way from Canada to Bermuda in 1934 and again in *Caplin*. My elder brother Donald, sailing with Lord Riverdale some 30 years later, was caught by an out-of-season hurricane in March, sailing from Charleston to Bermuda. I just felt that the third member of the family cruising this coast had better take the inland waters! The Atlantic, though, was prepared to bide its time.

Unfortunately the boat's old cruising licence had expired and I had been summoned to the United States Customs

Headquarters in Newark, because technically the regulations had been violated. We therefore had to sail back north to New York.

It was a stirring and moving sight to sail in bright sunshine, goose-winged, with the Statue of Liberty to port and the magnificent Manhattan skyline to starboard. To do so in my own yacht exceeded my wildest dreams, and the reality is much more impressive than photographs.

The night was spent in the expensive security-conscious Newport Yacht Club marina opposite the sparkling lights of Manhattan. The lady Customs Inspector at Newark was very helpful and issued a new cruising permit with the stern edict

"Be sure to phone in at each new port".

Formalities completed, *Independent Freedom* headed back to Sandy Hook, motor-sailing into a headwind. Just before the huge and imposing Verrazano Narrows Bridge, the foresail tore from luff to leech. My heart sank, but the tear was below the first reef so we tucked it in and carried on. At the marina we bunkered; *Independent Freedom* had more than eight times the fuel capacity of my old yacht. We spent the night comfortably at anchor, saving the $70 marina fee.

Wednesday 15 October. We motored out of the bay against the wind in pouring rain, hoisted the sails at the entrance, bore away around Sandy Hook and reached out through the Channel at a good speed. There was much more wind than forecast, so we reefed the mainsail, which eased the work of the autohelm.

We had a swift run down, with the New Jersey coast to starboard, while to port was Europe thousands of miles away. The yacht was goose-winged under a grey and dismal sky with continuous drizzle. However, it was so exciting to be sailing this fine yacht that the weather did not matter; between 09.00 and 15.00 she averaged over 7 knots.

We passed Atlantic City with its bright red lights on the buildings, running fast in the dark and drizzle, when just past midnight – chaos. The log notes '...the kicking strap on the foresail gave way, Chinese gybe, power off instruments, down sail, eye from mast pulled out, maybe batten broken'. Always happens at night!

The wind continued to increase, so we pulled the second reef in the mainsail. At 04.30 we rounded up hard onto the wind and beat into Delaware Bay against a vicious, short steep sea – wind against tide – occasionally being passed by tugs towing huge barges. A particularly heavy pound into a large wave broke the anchor pin which had secured the anchor in the bow roller, and the anchor was thrown on deck. The unstayed carbon fibre masts were bending – an alarming sight to the uninitiated. With occasional bouts of force 7, it was a long hard slog up to the Delaware Chesapeake canal, which we entered under power at 13.30. The sun had come out, and to see the fall-coloured trees lining the banks was very refreshing after the vast expanse of the river.

The night was spent at the wharf marina in Chesapeake City (the nearest grocery store was 7 miles away). The 25,000-ton container ships that slid past made less wash than the motor boats. We spent a lazy Friday morning watching the traffic, phoning the UK for a new sail and finding a repair yard in Chesapeake Bay.

We left in sunshine just after noon and motored out of the canal into the Elk River. We paid for our late departure with a nerve-racking hour in the dark, dodging the crab pot floats which are barely visible in daylight, let alone by torch light! Rock Hall seemed utterly deserted in the rain but the restaurant was full.

Friday 17 October. It rained all day, but only lightly. We had a good sail running down the bay, passing under the Chesapeake Bay Bridge, which is 4 miles long with a huge curve at the western end and the traffic humming above – utilitarian rather than beautiful. At 13.40 we luffed up hard onto the wind round No. 1 buoy and stormed up the eastern river overtaking boats. *Independent Freedom* was sailing like a witch.

Sunday 19 October. We left historic St Michael's with its museum-piece lighthouse in the harbour. The rain was pouring down, with a fresh breeze and gales forecast for southern Chesapeake Bay. The reefed foresail was hoisted and we averaged 5.5 knots, including an hour and a half on the wind, to Cambridge. We entered the harbour that evening ready for repairs on Monday morning. It was still raining, and I swear that American rain drops are larger and wetter than English.

The rain stopped during the night and it became cold. We moored at the yard alongside a motor boat painted in psychedelic colours, moving later to a jetty which was rather open to the harbour entrance. The Yacht Maintenance Company had obviously been around a long time, but the work was completed quite quickly. I had a bimini (not unlike the awning grandfather had made for *Caplin* in Balboa) made by the sailmaker who repaired the foresail, and we left on Thursday, all bills paid. Cambridge Maryland was not the liveliest place I've visited!

Solomon Island was reached that evening after a very cold afternoon at sea under power; we were in a hurry. The approach was made into the setting sun through a field of crab pots marked by black flags, not the most visible of markers! The coloured gentleman who took our money for the berth greeted us "Hey man does it always rain in England and everyone wears umbrellas?"

An F16 flew low over us the next morning as we plugged into a dead head wind and sea. A yacht we had seen with two poodles and dainty lampshades in the saloon put back into port. There were fish traps at the entrance to Great Wicomico River, and the anchorage in Mills Creek was empty when we arrived. Unfortunately the engine had not charged the batteries, so the peace and quiet of the anchorage was shattered by the generator.

We needed to get a move on; winter was almost upon us. We were up early on Saturday for our last day in Chesapeake Bay to more rain. However, once out of the river it was a reach down the bay in smooth waters. By noon the sun was coming out and the wind dropped, so the afternoon was spent motoring in a calm to Norfolk. What an eye opener it was passing the huge naval base – six aircraft carriers, including a couple of big ones and 25 other warships, all in commission, plus assorted tugs, barges and launches. I looked at my blue ensign, humbled in front of this awesome display of naked power, which so emphasized Britain's diminished state. And this was only one base!

The marina did not answer our VHF calls, so we moored

at the first convenient berth. They were quite happy to take my money! We were at the beginning of the Intracoastal Waterway with some 1,100 statute miles to make good, and only three weeks maximum to do it.

INTRACOASTAL WATERWAY

We had very carefully measured the height from the top of the mast to the water and found it to be 57 feet, which was sufficiently low for the waterway where the lowest fixed bridge has a height of 65 feet above high water. There were a lot of bridges to go under and I didn't want to hit anything. I spent the evening marking up the charts, which were not easy to read, with the courses to be steered and the times of the bridge openings for those that opened. I wanted to be well prepared for I did not want to go aground. With a wing keel it might be exceedingly difficult to get off again; the traditional methods like heeling the boat would not work. I felt that prevention was better than cure!

Sunday October 26 1997 (day 1). The first day on the waterway. We slipped our moorings and departed in the rain, motoring fast to catch up with a yacht which had passed southbound and had a mast at least as tall as ours. There was a massive naval dockyard to starboard and an officer on one of the ships alongside gave us a discreet wave while waiting for morning colours. The first bridge was open and the next bridge opened at the request of the yacht ahead, with us following close astern. Somehow I felt inadequate, thinking 'why should a bridge open for an insignificant British yacht', so I was extremely glad to be following an American one.

In the first hour, four bridges opened for us, the last one stopping the traffic on a major highway. We passed the marker for the Great Dismal Swamp route, noticing that it was closed due to lack of water, and entered the only lock on the waterway. It was 600 feet long and the fall was only about 2 feet. We passed under the first fixed bridge, which was 65 feet high so it cleared the top of the mast nicely, into the Albemarle and Chesapeake Canal. The untamed tree-lined banks of the wilderness were a change from the industrial backwater of Norfolk.

We put the clocks back one hour and passed from Virginia into North Carolina and the old slave states. It had rained solidly since we started and everything was wet and dismal. I soon found that it was important to keep in the middle of the channel or risk running aground. I was amazed at the speed the motor boats went, with appalling damage to the banks.

We entered the North Carolina Cut, and shortly afterwards went alongside the Coinjock marina where we were not made welcome, although they were quite happy to take my money, even if I was an Englishman! Things were not helped when we had a spill bunkering; luckily this went unnoticed, as we used detergent and water together with the continuing torrential rain to wash it off into the brown muddy water.

My first impressions of the waterway were that it was untended and run down; the banks were not piled and the water was grey or brown, but maybe this was a false impression, because of the cold unfavourable conditions, the continuos rain and overcast sky. We covered 50 statute miles in just under 8 hours, negotiating one lock and passing under 14 bridges, 11 of which opened; a satisfactory first day even though it had been wet.

Although warmer, it was overcast and dismal when we set off early the next morning. Once we were out of the cut, the North River proved shallow, but the banks were marshy and the view better. The wind was stronger as the land fell away and we entered the Albemarle Sound, a stretch of open water which proved quite rough. In Little Alligator River, Michel called the East Lake Swing Bridge which opened for us. This was the first time we had done it ourselves! It was a huge long bridge, the land barely visible in the drizzle.

In the narrows it looked like a flooded swamp and there were many colours on the trees – red, yellow, green, mauve and brown. Realizing we could just make the fixed opening time of the Fairfield Bridge, I increased to maximum power. We went through with another yacht which powered ahead when I slowed down. We passed under the fixed Wilkinson Bridge in the dark and anchored in Pungo River, laying out plenty of cable because there was a poor forecast. For a short distance the buoyage had changed from the (to our way of thinking) 'reversed' American system and was now the 'right' way round – red to port and green to starboard.

A yacht had run aground just past the bridge, which was making it difficult for a tug and barge bound south. It had been a long 12-hour day and the distance made good was 78 miles.

Tuesday 28 October (day 3). It was fun in the daylight to see where we had arrived in the dark, a small river with marshy banks. What a difference a bit of sun makes, but it was cold when Michel weighed anchor. Just after 08.00 we were sailing with the engine turned off and ran goose-winged down the Pungo River at 6 knots. While making for Pamlico River, reaching at over 8 knots in smooth water, it was fun until the shallow-water alarm went off and there was less than a foot under the keel. I had not been concentrating properly and had sailed out of the channel. The fact that other yachts did the same was no compensation!

The wind died soon after 10.00 and we motor-sailed into Goose Creek. The fishing boats had a flying bridge about 8 feet above the main deck making them look very odd, but no doubt it was efficient for spotting their catch. We met a tug and barge under a new fixed bridge in the Hobucken Canal, and had to pull in the sheets to let them pass. It was then out into Bay River and on to Neusk River. Even though sunny it was cold.

Whittaker Marina did not answer our VHF calls, so we entered the private channel without permission and berthed in very pleasant wooded surroundings. The marina had excellent facilities and I particularly liked driving the courtesy car – an ancient Buick. The next day was calm and sunny, and an electrician fixed the steaming light and rearranged the electrics so that there was a dedicated engine battery.

In the morning I phoned my broker at Admiral to check with Lloyds that the yacht was insured to proceed south of Cape Hatteras before November 1st, the official end of the hurricane season. She was.

It was sunny and calm when we crossed Neusk River and entered Adams Creek, where the banks were lined with rushes and evergreens. Some trawlers passed; they too made much less wash than the motor boats. Adams Canal had some houses on the bank and the country became more open.

The docks at Beaufort were empty as we hugged the wharves against a strong adverse tide; the Atlantic Ocean was just the other side of a narrow strip of land. The area was more built up and we passed an opening to the sea. In the afternoon we motored through a firing range but no flags were flying. A long way ahead we saw boats waiting for Onslow Swing Bridge to open, so we increased to maximum power and got through with them. There was no answer from Swan Point Marina, so we pulled into Hammoth Pool, where we saw boats anchored; there was nothing showing on the echo sounder as we scraped over the bar. There were egrets on the marshes – the first bird life we had seen. During the night we could hear the breaking Atlantic swell crashing on the shore.

It was raining when we followed a black ketch out of the pool, the rain clearing the decks of the black Carolina mud. Hard motoring enabled us to make the 09.00 opening of Surf City Swing Bridge. A refreshing smell of sand and sea greeted us as we passed the New River Inlet, with sails set. Some big houses stood on the starboard bank while the seaward bank was marsh. We didn't think we would make the Wrightsville Bridge opening, but the bridge keeper saw us coming and kept it open.

In the afternoon, we reached Fear River; the land around was very flat and the buoyage different from the chart. A 30,000-ton ship with a spoon bow passed, making very little wash. I had intended stopping, but the marina was full and so we left the river and went back into the waterway, ending a long day by anchoring in the tributary to Lockwood Folly River in the dark. While we were eating our kedgeree supper, the lights faded, but after Michel started the generator with jump leads, the batteries charged up again; apparently, something was wrong with the alternator.

Saturday 1 November (day 7). Started with 58-m.p.h. winds and thunderstorms just north of us over Wilmington. Due to the bridge-opening times, we started at 05.30, in the dark, and made way very slowly because the channel was so confusing. Lockwood Folly Inlet, which led out into the Atlantic, was difficult because of extra buoys, as was Shallotte Inlet, but it was then becoming light and clear ahead, although there were heavy black clouds astern.

At 08.40 we changed States, from North to South Carolina, and the scenery became much more interesting, with sand and gravel banks, and houses. We passed under lots of bridges including Nixon Crossroads Highway. Michel managed to fix the batteries. In Pine Island Cut, just after passing under the Hurrah Beach golf course cable car, where the banks were collapsing due to motor boat washes, the keel hit an underwater obstruction but there was no apparent damage. We passed under more bridges and then into the Waccamaw River which was the prettiest so far, with marshes, gravel and swamps, and trees in their fall colours. The Wacca Wache Marina had a berth for us after we bunkered, also a very useful courtesy car, so Michel was able to buy electrical bits for the batteries. I phoned the Customs, as I did from every stop where there was a phone.

It was raining when we manoeuvred stern first against the tide to clear the berth. We then motored down river through a cypress swamp. As the river widened it was difficult to tell the abandoned rice paddies from marsh. Once under Lafayette Bridge we were in the Winyah River which leads to the Atlantic, with Georgetown to starboard and a whiff of the paper mill. A Greek ship was being manoeuvered to her berth by tugs and a stiff breeze was blowing. We passed through a series of cuts, canals and rivers, and finally into Harbour River which was very shallow. A supply boat passed us cursing because *Independent Freedom* was in the middle of the channel but we had no alternative because the keel was already touching the bottom.

In the late afternoon we were amongst the marshes at Cape Roman Refuge and anchored amongst the rushes as the sun set. An optical illusion made it appear that a couple of boats anchored in nearby creeks were floating above the marshes. For the first time there was a great variety of birdlife – pelicans, sea gulls, egrets, cormorants, herons, hawks, terns and oyster catchers. We also saw a sea snake.

Monday 3 November (day 9). It was a lovely morning when we got underway and motored at slow speed for the 09.00 opening of Ben Sawyer Bridge. Lots of boats powered past and then had to wait! Once through, the race was on, out of the cutting with Fort Mountain to port, then across the main entrance channel to Charleston on a compass course. *Independent Freedom* overtook all the other sailing yachts, so became 'leader of the pack'! It was back into the waterway and we led the way through Wappoo Creek Basculle Bridge at the 10.30 opening into Stowo River, where we had to use the lead line because, even though the river was wide, the channel was narrow. We were still leading the fleet of yachts at the 11.40 opening of the John F. Limehouse Bridge, and into the tidal river at 13.00.

There was another a series of cuts and rivers, some very shallow, before we passed through the Ashepoo cut and up a river; an anchored Canadian yacht shouted that we were in the wrong place so we turned back and anchored in 18 feet. There was a beautiful sunset, but the peace was spoilt by a working dredger in the cut. We were past the half-way mark to Fort Lauderdale, having covered 515 miles at an average speed of 6.6 knots.

It was a beautiful morning when we left for another day of cuttings, narrows and canals, beautiful houses, much better scenery and lots of bridges. The South Carolina Yacht Club was a particularly imposing building standing in its own grounds. In the afternoon we crossed into the State of Georgia and across the Savannah River. Michel was particularly pleased with his radio work, getting the bridges to open!

In the evening a stupid mistake put *Independent Freedom* aground for an hour but, once afloat on the rising tide, we anchored at the entrance to Moon River.

The twists and turns and different entrances through the marshes and rivers made it more essential than ever to plan and mark the courses on the chart, or rather the book of charts. The tidal range was about 6 feet so the tides were, at times, quite strong.

Wednesday 5 November (day 11). A fine day. It was made more interesting when we found some lost marines in a speed boat with all their kit near Hell Gate. I showed them on the chart the island they wanted and pointed them in the direction they should take, but they still appeared lost! It was marshes and swamps all day, ending up a creek at the Two Way Fish

Camp Marina. The local people had such accents that it was difficult to understand what was said! They warned us that alligators infested the river, preventing a swim, but we did not see any.

It was glassy calm when we left on the ebb tide, making good speed down the river and into Buttermilk Sound, where it was necessary to navigate using the lead lines.

Mackay River was deep and widening when we shot the Lancer Island fixed bridge and out into St Simons Sound. It was wide and open to a calm Atlantic with the sun beginning to warm us. Once round the buoy in the sound, it was on the leads again into Jekyll Creek with marshes to starboard and trees to port. A fixed bridge had replaced the Jekyll Island Lift Bridge.

The wreck of a fishing boat ashore on Jekyll Point was a reminder of the dangers of the Atlantic which we were now entering. It was good to feel a swell again, and we could hear the breakers on the sand banks to port and starboard. I hoisted the foresail, the wind having picked up, and once round buoy No 32 in the ocean, it was a run back into Cumberland Sound. Little Cumberland Island was to port, a designated wildlife refuge with white empty beaches and woods behind.

The river narrowed with bends and then widened out into Cumberland Sound, where HMS *Triumph* was moored in a dock. Then, it was past St Mary's opening to the Atlantic and industrial Fernandina, under the railway bridge which opened after a train had passed, and through Kingsley Creek Cut which bypassed Amelia City. South Amelia River was all marshes again; we then sailed out across Nassau Sound into Sawpit Creek where we tried unsuccessfully to anchor. It was full power into the State of North Florida, where we were more successful in St George's River, an apt name for an English yacht's anchorage.

It was a dawn start to make the Jacksonville Beach Bridge opening, first passing under the Sisters Bascule Bridge, opened at Michel's request, and across St John's River with a tug and barge yard on the north bank. The two-laned Bascule bridge opened on time, holding up the rush hour traffic. The banks were now lined with houses and new buildings. Once through Palm Valley Bascule Bridge, it was back into the bush until we reached St Augustine. The inlet buoyage was most confusing, and there were breakers to seaward, but once across we only had to wait for the very pretty bridge to open. There were many yachts anchored nearby.

The fixed bridge after St Augustine was being repaired, and a barge restricted the channel; we were then out into open marshes. The wind was very cold even though we were so far south (less than 30° N). The Crescent Beach Bascule Bridge opened on demand and we were back into built up areas with houses to port and a condo ahead. Past Matanza's Inlet, where the Spanish massacred 300 French Hugenots, the Atlantic was only a few minutes walk across the sand. The Marine Land Marina proved as big a disappointment as did Marine Land itself, which was run down and mainly shut.

Saturday 8 November (day 14). The day started out cold as we manoeuvered stern-first out of the marina into the channel, and followed the markers south. It all seemed much easier here with houses and marshes, and that was about it. A car crash on Memorial Bridge delayed us until the wreckage could be removed. Our short day ended in the up-market Halifax Marina, near Daytona Beach (of motor car racing fame). Sunday was a day of rest and I hired a car.

After delivering the car back to the airport we left in the middle of the morning, making the 11.30 opening of the Conrad Bridge, but we then had to stop because I got lost after turning over too many pages in the chart book! We passed under the Smyrna Fixed Bridge, which had been hit by a tornado the previous day, and into the shallow Indian River. A very careful watch had to be kept to stay strictly within the channel or we would have run aground. Mosquito Lake was a wide expanse of shallow water after which a sharp turn took us into the lovely tree-lined Haulover Canal. We anchored outside the Marina at Titusville.

Tuesday 11 November (day 17). Armistice day started with dark clouds to the north but the forecast was OK. We made the 08.00 opening of the NASA Causeway Bridge, then passed two huge power stations and under the Canaveral Bridge, names more of the space age than mundane bridges. The river became much prettier in the afternoon and we moored in the

Vero Municipal Marina for the night.

We were away in good time under the bridge, overtaking the only other boat moving. It was a beautiful morning – the sky a light blue, flecked with white tufts of cloud, the sun a blazing white light warming the soul, and the mist rising in the still air, giving the islands' green trees an impressionist look above the ice-smooth water. Ahead, looming above the shroud, was an uninhabited condominium, symbol of the wealth hidden all through the islands.

Near an outlet to the Atlantic, there was a complete change; the water became green and alive over the sand banks, and the wind got up. Nothing of note until Jensen Highway Bridge, which opened early, but would not answer our VHF, so we had to wait half an hour. It was maximum speed to the next bridge which had announced 'We've gotta problem with the bridge', and remained open to let us through.

Across St Lucia we carefully followed the waterway route, not the inlet one which was different. Right in the middle of the channel *Independent Freedom* rode over a shoal but slid off again, her speed carrying her through. The sand with pipes sticking out maybe had something to do with it. Then it was back into the swamps, but once through Hube Sound Bascule Bridge houses appeared on the port bank.

We passed the 1,000-statute-mile marker and saw our first police boat – real sign of habitation, and the mansions on the banks were huge. After crossing Jupiter Inlet we were back into the waterway with more bridges. We were held up at one bridge because I did not have the right name for it, and it did not open at the official time. The marinas would not answer our VHF call, so we anchored off Peanut Island out of the channel, in sufficient water to allow for the fall of tide.

Thursday 13 November (day 19: last). Things started inauspiciously for our last day in the waterway. At 10 minutes past midnight I was awoken by a banging which turned out to be the United States Coastguards.

"You are anchored in the channel and must move!" snapped a beefy burly man.

"We have been here since 17.30 – almost 7 hours" I replied "and you saw us anchor. Why did you not tell us then?"

I asked, switching on the echo sounder.

"You must have moved you've gotta move!" the man said.

"Look at the depth – I am not in the channel!" I said pointing to the echo sounder.

"You're in the channel, move it!" the beefy man said, red in the face.

I thought of making an issue but realized that here was no point taking on the US Coastguards. I held my temper and we shifted about 2 feet and reanchored, watched by the Coastguard launch.

In the morning it was overcast and the day was made no better when we stopped at Rybovich Spencer Yard in Lake Worth to be told that they were 'no longer the Perkins engine agents' and we were too small to be worth bunkering. Welcome to the land of the super yachts!

We were then faced with a boring litany of 20 bridges that day, if our destination was to be reached. Our next excitement, if you can call it that, was when the engine stopped. Fortunately it was just after passing through Linton Boulevard Bridge, rather than before it. I was just able to turn and run with the wind while stemming the strong tide, still a bit close to the bridge for comfort, while Michel changed fuel tanks and bled the lines. We then realized that the fuel gauge had been wrong; the engine started again, running perfectly well when it had fuel! The tide was running strongly with us when we had to shoot Sunrise Bridge, a little too fast for comfort, with only one side of the bridge open and not much room. Our last excitement of the day was when the last of our 20 bridges would not open. It was becoming dark, there was traffic all around as it was the main entrance to Fort Lauderdale, and the fair tide was running fast. I turned and we had to wait an hour for the opening. It was then another 6 miles in the dark up the Dania Canal to Harbour Town Marina, which was so huge that we hired a car so we could get to the heads!

We had made it with time to spare – 1074 miles at an average speed of 6.6 m.p.h. and some 85 assorted bridges, all shot without major incident – very satisfactory! A pity we had been in a rush; perhaps a shallow draft motor boat and six months next time?

CHRISTMAS IN THE BAHAMAS

By now we had a list of refurbishments needed, and we decided to take a few days off while the work was being done. As might have been expected, America was no different from anywhere else when it comes to yacht overhauls, and nothing had been done by the time we returned, so it was two weeks of chase, chase, chase. I was really disappointed in Yacht Management, who should not have taken us on if they could not perform. However, that being said, their office was an exceedingly useful base from which to work, and Cherry the secretary was very helpful. I spent a lot of money, on an SSB radio, a wind-vane monitor, self-steering gear, overhauling the windlass, a new spray screen, mosquito netting to cover cockpit and all windows, servicing the engine, fitting a small winch, renewing the fresh-water pipe, and so on. West Marine the chandler did very well out of us as well. We found the tinned food to be inferior to that in England, but stocked up all the same.

Wednesday 10 December 1997. At last it was time to go and Tug Boat Annie's, the restaurant and bar, lost a good customer in Michel. I had been watching the weather forecast, and a nice window seemed to be opening. It would enable us to cross the Gulf Stream, which can be exceedingly dangerous in any strong wind, especially against its flow. At 16.30 we shifted *Independent Freedom* to the bunker berth in the Dania Canal. The United States Coastguards were close by when we had a bunker spill. We frantically cleaned it up with detergent, watched by two teenagers fishing, who said they would report us. I think they were looking for a buckshee but they did not get one, and apparently they did not split on us either. An hour later, waved farewell by the waitresses from Tug Boat Annie's, I thankfully left the berth and we motored down the Canal to the sea.

The very smart *Nieu Amsterdam* was alongside the passenger terminal when we passed. I had made a passage on the old *Nieu Amsterdam* from Cork to Southampton after completing the first Cowes–Cork Ocean Race, as crew on

Green Highlander many years before. Once a Greek tramp cargo ship was clear, we followed, and Michel hoisted the foresail.

Clear of the Fairway buoy and coastguards, we hoisted the mainsail and turned the engine off. The autohelm did not work initially, so we set the monitor, and after a bit of adjusting it performed well. I was exceedingly glad to be away and it appeared that we had plenty of time to make our date in Nassau. The wind was fair, SSW force 4, it was a beautiful night, cloudless with a bright moon and the yacht was sailing well. We were glad to be out of the confines of the Intracoastal Waterway, and felt a great sense of freedom. We were on our way round the world – not that I had told anyone of the idea, except Michel! The sea increased in the strength of the Gulf Stream and I had 30° of set on to maintain course. She was averaging 7 knots. Early the next morning, as we left the Gulf Stream, the sea went down and the wind headed and later increased. We took two reefs in the mainsail as the weather became overcast and the moon disappeared. The wind moderated a little after daylight and it was very pleasant sailing with almost no swell. The supply boat we had seen in the Dania Canal passed us, bound for the same destination.

After lunch, sailing in the lee of Great Stirrup Cay and Great Harbour Cay, with the water blue and depths of 8.0 metres, the fog came down. Later we were becalmed and Michel went for a swim. The wind filled in after dark from the SE and the sand was glinting in the moonlight off Hockes Cay. It was hard on the wind all night, and in North East Providence Channel it became quite rough; the yacht was shipping water and it was quite uncomfortable, but the self-steering gear worked well. Closer to land the sea calmed down. In bright sunshine, after permission was given, we motored into the harbour and moored at the Nassau Harbour Club Marina. Two uniformed ladies cleared us in, and we were free to explore this rich man's play ground, the Bahamas! The marina had a swimming pool which was a good start.

After considerable effort on my part, the charts ordered from Kelvin Hughes, which should have arrived in Fort Lauderdale, finally arrived in Nassau, and cost me another $200 to extract from Customs. We met my brother Edward and his family (wife Philippa and daughters Camilla, my God-daughter, and Olivia) at the airport, in a stretch limo hired for the event. Edward, like myself a member of the Royal Cruising Club (RCC), is my 'mission control', providing a base in the UK dealing with routine and emergencies with impressive effectiveness. A couple of days sightseeing and it was time to go, although I could not but be impressed to see eight passenger ships in Nassau, one of which was bigger than the QEII.

Thursday 18 December. We left early, motoring out of the sound. Once clear we sailed, but the sun was in our eyes so we could not see the coral heads. It clouded over when we altered course to the southwards, and we had a pleasant sail across the reefs. The dolphins playing round the bow caused great excitement.

Allan's Cay had rather more boats at anchor than we liked, so we motored round to the eastern side. Edward and Philippa went for a walk on the coral and we swam in the clear water. When it came time to leave in the morning, after an expedition ashore to see the lizards, the engine would not start. The batteries were flat. There was a light breeze but it was tending to put the yacht on a lee shore. The mainsail was hoisted head to wind. The anchor was raised by hand and as soon as it was off the bottom the foresail hoisted and backed. *Independent Freedom* gathered way and we sailed out of the cay and beat towards Oyster Island, coming up onto the leads for Highburn Cay. I tacked to just inside the entrance, then bore away for the dock which we had been told was empty. The sails were dropped off the slip and we glided with spring lines at the ready into berth 4.

Two days were spent there, and very pleasant it was too, while a battery was sent out to us from Nassau. The water was gin clear and the sand pristine. There was a barbecue site which we enjoyed, and a buggy took us up to the store. It was 45 miles to Sampson Cay which we sailed mostly close-hauled. The girls enjoyed the dinner, which was quite good, in a restaurant decorated like a ship's saloon. I was the only one to swim in the mini dock, but only until I was told there were sharks, so removed myself from the water fast! They looked huge when I looked down from the safety of the wharf.

It was fine the next day, so we could see the shallows and corals, with two girls keeping a lookout from the bow. Even so, we touched in the narrow channel on the way to Thunderball Club, where we picked up a mooring. The 007 Bond film of the same name was made here. We all swam and snorkelled, keeping out of the strong tide. Edward, Camilla and Olivia went off in the dinghy to swim in the cave, and ended up rescuing a couple who had managed to capsize their boat. After lunch we shifted to Staniel Club, mooring on the jetty. The club was quite full, and a festive dinner was enjoyed by all.

Wednesday 24 December. Christmas Eve was fine. It was nerve-racking, motoring out with only inches under the keel, but we had a pleasant sail to Black Point. With less water than charted round the Point, we picked up a buoy off a wooden jetty in the bay. While snorkelling, we discovered the buoy anchor was an old engine and the line not in very good condition, so Michel made fast our own line. Camilla and Olivia decorated the yacht. Christmas day was spent swimming and snorkelling, and the girls improved their sun tan. Dinner was eaten in the cockpit with a Christmas pudding made by my mother, so England was not forgotten.

Boxing Day was fine when we motored round the bay, with only about 3 feet under the keel. It was very rough through Dittiam cut, with a steep pinnacle-type sea and a strong ebb tide. Once clear of the cut, we hoisted the sails; it was then a dead beat down Exuma Sound to Farmers Cay. The shore looked most inhospitable, barren with no foliage, just the occasional cove and white beach. The flood tide sluiced us through the cut and we moored in a strong stream alongside a rickety pier. We walked to the airstrip and then to the village, all very poor. The restaurant was what might be called a little rustic, and the Bahamian owners appeared to be doing us a favour allowing us to eat! Michel got left on the jetty, letting go while we were manoeuvering in the strong tide! With Michel back on board, we shot out through the cut on the ebb tide and then motor-sailed down the coast. The electrics were playing up again and we kept the engine running in case it would not restart. The entrance to George Town, Great Exuma, is not easy, even with GPS, and there is not a lot of water in the huge harbour. A good lookout was kept from the bow. We made fast in the Exuma Marine Services marina, which had an extremely bolshie Bahamian manager.

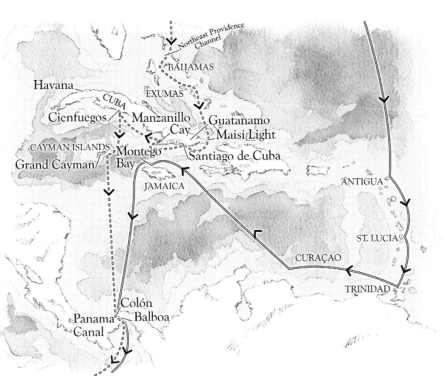

The tracks of Caplin *(dotted) and* Independent Freedom *through the Caribbean.*

EXCERPT FROM A LETTER TO ENGLAND

George Town, Exumas, Bahamas
I am sitting in what used to be the slave market overlooking the harbour, with the lights of yachts at anchor being the only ones visible, about to eat dinner.

The slaves are free and the market is now an hotel! This is the first fine evening in five days.

The yacht is tied up with a total of 21 lines in the marina, which is on the lee shore. At the worst of the gale we were shipping solid water on deck and bouncing around as though still at sea, with thunder and lightning to add to the noise. At one stage we thought the jetty was going to collapse, and kept 'anchor' watch, although what we could have done with no engine I don't know. The only redeeming feature of the situation was that it was reasonably warm. It would have been much better at anchor in the lee of Stocking Island but we were still waiting for spares from the States.

Edward and Philippa, and Camilla and Olivia, enjoyed their 167-mile, 9-port Christmas cruise over the Bahama Bank and in the Exuma Sound, despite our power problems. Luckily the weather was fine and we all enjoyed your Christmas cake and pudding! Edward brought out bits for the autohelm, but in the end they were not needed. Michel found a wire loose and once it was connected it worked fine. So much for the expensive American technician who said the gear wheels had gone. He probably kicked the wire loose himself.

Once the power problem is fixed we will clear out and sail direct to Cuba. The Exumas with their gin-clear water, white beaches and spectacular coral are fantastic. However, wherever there are settlements, and George Town is no exception, it all feels run down and unpainted, with lots of half-built abandoned houses. I hired a scooter today, a lot easier than a bicycle, and rode the 20-odd miles to the north end of the island which was fun. There was almost no traffic, no cultivation, deserted beaches and, in the settlements, unemployed youth just hanging around.

I have been disappointed at the amount of money I've had to spend on *Independent Freedom*. I bought a newer more expensive boat hoping not to have the problems that have beset us! C'est la vie! The rest of the world seems far away and somehow unimportant; I do not even listen to the news on a regular basis! The most important thing is the weather, followed by looking after the yacht. Everything else is of secondary importance, but only made possible because Lloyds is making money and my base is in secure hands.

    Love, Ian.

Eventually the spares turned up and the electrics were made to work but at considerable expense. We spent a few days amongst the other yachts anchored at Stocking Island, many of whom spend the whole winter in George Town. Volleyball on the beach, so intense that many of the not-so-young players wore bandages on their injuries! Fun for a few days, but for months on end? I listened every day to the forecast waiting for a window in the procession of cold fronts coming down from the States. Finally, Michel said we would be waiting for ever and that we should go.

CUBA: FASCINATING SOLITUDE

Wednesday 14 January 1998. We left George Town after watering and bunkering at the marina, and were glad to get away from the most disagreeable manager. We motored out of the harbour keeping a careful lookout for coral heads. Once into Exuma Sound, we set the sails and beat southwards in varying strengths of wind, reefing at times. For reasons best known to the Government of the Bahamas, all the navigational lights were out.

    We anchored overnight on Friday at the south end of Fortune Island, off Windsor Point, which was deserted, devoid of any living thing, human, bird or animal. The cabin is well insulated, so we could barely hear the waves breaking on the shore nearby, a black strip in the darkness. The foremast was moving, making its usual noise despite there being almost no movement now the yacht was head to sea.

    It was flat calm the next morning and we motored until we saw a pod of 15 whales – very exciting. A front passed and the wind filled in from the NNW giving us a fair wind. It gradually veered during the day to the NE and increased, giving us a fast sail south. The movement of the foot of the foremast was alarming, so Michel fashioned some wedges which helped.

The next day, in bright sunshine, we closed in on the coast of Cuba off the Maisi light on the eastern tip, reaching along the southern coast all day. It was grand sailing in the stiff offshore breeze in smooth water, at times only a couple of cables from the coast. The scenery was spectacular – the jagged mountains ridges, and green foliage reaching down almost to the sea. On the narrow coastal plateau triffid-like vegetation waved in the breeze. The sea was deserted – no fishing boats, no ships, no yachts and on the coastal road, which could be clearly seen, we saw just one lorry and a tractor with trailer.

It blew hard during the late afternoon and then the wind failed as the sun set, the sky blood red to the south, the mountains black to the north, capped with pink clouds. Michel took advantage of the calm and changed the alternator on the engine.

Unlike the Bahamas, all the navigational lights worked along the Cuban coast. The lights of the American base at Guantanamo stood out bright from the mainly dark coast. How contrary for them to have a military presence in a Communist country!

We arrived off Santiago de Cuba with much trepidation. The buzz when we left George Town was that it was not only American yachts (which perhaps should not have been there in any event), but all yachts, which were being thrown out of Cuba. However, we were met at the magnificent entrance, which has high steep cliffs with a huge fort on top to starboard, by a rather grubby launch and escorted to a berth, a T-fingered pontoon, overtaken by the gunboat which had been following us at sea.

The numerous officials smartly dressed in their uniforms were polite, and happily drank our cold Coca Colas; they searched and cleared us with no problems. They all accepted beers at the marina bar which was on the other side of the pontoon. This was the same in all the ports – no problems provided you obeyed the rules and avoided politics. We were always welcomed, despite our name – *Independent Freedom*! When we were anchored at Manzanilla Cay, three armed fishing inspectors boarded from a rickety boat and politely searched our fridge for cray fish. There were none – so no problem. (The evidence of the four cray fish consumed at Cabo Cruz, sold us by two enterprising divers, had long been despatched to the deep!)

The striking thing at Santiago, supposedly their second port after Havana, was the lack of shipping. We saw two small ship movements in eight days. The visit of the Pope did not help because nothing was allowed to move while His Holiness was in Cuba. Even the ferry boats propelled by oars were not allowed to operate, and there were no bridges over the river. We were told we could not leave until the Visit was over – detained at the Pope's pleasure!

Sailing amongst the cays on the south coast was a unique experience. We saw no other yachts for almost three weeks, and for ten days did not see another human being either, even though we were at anchor amongst the mangroves every night. We were on our own, there was no help available if anything went wrong. It was the complete silence at the anchorages unless there was a wind blowing, the emptiness of the wilderness and the lack of life, human or otherwise, that I found so fascinating. The plain unrelieved green of the mangroves was a real depressant, and when we saw any sand it was a red-letter day. The only signs there was anyone else on this planet were the navigational beacons and buoys.

One day we had a hard beat to windward, with both sails double-reefed in sustained force 6/7 and gusts of Gale force 8. The sea was steep but there was no current or swell and the yacht went like a bird dipping and swooping over the white horses in the bright sunlight, the occasional sea sweeping the decks clean. The rather eerie empty feeling enhanced by the proximity of reefs and breaking sea made for an exhilarating and interesting experience.

Tuesday 3 February. We nearly lost the yacht today. The mainsail was double-reefed, the foresail had been lowered and *Independent Freedom* was running at over 6 knots. Approaching our destination, Rabihorcado Cay, there was lightning all around us, the rumble and clap of thunder close by. I wore my rubber boots while hand steering. We rounded the north end of Rabihorcado to port and sailed into the lee, the white sand spit clearly visible in the gloom. We followed the pilot-book directions into the anchorage, but we ran into shoal water. A black cloud, criss-crossed with lightning and emitting great grumbles of sound, was working its way up-wind towards us. We were keen to get anchored and put up the dodger and bimini for protection from the spray and rain. Deep water was found and we anchored, veering all the cable.

The squall arrived with a crash of thunder overhead and the sizzle of lightning all around. I thought we were going to be struck. The wind veered to the west, increasing to Gale force 8, threatening to put the yacht on a dead lee shore. There was heavy torrential rain which reduced the visibility to almost nil. The sea rapidly increased and appeared to smoke as gusts of force 9 blew the tops off the waves, while sheets of rain flattened them. Independent Freedom started to pitch heavily, shipping seas forward. I steered due west into the wind, blinded by the rain so was unable to see the echo sounder, and almost deafened by the noise. Michel was below.

There was a slight lull and increase in visibility, which revealed breaking water all around. The echo sounder confirmed we had dragged and there was less than 3 feet under the keel. If we were to save the yacht and ourselves there was not a moment to lose. I started the engine and Michel fought his way forward to the violently pitching bows. The Lewmar winch does not have a pawl, confirmed by their agent in Fort Lauderdale, and the electric motor was not strong enough to hold the cable, let alone heave it in. The manual system is circular like a sheet winch, not a lever. How Michel managed to wind the cable in by hand, continually being swept by breaking seas, I do not know, but he did. I used the engine to motor up on the anchor to assist Michel. I could not see him because the rain had closed in again.

When the anchor was aweigh I headed southwest, watching to port for the shallows, although I think we would have been on them before we saw them. Once I thought we were clear of the shallows to starboard, hidden by the rain and spume, and in 4 metres of water, I headed west at 2,000 r.p.m. This would normally have given a speed of about 5 knots but we only made 2 knots. The yacht was pitching violently, shipping seas forward and water overall, the stayless masts whipping alarmingly as she slammed and pounded into the near-vertical seas. The wind increased again to force 9 as we went over a shallow 2-metre patch; waiting for the terrible sound if we hit the coral, my heart was in my mouth. Then quite suddenly we were in deep water and the seas became less vertical.

We rounded the north end of the cay, rolling violently in the now beam seas, and into the lee where we let go the kedge. We and *Independent Freedom* were now safe. The whole incident had lasted less than an hour but it seemed like an eternity. Michel made some hot soup to warm us up. Anchor watch was kept, and in the next 15 hours we shifted anchorage three times as the wind veered and then backed. We were glad to sail away in the morning.

Ashore it was like getting into H. G. Wells' Time Machine and going back fifty years. The roads were almost empty of traffic, and the few cars that I saw were patched-up American 1940 and 1950 vintage. Horse-drawn passenger carts clip-clopped their way along designated routes, the potential pollutant carefully collected in bags attached to the rear of the animals. There were no buses. The handsome Spanish colonial buildings, which had been built to last, were all in need of paint and a face-lift. The cathedral in Santiago had been smartened up for the Pope's visit and it looked magnificent. The people might be poor but they were overwhelmingly fit and cheerful, making the best of their circumstances.

Cienfuegos was our last Cuban port. Who should we meet but Gil Baty who had sailed with Lord Riverdale and my brother Donald when they were caught out in the hurricane off Charleston! What a small world it is! In Cienfuegos, Gil Baty was on *Gollywobbler II* with Anne Fraser, who was having problems; Michel helped with some of them and lent her our portable GPS. Gil cooked supper one night, and we had a jolly time and interesting cruising conversation. I had dinner ashore with them a couple of times before they went off on their cruise.

I went to Havana for a few days which was fascinating. The place was in a complete time warp. Michel did a diving course at a residential resort. I went for a dive but found that I preferred to be on the water not under it. However, I can understand the fascination and buzz.

To Panama: pirates and rum

Noon, Sunday 1 March 1998, position 21°58'N 80°28'W.
We were hard on the wind with a reefed main and foresail on
the way to Grand Cayman Island. Once the clearance party
had searched and cleared us we motored down the bay to the
entrance and beat out to sea. The weather forecast was
reasonable although I expected a weak cold front from the
States to pass over us at some stage. Michel had hurt his knee
and dancing the night away did not help, so he was now half-
crippled. Stephanie had joined us on *Independent Freedom* at
02.15 the day before, straight from the open-air night club. She
had been on the same course as Michel and they had become
pals.

On Sunday afternoon the wind moderated a little and we
took a reef out of the main. An empty dinghy was passed;
thank heavens it was empty, and not someone escaping. It
turned out to be a filthy night with rain, increased wind,
lightning and rough seas. Stephanie was a brave but not very
good sailor. In the morning we could see the black cloud of the
cold front approaching, so when the wind increased Michel
dropped the mainsail. The front passed over with heavy rain
and a strong force 7 wind. Once it started to moderate, the
wind veered slowly and the mainsail was rehoisted. By noon
there was a fair wind, a following sea but a head swell. In the
night it blew from the NE, force 7, and we had a grand but wet
sail.

Monday 2 March. The lights of Grand Cayman were raised at
04.00, and by 07.00 we were coming into the lee of the island.
I got in touch with port security on the VHF and they instructed
me to proceed to Spotts Bay. There were no boats or ships
anchored off Georgetown, and the waves were breaking over
the wharves and all along the sea front. A cruise ship, which
was hanging off, was also instructed to go to Spotts Bay, which
was not difficult to miss, because *Celebration*, a large cruise
ship, was anchored there. Once we had let go the anchor, one
of the tenders to the ship brought out a message from the
Customs, that I should bring the ship's papers ashore.

It was still blowing with an offshore wind, and there was a considerable swell running, but I rowed ashore safely and we were cleared. The Customs Officer wanted to come out to the yacht but baulked on seeing the dinghy with no engine! In the afternoon another cruise ship anchored close by. At 18.00, permission was granted for us to proceed to Georgetown and we followed a pirate ship round – she was painted in bright colours, a three-masted square rigger with gun ports. The 'Jolly Roger' flag was flying and the crew were dressed as pirates. They very kindly showed us a mooring buoy to pick up with their searchlight and then sent across some pirate booty in the form of rum! Little did they realize they'd got the wrong Tew; three hundred years earlier and they would have been consorting with one of my more colourful forebears, privateer Captain Thomas Tew – and who knows what mayhem might have ensued.

The next morning was fascinating – watching five passenger ships anchor close by including the new largest passenger ship in the world – more economic activity in one morning here than in the two months we spent in Cuba.

The marina in the lagoon on the north side of the island was spied out and directions obtained. We motored round the next day keeping close to the shore to look at the sights, found the right pass in the reef, which was well marked, and crossed the lagoon to the marina.

It required two weeks for Michel's knee to heel, and a considerable hospital bill which was unrecoverable under the medical insurance, by which time I was fed up! We saw the sights including Hell (a place where the ragged jagged black rocks were hellish), hired a car which was a necessity due to the location of the marina, and even went to the cinema to while away the time. Stephanie flew back to Cuba.

Saturday 21 March. We motored round to Georgetown on Friday and left the island on Saturday. The weather forecast suggested a weak cold front would pass tonight or tomorrow. The wind died in the afternoon and we motored, the swell gradually reducing. In the late afternoon a school of dolphins played around the bow for half an hour, leaping out of the water. A light breeze got up the next morning but the engine was still needed for a lot of the time, and there was a strong adverse current.

Monday 23 March. At 05.00 the front passed over us and the wind increased to gale force at times but it was a fair wind. The mainsail was lowered and *Independent Freedom* ran fast under the double-reefed foresail only. Later, we hoisted the mainsail with reefs and then lowered it for the night. The sea got up and the confused swell became more regular. It blew hard and was rough for the next four days. The best day's run was 167 miles at an average speed of 6.7 knots.

Colón, Saturday 28 March. The coast of Panama was raised just before midnight on Friday. Early on Saturday morning, after receiving no reply from port control, we entered Puerto Cristóbal under sail and anchored off Colón to await our trip through the Panama Canal.

Caplin: Caribbean to Panama Canal

(The following account is from the Mate's recollections some 60 years later, the log having been lost in a fire.) *Caplin* arrived in the Caribbean at the end of 1938 and Skipper and I spent a leisurely time recovering from the Atlantic crossing and enjoying the area. From Antigua we sailed south, calling at St Lucia and then, celebrating Christmas on the way, Trinidad, where my cousin Mervyn was stationed. He was in the oil business, and entertained us. We returned the hospitality by having tea parties on board. We cruised along the coast of Venezuela; I remember calling at Curaçao where there was a rum industry. We visited the molasses factory – what a smell!

From there we sailed up to Jamaica. The Montego Bay Regatta was on: *Caplin* was a cruiser, not a racing yacht, so we didn't really want to enter, but they were very keen we should. We were really quite famous by then, and they made a special class for us so we could compete. They were determined to give us a trophy, and I have it still: a lovely wooden tray, inlaid with the various woods of Jamaica. The inscription reads 'Montego Bay Annual Sailing Regatta Foreign Cruiser Race 1939'.

It was in Jamaica that we were given Dopey, our ship's cat. I loved him dearly; he was very fond of flying fish, which were quite delicious. Sometimes they would leap on board and then we would collect them up to eat, but after Dopey arrived we had to be pretty fast or he'd eat them first. He had a cat box on the counter, which he would use perfectly but sometimes a bit of spray would come over and then he'd leap out of the box! He wanted to be with us all the time and several times when we went ashore he must have tried to swim after us because when we got back we found him in the water, clinging to the bobstay.

From Jamaica we sailed down to enter the Panama Canal. Skipper was a very careful man, and described himself as timid. He wanted to haul *Caplin* out at Balboa and inspect her thoroughly before setting out across the Pacific. He had also decided, after our Atlantic crossing, that a third member of the crew would be a good idea for crossing the Pacific, and had chosen a young Navy man out of Pangbourne Naval College, Lionel Thorold, who would be joining us from the *Corrientes* when she came through the canal.

Before entering it, though, we had to consider money. Skipper was worried about the cost of using the Panama Canal and if we couldn't afford it we would sail round Cape Horn. It turned out that the charge was a few cents a ton, including an expensive pilot, so the cost for *Caplin* was peanuts. There were lots of locks; we were tied up alongside one of the huge merchant ships. I do remember the alligators in the water, like small crocs, about a yard and a half long. They just lay there basking. They were in the canal itself, not just Lake Gatún – there were hundreds of them.

When we got to the lake, Skipper wanted to hoist the sails – he was always reluctant to use fuel if he could sail – and the pilot (they were all Americans) was horrified; he said "What if some of my buddies see me in this wind-boat?" We did sail, though.

INDEPENDENT FREEDOM: PANAMA CANAL

Sunday 29 March 1998. Associated Steamships, Lloyds Agents, have proved to be very efficient. They dealt with all the paperwork, delivered the spares and produced the extra linesmen needed. Michel picked them up from the Yacht Club and they were onboard at 04.40 – Carlos, Ninas and Rudolf. Shortly afterwards Pilot Pedro boarded, and we commenced our transit through the Panama canal with two other yachts – a fantastic experience.

We passed through the Panama canal today, motoring fast enough to complete it in one day. I think it is a man-made wonder of the world. What vision to have built such huge locks before the First War. Two other yachts motored in company with us, rafting up in the locks under the direction of the efficient and charming pilots. When anchored off the canal maintenance base, our pilot encouraged us to have a fresh-water swim. Our linesmen enjoyed the bathe as much as Michel and I.

The last lock was the most exciting; *Independent Freedom* swept out at huge speed on the current as the fresh water mixed with the salt. We felt the first waters of the Pacific – a new ocean, a new sailing world.

To my utter amazement, as we passed under the huge Bridge of the Americas joining North to South, a surf board fluttered down! A quick alteration of course and a fast hand had it quickly on board. The youngest linesman, a 'first tripper', left the yacht happy as a sand boy clutching the board!

THE PACIFIC:
IN GRANDFATHER'S WAKE

CAPLIN: PREPARING FOR THE PACIFIC

BALBOA: ARRIVAL OF LIONEL

Friday 28 April 1939. The deck has had its first coat of paint and *Caplin* looks much smarter. We are delaying beaching her on account of the wash from countless US Navy launches. We have been spending most of our time doing odd jobs on board.

Sunday 30 April. Busy on board all day putting up extra shelves. We now have the port bunk tidy and with much spare space, including a special shelf for the typewriter, atlas, charts and so on. We found out when the *Corrientes* was coming through the Canal, so the Mate went ashore with the two American boys and finally brought our new third crew member off to the ship at 03.00. He is shaping fine – real name Lionel. We call him that or Rupert alternatively. He does not talk too much, is yacht trained and anxious to please, and appears to be just what we want.

Wednesday 3 May. We had a morning with the chart catalogue yesterday. I have made out a list for our route across the Pacific as far as Singapore and also to New Zealand. The US Navy is still here, and their stream of launches makes such a wash that we dare not beach *Caplin* until they are gone. Mate was rather battered yesterday; dentist and typhoid inoculation and vaccination. She actually turned in about 21.00.

DANGLING OVER THE DOCKSIDE

Friday 5 May. There is rather a tragedy with *Caplin*; her keel bolts are corroded. We have to be lifted ashore at Balboa to have them renewed – much expense and possible delay. We motored to the docks this morning and have been waiting all day to be hoisted out. No hurry – they are very busy; if they do it at their convenience between other jobs the charge will be reasonable. If we insist on not being kept waiting, men will be specially brought round and we shall be charged for it.

Wednesday 10 May. Life has been one hectic rush and we turn in just dead tired; haven't had the gramophone for days. Tonight we finished work in time for supper about 19.30. Mate was hard at work all day painting the dinghy; she just rolled into her bunk and was asleep in two minutes.

Poor little *Caplin*, seeing her dangling over the dock side hung by a couple of wires – what if she had dropped? But of course the Americans are much too efficient for that. The heads of all the keel bolts had corroded off. I had a faint suspicion this might happen, and wasn't going to sail across the Pacific without being sure. It will cost the best part of $200, as the new bolts are made of Monel, a special very costly metal alloy. The work has been done extremely well. Now we are back in the water again; all the ballast and water tanks had to come out, but we got them back this evening and our cabin is cosy again.

CHARTS, STORES AND PAINT

Friday 12 May. I got the charts yesterday – a huge roll – and five books of sailing directions. Lionel has been very assiduous painting the side and varnishing, so *Caplin* really looks like a well-kept yacht. We cannot be smart, but I do like the ship to be fairly tidy and not the battered wreck that most of these ocean voyagers look. We have had an awning made which stretches between the masts and has a couple of poles to spread it. It makes it cooler below and more pleasant sitting in the cockpit, and the Mate has her ventilator. She and I spent all yesterday afternoon at the Commissary ordering our stores.

I shall probably get a shock when the bill comes, but I put it out of my mind till it does. We have got some fish hooks and lines to trade.

Saturday 13 May. We all lunched with Mr and Miss Adams (at the Legation) yesterday. He heard of us from the Commander of the *Orion* and kindly asked us up.

We have finished painting *Caplin*'s side. Her bottom is painted with brown anti-fouling paint and we have brought this brown about eight inches above the waterline. It will alter her appearance a little, but I've not seen her 'from afar' yet, as one might say. We got eight five-gallon cans and painted them – for extra water. Our awning is a great comfort.

All the morning I have been traipsing round Panama and Balboa getting my papers fixed. I went to see the Ecuadorian Consul – everyone directed me the wrong way, and I spent an hour-and-a-half driving round Panama in buses. When I got to the office it was too late, and anyway 'pleasure visit only' had been left out of my application, and I had to return on Monday with it properly made out. Am now back on board black with rage.

A huge pile of packing cases containing our stores is on the dock – we are alongside – and it has been deluging with rain, but it doesn't matter as they are covered with a sail, and anyway we are too tired to start storing them. The awning is lovely; it keeps the cockpit dry and not too many leaks in the cabin.

We have to pay about $25 to visit the Galapagos – we are nearly broke, with the expense of the dockyard and the huge supply of stores. Lionel has a few pounds and so has the Mate, so we shall pool our resources and sail away for Tahiti with about five pounds left.

Monday 15 May. We all got up at 06.00 yesterday and spent the day stowing our stores; we took up the cabin table to give us room and everywhere was littered with tins by the thousand. By tying up the legs (two massive wooden parts for keeping the ship upright when beached) and flooring the bottom (of the locker) I made quite a lot of space under the port cabin seat. Both sides are now crammed full. We took the sails out of the quarter berth and have stowed beer and about six months of Klim (dried powdered milk) there. A few tins have overflowed into the shoe lockers in the fore cabin, but everything has been put away. Spare rope – three coils of it, different sizes – is under the cockpit. For water, we have eight five-gallon cans which we have painted; some will go into the quarter berth and a few under the cabin table. Quite a weight, all this, and the water is now well over the copper, but *Caplin* has rather excessive freeboard.

Incredible rain yesterday and water ran right through Mate's mattress, wetting the sail beneath, but I think I have found the leak and fixed it.

The only sign of a long voyage are the four water cans – painted green – lashed at the fore end of the cabin. On deck the dinghy has a big cargo of ropes and fruit, and boxes of fruit are lashed on the counter. The dinghy also has several spare five-gallon tins of gas and kerosene.

ESCAPE FROM THE GULF OF PANAMA

Tuesday 16 May 1939. We aimed to have everything ready on the Monday and thus have nothing to do today. However, on Monday night the radio would not work, and I had quite a time running around the dockyard to get someone to fix it. I got a man to come down, but he could not do anything, so there it is – a useless white elephant and I'm altogether disgusted with it. It doesn't really matter as I have the two watches.

Then we had a string of visitors, to say goodbye but hindering our preparations for sea. Mostly they brought gifts – fruit and candies for the Mate. Miss Adams among others, with a huge water melon and several pineapples – she saw we were busy and would not come on board. People were so kind to us. Then we heard the *Ethie* was at Cristóbal. Captain Hearn came down and took the Mate off to try to get a message through; bad luck missing them just like that. We had to turn the ship round to get the dinghy on board and lash everything down. Then Captain Hearn carried us off to lunch – they were so slow and I got really impatient; we got back to *Caplin* within half a minute of the time of our departure and found our pilot – a friend of Captain Hearn – waiting for us and looking rather worried at no sign of life in the ship.

Captain Hearn came with us for the jaunt too; we cast off our lines and motored away down the channel, myself feeling very much rushed. Cries of horror from the cockpit and a spout of water coming up the drain holes. *Caplin* was so low in the water that the drain hole was below water level and water was coming through the wrong way! Going ahead with the engine makes her settle an inch or two by the stern. Mate stuffed a rag in the hole and stood on it, while Lionel cut a wooden plug.

About an hour's motoring – no wind – and the pilots left us with many good wishes at the seaward end of the channel. We kept the 'Broken Heart', our name for the engine, beating till off Taboga Island, then stopped and made sail. We drifted in a calm for half an hour. Then there was a light air on the beam, gradually freshening to a good breeze.

Caplin romped ahead all that night through the smooth water, making over 7 knots at times. By 05.30 this morning we had run 90 miles and had Cape Mala abeam; just marvellous luck to get clear of the Gulf of Panama like that.

The Gulf of Panama is the worst place in the world for calms. The early navigators sometimes drifted for months, dying of hunger and thirst, with their ships fouling with weed.

Since then we have had calms and variable winds, but it was never calm for long and we have averaged 70–80 miles a day. Yesterday at noon we were half way – roughly 420 miles to go. If only our luck holds we shall make a marvellous passage.

Lionel has been noisily seasick from the start; he has got a bit better the last two days and I hope is really recovered. Till yesterday he could keep nothing down, except once or twice a cup of Bovril. He has been able to keep his watch and is plucky over it. He managed an egg at supper last night.

We've had a good deal of rain; yesterday the parral (the wire keeping the gaff jaws to the mast) broke and we had to get the mainsail down; Lionel was able to come up and help. There has been more trouble with the gaff jaws not riding square and chafing the mast. I've bound it with rope which I hope will stop it. Yesterday we saw a water-spout – an evil-looking finger coming down from the sky a mile or two away.

INDEPENDENT FREEDOM: BALBOA

Tuesday 31 March 1998. We only spent two days moored to a buoy off the Yacht Club, as opposed to the weeks *Caplin* had spent. There were no Navy launches to create washes, but plenty of commercial traffic. The weather was fine. We visited the Admiralty chart agent where my grandfather had purchased his Pacific charts; mine had been flown out from the UK. There was a huge supermarket in Panama City where we purchased our stores, and two or three yacht chandlers. Unlike my grandfather, I did not have to worry about the availability of cash; I had the joys of plastic money!

The Balboa Yacht Club provided a lively social life and meeting place for other yachtspeople. I sent, and paid for, a fax to 'mission control' – my brother Edward in the UK – but he never received it. Michel sampled the night life of Panama City – a final fling before the rigours of the Pacific! We took bunkers alongside their pontoon and departed for Isla Taboga late in the afternoon. I kept close to the channel buoys, well out of the way of commercial traffic. The services of a pilot were not required!

CAPLIN: BECALMED HALFWAY
TO THE GALAPAGOS

03°N 083°W, Monday 22 May 1939. I've had a headache since we left – nothing serious, but probably a mild form of indigestion. Four years ago I had the same trouble and at last consulted our doctor, who gave me some powders, since when I've practically never had the problem. Generally I carry around some of his medicine with me but the last year I've been so well that I've not bothered. I've got the prescription with me, though. However, this morning I'm feeling fine – never have been seriously ill. We are becalmed about half way to the Galapagos, rolling a bit. The sails are flapping and the main boom tugging and rattling its sheet; also it's raining. I relieved Lionel at 06.00 and he is now asleep in the starboard bunk.

INDEPENDENT FREEDOM: AWAY FROM THE AMERICAS

Wednesday 1 April 1998. We left Isla Taboga under sail in fine weather with a fair wind. We passed between Isla Brava and Isla Taboga, where friendly fishermen waved from their boat. A huge school of dolphins followed us for over an hour, leaping and cavorting around the yacht. Michel had his music on loud from the cockpit speakers – perhaps the dolphins were attracted! He encouraged me to sail between Isla Toque and Isla Bona where there was an abandoned mining works and loading point. There was a village and church on Isla Toque, where the fishing canoes came from. It was very hot indeed.

Like *Caplin*, we were lucky and had a marvellous fast sail in smooth waters past Cape Mala, making 176 miles noon to noon, an average of 7.3 knots. It was an exhilarating start to our Pacific crossing. The wind was taking off as evening approached on Thursday. There was still quite a sea running and a long moderate swell.

VESSEL IN DISTRESS

Thursday 2 April 1998. At 17.55 we came upon the *Morgan C* of Punta Arentas (Costa Rica), a fishing vessel. She was drifting beam-on to the sea, with a man on top of the bridge waving a white rag up and down, obviously in trouble.

Well, it is a distress signal! Michel quickly let go the ropes holding the booms out so freeing the sails to swing as we came about; we rounded up close in the lee of the heavily rolling boat. She was about 50 feet long and had her anchor down, not that it was doing her any good, miles into the deserted Pacific! Michel discovered, with no English spoken, that they wanted a battery. It was too rough to go alongside, so I told them to launch their dinghy. In the back of our minds was the thought that if we kept our distance we could not be 'taken over' ourselves, an unworthy thought as it turned out!

With some difficulty, because of the conditions, we lent them a house battery, transferring it by the dinghy. It was used to send a radio message and then returned. The *Morgan C* was drifting to leeward quite fast, and I told them we would stand by until rescue arrived. During the night we shone our searchlight into the sky every half hour to assist the rescue boat if it was nearby. The drift during the night was 16 miles on a course of 232° true which, if maintained, meant the *Morgan C* and her five crew would drift past the Galapagos.

Shortly after daylight the bird which had been with us all night flew away and we started the engine. I closed in on the fishing vessel, close enough to hand the Captain a note with our position. Soon afterwards their dinghy was launched, and Captain Ramon came on board. With Michel's help he spoke on our SSB radio. We understood the rescue boat from Punta Arentas, some 240 miles away, was due and should have already arrived. The Captain returned to his boat and sent across a delicious filleted tuna for breakfast. At 08.00 a fishing boat arrived from the SW; she must have passed us during the night, and she took the *Morgan C* in tow.

Friday 3 April. By noon our position was 29 miles NE by N of *Caplin*'s position on 22 May 1939, and *Independent Freedom* was sailing fast on a broad reach.

(The great difference between 1939 and now is GPS; I knew the position of the yacht all the time whereas my grandfather was dependent on the sun and stars when visible. His defunct radio was to have been used to take time signals and check the accuracy of his watches. Their day revolved around position finding, because the Mate took sights as well. The beginning and end of the day were most important for star sights, not just a comment on the beauty or otherwise of the sun rise or set! For them, landfall was an exciting and sometimes nerve-racking event depending on the accuracy of their navigation.)

OUR OWN EMERGENCY

Saturday 4 April 1998. We were motoring in light conditions when we had a panic. The boat was filling, with water spraying the engine compartment from the revolving propeller shaft. We put the engine out of gear, manned the mainsail and tore up the floor boards.

"It's fresh" I shouted to Michel who was pumping like mad

in the cockpit. The fresh water hose which ran past the engine had broken, draining the port fresh water tank into the bilges. What a relief it was not sea water! There were still 60 gallons of fresh water in the starboard tank and eighteen in reserve on deck. The pipe had been repaired in Fort Lauderdale.

That evening we passed a turtle close to a floating log There was a big swell running, great rolling hills of water. Just after midnight on Monday, a gorgeous moonlit night, Michel called all hands on deck; it was frightening to have a whale surfacing close by. During the morning a pod of these huge creatures passed – not something to collide with! The day's run was only 41 miles. How much 'El Nino' was affecting the weather I do not know, but we had our fair share of calms, squalls and rain!

Fuel was a concern because it was not clear from 'The Pacific Crossing Guide' if fuel was available in the Galapagos (it is) so we motored only in the calms, and only during the day; it was not possible to see the many floating trees at night.

00°38'N 85°37'W, Noon, Tuesday 7 April. It is overcast and raining, hot and humid. The wind is E, force 4, and the yacht is sailing well. Only 305 miles to go with 598 sailed 'away from the Americas'!

CAPLIN: CALMS, LIGHT AIRS, THEN SE TRADES

Calms and light airs from all directions for the last few days. *Caplin* ghosts along, making perhaps 50 miles a day, but yesterday after 48 hours without sights we found an adverse current of 40 miles. However, a slow passage was almost expected and we have done very well; over half way and less than 400 miles to go.

I have been reading up about the Galapagos in the 'Sailing Directions'; apparently they have been developed and settled a bit in the last 10 or 15 years, and a schooner runs every two months, so almost certainly we shall be able to send letters there.

Lionel is not well yet; he eats a bit now but is still occasionally sick; I don't think he feels too bad between. He is plucky over it but now, after a week at sea, it is getting a trifle serious. and it's not as if we have had any bad weather or violent motion. *Caplin* is now gently bowing to the swell.

Rain is pouring down and wayward little airs come from varying directions. Lionel is lying in the starboard bunk with a book. Mate is draped in a cape, sitting in the cockpit and handling the ship. Incidentally, with plastic wood and linseed oil the decks are now practically tight.

Dopey is fat and sleek and grows every day. She was a kitten we procured in Jamaica, aged 2 weeks, and became extremely companionable, though rather rough. She is all over the ship and climbs right up to the sheer pole, giving us heart spasms – what a word – that she will fall overboard, but we cannot do anything about it. She loves the dinghy, in which she can hide among the ropes and fruit boxes.

The shelves I mentioned were made from battens fixed to the beams in the fore cabin. This makes a narrow space or pocket between the deck and the battens in which to stow the new charts and the big atlas. Some more battens behind the toilet make a space for magazines, of which we have been given a hundredweight. Opposite the Mate's bunk, near the bookcase, is a shelf for her typewriter.

01°03'N 085°44'W, Thursday 25 May 1939. After a week of light airs we picked up the SE trade wind 36 hours ago, and have been sailing steadily between 3 and 5 knots ever since – fairly smooth but with the wind on the bow *Caplin* jumps a bit. At noon our position was 01°03'N 085°44'W, just 240 miles from Galapagos. If the wind holds – which looks likely – we shall make the passage in eleven days. It might even be a record for a sailing ship – good old *Caplin*! She sails herself and it is a lazy life. We read quite a bit; at night we keep two-hour watches. Yesterday it was calm enough to have the gramophone after tea. Lionel is better today; it is the first day that he has not been sick at some time or another. Mate takes her sights every day.

Wreck Bay, San Cristóbal, Galapagos

Sunday 28 May 1939. The trade wind continued and yesterday at daylight a little hump appeared ahead on the horizon. Some little confusion at first, as the highest part of the island was hidden in clouds, but it was all clear as we neared the island. We ended the day with a jolly beat into this bay just before it got dark. 'Gerbault' makes a great song and dance about the difficulties of entering this bay. A large sunken reef (Arrecife Schiavous) blocks the entrance, leaving a fairly narrow channel on the north side, but it is adequately charted and presents no difficulty to an ordinarily competent navigator.

The Ecuadorian army appeared in a shabby boat with three soldiers, one of whom had to stay on board till the morning when the Commandant appeared to look at our papers. However, he was quite a civil young man and enjoyed the food we gave him. He slept in a sail on the forecastle. We met Karin and her husband Sr Cobos, the owner of the island, and tomorrow we go to visit them at the settlement four miles inland. Karin has been made famous by Robinson's book; apparently he fell in love with her and describes a romantic parting.

Mate and I went exploring in the dinghy this evening and got some tiny pink cowries. There are a few ramshackle houses on the beach for the guard (30 or 40 men) – no cultivation but all the ground is covered in dense scrub – no flowers – and I'm not enough of a botanist to appreciate it. Each island has a number of endemic forms, and it was the flora and fauna of these islands that started Darwin on the 'Origin of Species'. Jolly to be quietly at anchor, but we have made an amazingly good passage – 11 days only. Lionel continued being sick from time to time, but he is all right now. Hope he gets his sea legs, or he will probably leave us at Tahiti. We propose stopping here for 2 or 3 days and then to spend 2–3 weeks exploring the other islands, then off to the Marquesas – 25 to 30 days.

INDEPENDENT FREEDOM:
THE MOST AMAZING SHOOTING STAR

02.30, Wednesday 8 April 1998. The log reads 'I saw the most amazing shooting star on a course of about 060° true, first noticed at an altitude of about 25° to the west of the Southern Cross, about 7° long with a very bright 'engine', brighter than any star or planet in the firmament, pushing a myriad number of small stars with a bright one in the middle, about half the intensity of the 'engine', shaped like a gigantic disintegrating rocket moving very fast; a jumbo jet appears positively pedestrian, I would say ten times the speed of a jet plane. As it moved across the sky so it fell in altitude, finally disappearing behind a cloud at about 10° altitude.' I have never seen anything so spectacular in the night sky in all my life.

At 18.00 the same day we crossed the Equator at Longitude 86°33'W, motoring in a calm.

According to the Pilot Chart, south of the Equator the wind direction is only from the east to south quadrant. Until we reached the Galapagos the wind was in every direction except that quadrant, including WSW, force 6/7, when we reefed, and on Thursday it rained all night!

It was satisfying on Friday evening to plot our position on British Admiralty chart 1375 'Galapagos Islands'. Early the next morning the southern end of Isla San Cristóbal could be seen in outline from the light of the full moon.

We closed Roca Este, a group of rocks, and tacked close inshore along the east coast. It was deserted, devoid of any life, human or otherwise. The green vegetation stretched from mountain peak to the sea; no brown as reported by Darwin.

The wind failed just after lunch, so we motored. From the chart there appeared to be a channel to the south of the reef blocking the entrance, Arrecife Schiavous. I steered a course to pass through this short cut, but something was wrong. There was a strong current and breakers were ahead where there was supposed to be deep water. Maybe 'Gerbault' had something, despite my grandfather's dismissal! With only a metre under the keel, we reversed our course, and the reef was left to starboard as we entered Wreck Bay.

Independent Freedom anchored amongst the other yachts and the cruise ship *Galapagos Explorer* rolling in the heavy swell. A far cry from when *Caplin* arrived in 1939! I reported to the Port Captain at the naval base, but was told to come back on Monday. No guards sleeping on our sail!

Caplin had taken 11 days for her passage with no motoring. We had taken nearly 10 days including two days of motoring at slow speed. Just goes to show what a fast boat *Caplin* was! They spent almost 3 weeks exploring the unspoiled Galapagos.

The tracks of Caplin *(dotted) and* Independent Freedom *through the Galapagos Islands.*

Caplin: Cruising Around the Galapagos

Floreana

From San Cristóbal (Chatham) we sailed the 55 miles to Floreana and anchored in Post Office Bay, so-called because there is a barrel in which the old whalers used to put their letters, and homeward-bound ships would call to take the letters. The barrel has been renewed from time to time and still exists. The bay is uninhabited; there are some jolly sand beaches backed by gradually rising ground with fairly thick scrub. Quite a few flowers but of course all new to me. A trail runs up to the settlement – about 3 or 4 hours rough going. In the barrel was a book with names of visiting yachts and their crews, and several letters which we have taken to post in Tahiti. Some names we knew, which was rather fun. The custom of leaving letters is now chiefly romance.

I walked up the trail for half an hour while the Mate sought shells. Later, all three of us came ashore with the Mate's machete and cleared the scrub round the barrel so it could be seen from seaward.

Next day we motored 3 or 4 miles to Black Beach anchorage. There was one hut and a flag staff flying the Ecuadorian flag. Landing, we made the acquaintance of the family in the hut: a man from Ecuador but born in the Galapagos, mostly Spanish; his wife, mostly South American Indian; their 17-year-old daughter Marta, who would be pretty enough (after a long sea voyage, a rather indecent reference to Pericles IV-6) and José, a 10-year-old adopted Indian boy, chiefly a huge grin. Zabala (the man) was the representative of the Government, so I showed him my papers and a letter from the Commandante at Chatham – all in order and a charming family, delighted to see us.

They provided a donkey for Mate and took a photo – hope it comes out! They sent José with us as guide, and off we went leaving Lionel to look after the ship. An hour's steady tramp, steadily rising through the usual scrub, brought us to a garden where the Ritters had lived. Bananas, limes, flowers and running water.

After an hour we got to the neck between two mountains – grass and trees and then a mile or two of thick jungle of wild oranges, guavas and lemons; sixty years ago it had been a plantation. We passed a pond with feral duck – so tame that José waded after them and killed one throwing a stick. Then we saw a huge wild bull – ex-Friesian. We were rather scared of it, but José just shouted and waved his arms at it. The bull gave us a friendly glance and then slowly walked away. Pigs, cattle, donkeys and dogs were probably introduced by pirates and have gone wild. The trees were festooned with

Sixty years after the voyage recounted in this book, Caplin *is still sailing. Picton, March 1999; the author at the helm*

Cdr Graham and daughter Marguerite, with Dopey the cat, preparing for a voyage spring-clean; probably in Jamaca

ater

Gibraltar

Canary
Islands

e Verde
nds

Independent Freedom *under sail in Tonga*

The author in Hell, Grand Cayman

Running south to Panama

Independent Freedom transiting the Panama Canal

Morgan C in distress in the Pacific – a bit deep to anchor!

Independent Freedom: *landfall at Hiva Oa, Marquesas after 23 days at sea*

Hoisting aboard Independent Freedom's *new engine; Marina Taina, Tahiti*

Caplin's mate (the author's Aunt Marguerite) before the mast

long hanging mosses and lichens – all very romantic.

Eventually we came to a clearing with a very roughly thatched shelter and found a solitary middle-aged Englishman – Dudley. He had only been there a month, and most of his equipment had been stolen in Ecuador. A schooner runs from Guayaquil every 3 or 4 months. He gave us cocoa and we then went on a 10-minute walk to the next family – a Conway man and wife, youngish American. They had been on the island 18 months and had a lovely garden – all sorts of vegetables and flowers, but only a thatched shelter to live in. They seemed very happy, evidently hard workers. They gave us a quite delicious roast wild pig, but the flies and mosquitoes were swarming. It was not very hot, especially there about a thousand feet up. One could see the attraction and romance of their life and the joy in making a garden and home, and being quite independent.

To complete the social round we continued for half an hour to the Wittmer family. A German, his wife and several children – he young-middle-aged and she a little younger. He was a cheery little man, less villainous than I expected from his photographs. His wife was a pretty woman, exuding ordinariness and respectability, and a great chatterer. She talks fair English but with him we effected communication in Spanish. They had been there 8 years and had made themselves very comfortable; there were masses of fruit and vegetables, pigs and poultry, and a house – entirely self-supporting. They seemed very happy too. We then proceeded back, getting to the beach just before dark. I enjoyed the tramp, but was thankful the Mate had the donkey to ride; she had been desperately tired on the return from Karin's at Progresso.

We stopped two more days at Black Beach so that all four families could visit us, but the Wittmers are such bad sailors she would not come out to the yacht, so we met and had a meal at the Zabalas'. The Zabalas then fetched water for us on his donkey and brought us masses of vegetables and fruit, including a sack of oranges and sweet potatoes. They did not want money so we traded odds and ends – a butter dish, some flour, a pair of scissors and a sail needle, old clothes, soap and baking powder. They were very pleased with what we gave them – which was not much – and were not at all grasping. One evening we took the gramophone ashore to their hut. Wished I could paint a picture of their rough shack and the dark Indian faces of the women in the light of the dim oil lamp. Both had the friendliness and charming manners of primitive people.

CONWAY BAY, SANTA CRUZ

Tuesday 6 June 1939. We have now sailed away to this island (Santa Cruz) – a big one 20–30 miles across. On one side is a settlement of perhaps seventy people but we have avoided that, as the anchorage looks bad. Here we are in a sheltered bay on the lee side of the island. The wind was very light, so we just saved daylight by motoring for 3 hours. It is entirely uninhabited and we are longing to go ashore and explore.

It is gradually getting light. To the southward is a lump of an island – an old volcano, which shelters the bay. There is no wind and we are rolling gently to a very slight swell. The beach is rocky, alternating with little sandy bays. Behind, the shore rises gradually to high hills all covered in low trees and scrub. I must finish writing and get the dinghy, which is now full of fruit, unladen so that we can launch it – then breakfast and go 'truly exploring' with a vengeance. There is a rough plan of this bay surveyed in 1836. I think that was the *Beagle* with Darwin on board. Wish I had books and knew more botany, so that I could appreciate the marvel of the local flora! We saw several wild donkeys yesterday grazing on shore.

We had a jolly day on the beach at Conway Bay. Saw a sea lion on the rocks, so tame that I could have touched him or her with the oar. The birds are tame too – several little things the colour of sparrows; one actually perched on José's head, and one on my back as I was lying down resting today, a lovely little chap with a brilliant red head and breast. In one bay a pelican – like the ones at Jamaica – came up to us on the beach, until we were actually afraid of its long bill and we had to push it away with an oar. We bathed and conched (looked for shells) and explored in the dinghy, but the scrub was so thick we could not get inland or find water.

SAN SALVADOR

Thursday 8 June 1939. Yesterday we sailed to James Bay in James Island (San Salvador). This is an entirely uninhabited one and big too – perhaps 20 miles each way. The Conways lived here for 3 months and gave us a plan showing where their house was and a stream. There was a ruined hut on the beach, and we found a trail and the stream after a bit of a search. We now have a carefully blazed trail up to it. There are lots of small trees and bushes, but not quite so impenetrable as the last beach. We saw wild goats and donkeys. Today we carried our clothes up to the stream to wash them and picnicked; it was rather like a stream in Devonshire, but not such lush vegetation as the soil is poor and dry.

We carried our .22 rifle to shoot a goat, but did not find one, and the automatic in case we are attacked by the donkeys or wild cattle – most romantic going armed, but I don't think there are cattle on this island. I brought down a five-gallon can of water on my shoulder. I was very glad to find it so that we could start our long voyage with tanks all full. Water is very short in the Galapagos and it was necessary to avail ourselves of every chance of getting any. *Caplin's* normal capacity was 60 gallons, but the extra cans had raised this to 100. This was rather more than 60-days supply for three persons.

We have quite a good anchorage, a few hundred yards from a sandy beach. There was a little surf, and at our first attempt at landing, the dinghy broached-to and swamped. There was no danger – quite a tiny surf really and shallow water –we were just not taking it seriously. Now we land carefully and quite easily, keeping the dinghy head on.

These islands are mostly 20–40 miles apart and are not all visible. The wind blows constantly from the S or SE (the trade wind), and our anchorages are all on the lee side of the islands. I don't much like leaving the ship alone for a long time, and am always glad to come back and see her mast over the bushes; though I would not leave her alone at all unless I thought it quite safe. We are about 30 miles south of the equator, but the nights are deliciously cool – nothing like so hot, even by day, as at Balboa.

The Conways had brought us half a wild pig so we have

been living on pork mostly. Mate fries it first and then stews
it – most tender and palatable. We dry salted some and it kept
for a few days, but some we put in lime went bad.

Saturday 10 June. Mate had evidently rather over-exhausted
herself scrubbing all our clothes in the hot sun. She barely ate
any supper and soon after I had gone to sleep, she woke me
in great distress with a violent sick headache. We had finished
our aspirins and had forgotten to get any more, but I got out
the medicine box and hunted through it. I found a packet of
amonal tablets that had been given us, and gave her a couple
which sent her to sleep in a few minutes. When she woke next
morning she was all right. Yesterday Lionel and I walked 2 or
3 miles to the top of a crater. The rim was a circular rocky wall
and 250 feet below us was a lake surrounded by vivid green
vegetation. The lake is salt and at one time had been worked
for this. There was the remains of an old motor winch and
various wires at the top. Mate had spent the morning
conching, and found a seal on a rock that was so tame she
could have patted it. Some of the rocks were swarming with
marine lizards – curious black creatures that waddle about and
dive into the sea to eat weed. We killed one and boiled it, but
could not bring ourselves to eat it, though they are supposed
to be edible.

It is fun exploring this uninhabited island, and as we have
found water we can stop for a few days. It is important to start
with our tanks brim full. Water is generally scarce and difficult
to get in these islands – at least near the sea. In the interior
there is usually plenty. The small birds sing very sweetly –
unusual in the tropics. I wish one of us could paint. The view
from the top of the crater was 'very good'. Bright blue sea,
with a mountain on one side and the black lava river half a
mile or more wide on the other, and all the foreground olive
green scrub – not particularly beautiful but strange.

In James Bay we shifted a couple of miles to another part
of the bay. All quite uninhabited, but there were traces of a
recent visit in the shape of empty cans and cartridges. Lionel
reported goats, so later the Mate and I went ashore again and
saw a group of three grazing. I crawled up very carefully
through the bushes and at about forty yards fired at one. Did

not think I would hit it with the 0.22 rifle, but they are a bit shy. To my surprise it fell straight in its tracks. Hit in the neck and practically dead, but to make sure I put a shot through its head with my pistol. I dragged the carcass to the beach and skinned it, while Mate went off to get Lionel to help. I am no hunter nor butcher, and it was rather grim skinning, cleaning and cutting up the carcass. I had the kidneys for breakfast next day. Mate cooked the meat by frying and stewing till it was quite tender and we had several meals off it; but did not really like it very much. To a novice, butchering a carcass rather puts you off eating it, and goat's meat is rather too rich and strong-tasting. Nothing like the wild pig we were given by the Conways.

ISABELA

From James Bay we sailed northward round Isabela Island to Tagus Cove – 80 miles; we were becalmed most of one night and then motored for nearly 12 hours. Our normal petrol capacity would take us about 60 miles with 15 hours motoring. At Panama we embarked another 10 gallons which was loaded on deck. The carrying capacity of a small yacht is so limited that every item has to be carefully considered. The cove is formed by an extinct crater, one side of which has been broken or rather washed away and forms the entrance – about a mile long and a mile wide – the snuggest anchorage in the Galapagos. High scrub covered cliffs all round, and landing was only possible at a ravine at the head of the cove, but we could not beach the dinghy there, so one of us had to lie off with the boat while the others jumped on to the rocks.

It was, in a way, the least attractive of any of our anchorages as there were no lovely sandy beaches, but the interest of the place is that it has been the custom of visiting ships to paint or cut their names on the rocks. Some big yachts and men-of-war had made a job of it and had painted letters 6 feet wide on the hillside. I had hoped to find old names, going back perhaps a hundred years, even possibly the *Beagle*, but we found nothing over 10 years old. There were perhaps fifty or a hundred names all plastered round the shore in white paint. Several names we had heard of – *Philante, Arto, Yankee* and *Svaap*. Mate painted '*Caplin*, R.C.C. 1939' while I held the paint pot. So, if we come to grief on this voyage that will be the last record of us!

This island, Isabela, is seventy miles long. There is a settlement of seventy people scattered within a few miles of each other at the southern end of the island; otherwise it is uninhabited.

Off Tagus Cove, separated by a strait two miles wide, is Narborough Island, perhaps 10 or 15 miles wide and 4000 feet high; just one gigantic volcano. An amazing sight, nearly all black lava which has run down in a stream from the top and spread over the plains – like a nightmare. In one or two places are patches of green, but mostly a black inferno. What a place for a penal settlement! All the criminals would go mad or die off. If only one was an artist; photographs would show nothing of it. Isabela has similar lava streams and one of its volcanoes is still active, though we saw no signs of its activities, but Narborough is the grimmest sight, the most hostile that I have ever seen.

There was fresh water marked on the chart a mile from Tagus cove, so we sailed out next morning and I lay off in the yacht – no anchorage – while the others went to prospect in the dinghy. I saw the Mate scramble ashore at the foot of a likely-looking ravine; later she came back, so Lionel landed and she rowed out to me – full of the bird and animal life she had seen. I left her to look after the ship and rowed in to the rocks.

Several sea lions, including a family group – father, mother and two children. Father looked such a pompous old fellow. A pelican swam up to within a few feet of the dinghy and the rocks were swarming with the marine lizards; one was 3 or 4 feet long, but mostly tail. Evil black things they look. I could have knocked them over with my oar and felt it unenterprising not to secure some to eat, but the one we had cooked looked too grim in the saucepan. I rowed into a cavern. There were several more sea lions on the rocks; one I poked with my oar, which he feebly snapped at and then lumbered into the water. Masses of birds too, though I could not see the penguin which the Mate had reported.

Lionel managed to fill two five-gallon cans with water;

it was muddy, but would keep us alive at a pinch. Not too easy embarking them as there was, as always, a slight swell and no beach, only rocks to jump from. As well as the big lizards there was a group of five baby ones. Mostly they sat absolutely still on the rocks, but if one got too close they lumbered away with an ungainly stride; and in the water, too, they appeared to swim very clumsily. They are supposed to live on seaweed and are the only marine lizard known.

It was noon by the time we had finished watering; but there was very little wind, and by 17.00 we had only drifted some 4 or 5 miles, so we motored back to Tagus Cove, rather than spend a night drifting close to the shore.

Yesterday we made a new start. Again very calm weather, but we had open sea ahead by dusk, and by daylight had made good 50 miles. However, it was calm when I came on deck at 06.30, and for some hours we had no steerage way. Calms are not so bad when one is out of sight of land, though one has to think about the water supply. We had really quite a big margin, 60–70 days with normal expenditure, and perhaps double that if we went on a short ration. I expected the voyage to take 25–30 days.

INDEPENDENT FREEDOM: GALAPAGOS

ACADEMY BAY, SANTA CRUZ

Thursday 16 April 1998. Although the authorities gave us a 30-day stay in the islands I am afraid we were not as adventurous as *Caplin*. The weather was inclement to say the least – El Nino, we were told. The continuous heavy swell in both Wreck Bay (San Cristóbal) and Academy Bay made me uneasy thinking about leaving the yacht. There were many other anchored yachts and charter boats, threatening a real risk of collision in the rain squalls. Thus the Galapagos became a refuelling and water stop with unexpected goodies from the supermarket in Academy Bay. What a difference in two generations!

The frolicking sea lions and seals were fun to watch when they were not asleep, sometimes from a dinghy. Ashore in Wreck Bay the township was rather seedy, not helped by the rain. In a bar where we were able to fill our water cans we met the crew of *Mangoe* – an American yacht. The two of them were keen divers so teamed up with Michel to go diving. Peter, a presentable young man, East German, attached himself to us and we all hired a boat. Leon Durmiente, a huge split rock some 10 miles from Wreck Bay, was the diving site. They dived in the 50-foot split while I snorkelled the swell rushing through the gap. The open diving boat had no radio and kept breaking down. On the way back against the wind and sea it was also very wet, and I began to wonder if we were going to make it! Once back on the coast we stopped to go for a walk and passed dead seals starved of their natural food due to El Nino. In the evening all foregathered on board *Independent Freedom* for supper.

Last Monday clearance was obtained and the trip to Academy Bay was made with a crew swap from *Mangoe* – Peter, and the son of the teacher from San Cristóbal, Erwin. There was much mutual photographing of each others' yachts before it became dark, with a fine moonlit night. Anchoring in the bay was an obstacle course with all the unlit yachts and boats.

In the morning we shifted closer to the shore, just outside the surf line, to shorten the dinghy trip to town. The fuel we had taken in cans from Wreck Bay was contaminated and we had to change it. Luckily none of it had been put into the tanks. Unlike *Caplin, Independent Freedom* carried plenty of fuel, 120 gallons in two tanks with a reserve of 25 on deck. Of course *Caplin* had no fridge and so, unlike us, did not have to charge up the battery every day. On the other hand, they had no supermarket to shop at, hence their hunting expeditions for fresh meat.

Ashore the wet weather did not improve the dowdy town but we had a good meal in a restaurant. The Darwin centre was interesting and the giant tortoises did not lose their appeal in captivity.

Peter was still on board and Michel decided he wanted a crew. He seemed a cheerful enough fellow and, although he had never sailed before, appeared willing to learn, so I agreed he could come with us to the Marquesas

It was apparent, despite 'El Nino', that the trade winds

were blowing further south. In the evening we departed from the Galapagos, bound for Hiva Oa some 3,000 miles away.

CAPLIN: GALAPAGOS TO MARQUESA ISLANDS

Thursday 15 June, 1939. It is 16.30 and we are about 60 miles west of Isabela Island, the last of the Galapagos, on our way to the Marquesas, nearly three thousand miles away. The sun shining, but it is pleasantly cool – a very light wind on the port beam and the *Caplin* is ghosting along at about 3 knots. A very long swell rolls up on the beam, but the sails steady the ship, so that my cup of tea rests quietly beside me on the table. Lionel is sitting in the cockpit with a book, nominally steering, but *Caplin* knows the way and does not really need attention. Mate is fast asleep in her cabin. Dopey the kitten, sleek and fat, and grown out of all recognition, sleeps beside me on the cabin cushion. A low gurgle from the galley reminds me of the slowly boiling joint of bacon. Mate and I had been discussing Lionel. He has almost everything we could have chosen for a companion – likes music, can sometimes beat me at chess, always willing to do more than his share, interested in books and can talk. He was seasick this morning, but it does not seem to incapacitate him at all. However, I have grave doubts about what he would be like in bad weather.

Monday 19 June. We are about 600 miles out now; the first day or two were light airs and slow progress, then there was a fresh beam wind and roughish sea. For the last three nights *Caplin* has kept her own watch, steering herself with the tiller lashed; today is smoother, with less wind – just abaft the beam, so we've set the second spinnaker. *Caplin* has still been steering herself but I thought it better to keep watch tonight. I've got the first watch and I'm sitting in the cabin writing this. Half my mind is on the feel of the ship, in case I need to go on deck and adjust the tiller lines if I feel she is off her course. The lurch of the ship makes writing difficult.

We have supper at 18.00 to save daylight and for the last few evenings I have been reading aloud afterwards. Tonight we finished 'Pride and Prejudice'. It has been a pleasure reading

it, because the Mate has really enjoyed and appreciated it.
Lionel, too, chimes in with correctly appropriate remarks. He
eats breakfast and vomits regularly, but keeps some of his other
meals down. Between vomits he seems all right and can do his
work, but I hope he won't die on us! The day we left
Galapagos, Mate said "It's no good playing the theme song
here" – one of Tambers very sentimental love songs.

We are pretty much alone now, the Galapagos behind us
and the next islands over 2,000 miles ahead. I am wondering
if there is any ship within even a few hundred miles. Our
radio does not work – it went wrong just as we left Balboa.
Mate is a perfect brick over the cooking, and takes a lot of
trouble at providing vegetables etc. We have been long
without bread and fresh meat; also the butter is finished now
and the few remaining bananas are over-ripe. Breakfast today
was cold bacon, porridge and ship's biscuit. For lunch we had
spam, a sort of tinned ham or bacon, quite good with potatoes
(sweet ones), tinned beet, peas, and a trifle of asparagus left-
overs. For supper we had tinned kippers and fried potatoes.
We have only about two more meals of potatoes and will then
use rice. We have ample stores, though with 3 weeks at sea
ahead of us, our meals may get a bit dull. Dopey is much too
venturesome now and is all over the ship; we fear she may fall
overboard.

Monday 3 July. We should sight the Marquesas tomorrow
evening. We have had a splendid passage; the wind was rough
and strongish but it was thrilling with the ship straining ahead,
day after day through rough seas, with a strong wind behind
us. Its direction (SE) never altered, though it varied slightly in
strength. We rolled nearly all the time and occasional splashes
came over the stern, but the sea, though big and surprisingly
irregular was never actually dangerous. It was fairly
uncomfortable but we did not mind that as we were so
excited over the magnificent day's runs. We had a regular
routine; I generally took the 20.00 to midnight watch, Lionel
midnight to 03.00, and Mate 03.00 to 06.00, when I came on
again. Concerning food, I got breakfast and Mate the other
meals, and for sleep, Lionel rested in the forenoon, and Mate
and I had a sleep in the afternoon. All this made the days pass

very quickly. Every day we got sights and so kept a close track of our position. Our course was a little north of Robinson's and our best day's run was made just 60 miles north of his best one.

We sighted Hiva Oa in the Marquesas over the bowsprit at the appointed time, 21 days out. Here are some statistics of which I am really proud: Tagus Cove in Albemarle Island to Hiva Oa: 2924 miles in 21 days and 3 hours, average speed 5.8 knots; best week of seven consecutive days – 1172 miles averaging 7 knots (with the current helping); and best day's run 185 miles, though Mate's sights made it 188 miles, which is the same as Robinson's best day. It was fine sighting land, just when and where it should be; the new watch had done very well since we lost use of the radio.

INDEPENDENT FREEDOM: GALAPAGOS TO MARQUESA ISLANDS

Thursday 16 April to Sunday 10 May 1998. For the first couple of days out we had calms, variable airs, squalls, rain and a confused sea with a heavy southerly swell. On the third day the SE trades set in. At 18.00 we put the first reef in the mainsail, and later a reef in the foresail. It was great to be sailing, the yacht quite comfortable in the sea and heavy swell.

Michel and I always keep deck watches at sea, with the autohelm or wind-vane monitor steering. It might appear that, with three on board, too much sleep rather than a lack of it would be a problem. However, Peter turned out to have poor eyes and he suffered from headaches, or so he said. I tended to be around when he was on watch, especially when the yacht was sailing fast. We kept the usual 4-hour ship watches at night, alternating every 3 days, so we all had a fair share of the 24.00 to 04.00 one. No one liked this watch. I liked to be up at dawn to welcome the new day.

The concept of personal responsibility seemed to escape Peter; this may be a product of the East German educational system. Initiative as far as doing things for the boat was nil, but he displayed plenty where his own comfort and pleasure were concerned. He was good at chess, not having the sense to let me win occasionally; he so consistently beat me (29 times) that I gave up playing. Even so, he was a pleasant enough companion and was not seasick, unlike poor Lionel on *Caplin*. I helped him with his English lessons most days.

One night during the 20.00 to 24.00 watch the vital necessity of keeping a proper lookout was brought home to us, even though we were in the middle of the Pacific. I had to alter course for an overtaking ship, even though we were showing the proper navigation lights and flashed our searchlight towards her bridge. We had a similar experience during the daytime, when a ship passed less than a cable away across our bow. The nighttime overtaking ship eventually answered our VHF channel 16 calls after she had passed, but the one which passed us in daylight did not answer at all.

A radio net had been started for this voyage, the controller passing the net on to another yacht when they reached their destination. After a week or so of listening we joined in. I must admit it was comforting in a way; one felt less alone in the vast expanse of the empty Pacific. Certainly Michel enjoyed the radio work. *Caplin* had a radio to obtain time signals, so necessary for obtaining their Longitude, but it had broken down. In the evenings they read aloud for entertainment, whereas we had a stereo system with loud speakers in the cockpit, and Michel and Peter had individual Walkmen. In *Caplin*, they ate three hot meals a day, but we happily made do with one, and snacked on too many biscuits. We only turned on the fridge when the engine was running, so it kept the soft drinks and the tinned New Zealand butter cool. We did not have to steer, which was better than having an additional crew member, because the auto pilot did not eat drink or talk – it just used up the batteries!

The next week was fast rough sailing, the wind mainly SE, force 5/6, but one day force 6/7. The best day's run was 183 miles at an average of 7.6 knots. It was wonderful sailing with, at times, clear blue seas with white horses; the yacht very comfortable with reefed main and foresail. The sea was moderate to rough, and a heavy southerly swell was running. We saw a sperm whale and dolphins one day. There were some beautiful sunrises and sunsets; photographs do not do justice to the myriad colours. At other times, the vessel was rather wild, sailing very fast and shipping water forward. Oh the dream come true! But it was not to last, and the reefs had to be shaken out. The heavy southerly swell persisted all the way and the SW wind varied from force 2 to force 5.

Michel, using an expensive fishing rod purchased in the States, caught a two-pound marlin amidst great excitement, but he considered it 'cradle snatching' so put it back; the only fish caught on the voyage! The light reaching staysail was set between the masts for 2 days in addition to the main and foresail, which were often goose-winged. As the masts were stayless, there was no chafe and the sails could be set at right angles which was very efficient. The only gear failure was the American kicking-strap bolt fitted at Cambridge, Chesapeake Bay, up until a couple of hours from the Marquesas, when the main-sheet shackle parted.

CAPLIN: DISAGREEABLE RECEPTION IN THE MARQUESAS

Thursday 6 July 1939. Yesterday we sailed into a bay where the Commissaire was supposed to live; it was not too well sheltered and we rolled badly. No one came out, so after tea Mate and I went ashore, landing badly on rocks with a breaking swell. We walked a mile along a long path with the usual tropical greenery and came to a village where we met 'Bob', an English trader. He gave us a drink, told us that the officials were in the interior and that we had broken the regulations in landing.

Today we waited again till the same time and then Lionel and I went ashore, meeting with a very hostile reception from the French Commissaire and a doctor. Apparently we had broken their regulations in landing, had come to the wrong port of entry, and had no French visa to our papers. Without being actually rude, they were most disagreeable. This was the first such problem since sailing half way round the world, and I am always so careful to have my papers in order! They requested that we leave at 06.00 the next day. I was furious, but it was no good saying anything.

In the meantime we had heard that the annual fete here took place in a week's time and we thought it quite likely we

The Marquesas.

could have met the *Achilles* and Dick (who'd sailed with us as
far as Bantry Bay) here. Our anchorage was vile, a heavy swell
was rolling into the bay and breaking with alarming noise on
the shore. We rolled abominably all the time, so I was really
quite glad to go on, though I was sorry not to have seen the
other islands in the group.

INDEPENDENT FREEDOM: A BETTER RECEPTION IN THE MARQUESAS

Sunday 10 May to Friday 22 May 1998. Hiva Oa was in sight at 03.00 and daylight revealed the green rugged tortuous sides of the mountain. At 11.00 we anchored in Atuona harbour amongst many other yachts, a friendly German running our stern anchor for us. We had sailed 2,872 miles in just under 23 days at an average speed of 5.2 knots with 33 hours motoring. *Caplin* sailed it in just over 21 days, and 52 miles further. Our best week's run was 1,042 miles, whereas *Caplin*'s was 1,172 miles. It all goes to show what a fast gaff yawl *Caplin* was!

We were rather better received than my grandfather, clearing with the Gendarmerie without trouble. At considerable expense, I phoned my brother Edward ('mission control'), who thought we were in Costa Rica! He had not received either of the faxes I had sent, and paid for, the first from the Bilbao Yacht Club and the other from the bank in the Galapagos.

We loaded water into the cans and purchased some stores, and I had an expensive haircut by a pretty young woman. A considerable swell was running into the crowded harbour and it was raining heavily so we were glad to leave Atuona. Gauguin's grave remained unvisited by me. It was quite a performance to get under way, watched by the surrounding yachts, but we made it without incident.

We motor-sailed close to Pointe Teaehoa where there was a confused lumpy sea, the swell breaking on the rocks which were steep-to. The valleys and hills were covered with lush green vegetation. We crossed the Canal Haava close in along the shore of Tahuata Island, passing the supply ship to Hiva Oa. A few blow holes were shooting spray high into the air. We entered Baie Vaitahu but there were too many yachts there, so we turned back and motored into Hiscox's third most beautiful Polynesian anchorage, Hana Moe Noa, and dropped anchor in the middle of the empty bay. The strikingly craggy cliffs and hills were very green and the 1,546-foot-high peak was covered in cloud, with rain falling on the lower slopes. The swell was breaking with a roar on the deserted yellow sand beach which was backed by palms waving in the breeze.

A couple of days were spent cleaning the hull, snorkelling, repairing broken battens and checking the engine. When more boats came in it was time to move. We sailed the few miles to Vaitahu Bay, landing at the jetty. We looked in at the store and the church, returning to the yacht to be blown out to sea under bare poles by a vicious squall sweeping down from the mountain. Continuing under a double-reefed foresail to Hanamenu Bay on the north side of Hiva Oa, we left the imposing volcanic sentinel in the middle to starboard and anchored off the black-sand beach. It was backed by palm trees and surrounded by steep green-clad mountains. Ashore there was a horse, an abandoned home and a small river.

I thought it was a good idea to use the fresh river water to wash clothes, but should have waited until a port with a laundry. I was eaten alive by bugs, yet Michel, who is normally ferociously attacked by any mosquitoes in the vicinity, and Peter, were left alone!

A week after arriving in Hiva Oa we sailed to Ua Pou looking in at Baie Vaiehu with its spectacular cliffs on the way, and dropped anchor inside Motu Koio, in the Baie Hakaphietau. It was pretty with the famous rock spires soaring up into the sky at the top of the valley. Michel christened it King Kong island after the film!

It was quite difficult landing from the dinghy in the swell. A political rally was being held in the open air above the jetty. There was a small store and a telephone alongside the steep road. I returned to the yacht while Peter and Michel climbed up the valley, swimming back on their return.

Peter had overstayed his welcome, and after discussions with Michel, I asked him to leave. He burst into tears and was most reluctant to go. The next day we had a fast rough sail in bright sunshine, wind ENE force 7, to Nuka Hiva, anchoring close to the dinghy dock, adding a stern anchor to hold her head to the swell.

Peter was signed off at the Gendarmarie and I obtained my 'white' paper. I did not want to be liable for his 'bond' when we reached Tahiti, the bond costing US$ 1,100 per head. Apart from a couple of good meals ashore, and a night of Polynesian dancing, Nuka Hiva was not very attractive.

Friday May 22. My fifty-fifth birthday was celebrated by leaving the Marquesas for the Tuamotu Islands. I was some eight years older than my grandfather was in 1939. He sailed straight through the Tuamotu Islands then, obeying his orders from the authorities, and I had intended doing the same. However, other people suggested we were crazy not to visit them. I did not have any charts and there were no plans in the 'Pacific Crossing', so I borrowed some and made sketches. That, combined with the Admiralty Sailing Directions, proved adequate.

Caplin: through the Tuamotus to Tahiti

Papeete, Tuesday 25 July 1939. We took about a week coming here – rather anxious coming through the Tuamotus. There were two atolls on our route which we had to avoid, but we did not sight them as it was night. Next night I got star sights and a fairly reliable position, but I was not absolutely sure of my time, as we had got no radio time signal at Hiva Oa. We sighted the next island – you can only see them at five or six miles, and then only tops of trees pop out of the water, but there was an unexplained discrepancy in my morning sight and I was not absolutely certain if our island was the right one. We left it to port and there was another just visible from aloft about ten miles away. We sailed through this pass between the two islands. About thirty miles ahead was another pass, five miles wide between two more islands. We sighted our next island an hour before dark.

I expect I am muddling this frightfully – shall try to get it straight. The first pass was ten miles wide between two islands then, thirty miles on, there was another pass five miles wide between two more, all looking exactly alike. We had sighted the first island and got through the first pass by about midday. There were some rain squalls, during which it was very thick and the wind was inclined to take off.

If we did not sight the islands of the second pass before dark we were in rather a muddle, tangled up among islands during the long night. Also, a discrepancy in my morning sight and a doubtful latitude at noon when the sun was nearly hidden in a cloud made me a little doubtful whether we were not in an entirely different pass fifteen or twenty miles away. If this was so we would be steering not for a pass but right towards a reef thirty miles long. The chart was also rather vague. The plan of the second pass showed a different shaped island from that depicted on the general chart, also in a different latitude and longitude.

As we approached the second island it did seem more and more likely that we were in the right pass, but I was still not quite sure. Two of us kept on deck peering through the dark and listening for the sound of breakers – 19.00 and 20.00 and sailing by compass but unable now to see the land and I was ready at any moment to see breakers ahead. But with each mile we sailed in clear water it was more sure we were in the right pass. At 21.00 we were at our nearest point to the island to starboard – which we had never seen, but we could now hear the surf on our starboard beam and by this time I was sure we were right, so was able to get a few hours rest while one of the others steered.

We now had a clear run to Tahiti, which we made quite easily a couple of days later. A patch of calm delayed us and we spent a night very slowly drifting along the shore and were off Papeete at daylight. A pilot came out, and after some delay (bureaucracy from having called at Hiva Oa) we got Pratique. Police and Customs officials and various forms to fill in, but all very civil.

Carried off to lunch!

A few minutes after we had anchored – close to the waterfront, with a stern line to shore – a voice called down the hatch "Mr Macpherson would like to speak to you".

I had just been reading his cruise through the East Indies in our journal (Journal of the RCC), and I had met him several times in England – he is the Macpherson of the Naval prints, but that is a long story. I had not the slightest idea he was in the Pacific and it was just grand being hailed by a friend! He carried us off to lunch ashore etc. – how we enjoyed the fresh food!

Tahiti is seven thousand feet high, and masses of coconut palms and just the South Sea Island of the picture postcards; it was just lovely in the sunrise. The harbour is surrounded by a reef with a narrow pass and is as smooth as a millpond. We are among a line of schooners, anchored off the waterfront, with our sterns to the shore.

INDEPENDENT FREEDOM: MARQUESAS TO TAHITI

Friday 22 May1998. There was little wind when we left Nuka Hiva so we motored along the coast to Baie De Tae Oai, or Daniels Bay, with its impressive scenery and waterfalls. Although there was a considerable southerly swell running, it remained windless for the first three days. A gaff cutter, the only boat we saw, took its sails down in the calm. On the last night, when there was a decent breeze, we were under reduced sail for our daylight arrival.

TUAMOTU ISLANDS, DARWIN'S 'DANGEROUS ARCHIPELAGO'

Manihi Atoll, Wednesday 27 May 1939. On Wednesday morning it was "Land-ho!" or rather "Palm trees-ho!" as the first of the Tuamotu Islands was sighted. Darwin called them the Dangerous or Low Archipelago; they are curious rings of land just rising above the edge of the water. These low islands bear no proportion to the vast ocean out of which they abruptly rise, and it seems wonderful they are not overwhelmed by the all powerful and never tiring waves of that great sea, miscalled the Pacific. I closed the reef surrounding Manihi Atoll, skirting along it to the pass. What a difference from the volcanic Marquesas – no green mountains, just sand, reef and palm trees.

The Admiralty Pilot gave a formula based on the moon for the tidal predictions which seemed to coincide with the time of high water given in the Admiralty Tide Table. *Independent Freedom* entered Passe Tairapa an hour after the outflow had begun; it was strong. The pass was well marked, with a green post to starboard and three red ones to port. A small ship was alongside the jetty on the starboard side, and on the opposite side a man indicated that there was 10 feet of water and I should to keep to port. I did so, steering close to the reef, and found a counter current. At the end of the pass there was a huge surge of bubbling running water; the engine laboured as though we were going uphill. The yacht inched forward and then, suddenly, was out of the current and in the deep lagoon.

It was too deep to anchor off the village and anyway it was a lee shore. I followed the reef round and anchored in the lee of a motu (islet), off a white sandy shore shaded by palm trees washed by crystal-clear water from the deep blue lagoon. It was fine and sunny. For the first time in two months there was no swell and we lay quietly. This was tropical paradise!

A very pleasant week was spent here swimming, snorkelling and walking ashore, and Michel enjoyed diving. There was a luxury thatched bungalow hotel two-and-a-half miles away, where the food was very good and the Polynesian dancing colourful and lively. They would even send a water taxi if asked! The weather was perfect and for the first few days we were the only yacht.

When we left for Ahe, a day's sail away, Michel had to dive and free the anchor from the coral; the shank had been bent through thirty degrees. The pass and channel to the village were well marked and lit, but bore no resemblance to our sketch! The village was small, and the faded paint on the clapboard houses and two rather rundown stores reflected the fact that there was no hotel or landing strip. There were no gardens, no colour, although the children seemed cheerful enough. It was only a hundred yards' walk to the reef surrounding the atoll, the Pacific pounding away and not a soul in sight, the view unchanged for centuries.

It was very pleasant for a day or two, but I do like a bit of life now and again! The supply coaster from Tahiti came in on Thursday morning; that was the excitement for the week. Boats came in from the black-pearl farms and the wharf was crowded with people collecting their goods. I was able to buy twenty frozen baguettes from the Compradore. They were delivered to the jetty direct from the hold of the ship, and I resold some to one Spanish, one French, one American and one English yacht in the anchorage.

Rangiroa

We left at noon on the same day under the foresail only, sailing out of the lagoon in a 25-knot squall. It was rough outside with a heavy southerly swell. Two reefs were taken in the sail to slow down for a daylight arrival at Rangiroa. It was a fine bright night but when the moon set it was very dark. At 05.00 I sighted the leading lights, and as it became light we skirted the very heavy outflow which had breaking seas. Full power was required to make it in, close to shore on the port side of the pass. Michel spotted forward as I steered as close to the reef as I dared. There were heavy breaking seas close to starboard. It was a little hairy at times, when we were swept backwards relative to the land while motoring forward at 7 knots. A small crowd had gathered ashore to see if we would make it! We did eventually, and anchored off the Kia Ora hotel.

This was more like it. A first-class French-run restaurant to eat in, a glass-bottomed bar over the water to watch the coloured tropical fish, with *Independent Freedom* in sight at anchor in the clear water, which was wonderful for snorkelling and diving, and fine warm weather. We hired bicycles to ride along the flat road to the other pass, where there was good surfing and, if you wanted to get away from it all, a walk on the reef with the Pacific swell breaking and no one in sight! Michel went diving and was thrilled with the hundreds of sharks he swam with. Eight days were spent in this paradise and we regretted leaving.

Passage to Tahiti

Saturday 13 June 1998. The passage to Tahiti started well enough, close-hauled along the shore past Tikehau Island. In the afternoon it clouded over with drizzle, and the wind was cold. Early the next morning we had taken in two reefs in the main and one in the foresail, and by daylight were fully reefed with three reefs in each. It was blowing a full gale with a rough head sea and heavy swell. The yacht was pitching and occasionally pounding – shipping water overall with the lee rail under water at times.

It blew hard all day, but *Independent Freedom* made steady progress at between 4 and 5 knots and, considering the conditions, it was really very comfortable. In the evening the wind eased a little, so one reef was shaken out of the foresail and we were then able to overhaul a yacht nearby! I had to tack during the night to miss Marlon Brando's Tetieora atoll. In the morning with majestic Tahiti in sight, an island which is classical to the South Sea voyager, the wind went light.

Monday 15 June. With permission from Port Control, we followed a morning ferry through Passe de Papeete into the harbour and moored stern to the quay as *Caplin* had done 58 years ago. Unfortunately, no fellow RCC member to carry us off to lunch ashore!

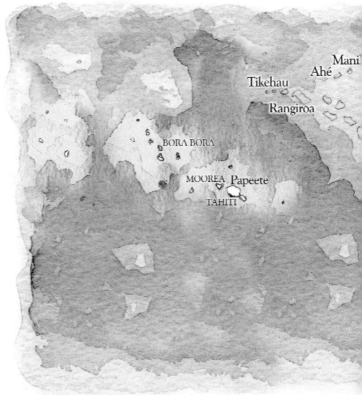

The Tuamotus and the Society Islands

CAPLIN: TAHITI AND MOOREA

PAPEETE: PLANS FOR THE ROUTE HOME

Monday 29 July 1939. We are getting involved in a social round, just as in Jamaica, but I cannot give a day-to-day account of trivial details. The annual fair was on when we arrived and troupes of dancers in their native dress competed for prizes. Most interesting, but not exactly beautiful, though the dresses of bright yellow raffia are picturesque. We took a bus ride to the other end of the island – all day along the coast through coconut groves and the usual tropical trees. It is

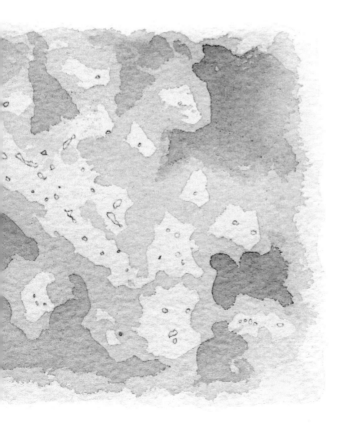

difficult to get all one wants done, and for our first week here we worked pretty continuously on the ship, painting and varnishing, so that she does not disgrace her flag like two other yachts close by, one English and one American.

We propose sailing from here in two or three weeks for Bora Bora, Rarotonga and Tongatapu. Then possibly to Suva, Fiji and down to New Zealand for the summer season. The plan is to go north by New Caledonia in March and through the Torres Straits and Dutch East Indies to Bali, leaving the latter at the end of June and crossing the Indian Ocean via Christmas Island, Cocos Island and Mauritius. We propose spending Christmas 1940 at Capetown, and then on home, aiming to arrive in England in May 1941.

THE LOVELIEST BAY IN THE WORLD

Paopao Bay, Moorea, Wednesday 9 August 1939. This is the loveliest bay in the world – a couple of miles deep and half a mile wide, surrounded by quite fantastic mountain peaks up to three thousand feet. The foreshore is lined with coconut palms, then tropical jungle, with the needle-like mountains behind. We meant to stop a couple of days, but have been here a week. Moorea is an island ten miles from Tahiti, and is itself about eight miles across. We are glad to get away from the rather jaded town of Papeete. I've been doing a little writing and the Mate has been typing for me, and we always have some work about the ship.

Saturday 12 August. We have finished breakfast and the morning chores. Lionel is filling the water tank and the Mate is preparing some raw fish for lunch – actually steaks of a bonito some friends caught yesterday. You soak it in the juice of limes for some hours, after which it has the appearance and texture of having been cooked. We are enjoying the peace of this bay; it is still the loveliest in the world. We have been for some walks, and the Mate once got a pony to ride. We are going back to Papeete in a day or two to meet the mail steamer.

We have borrowed a few books from the *Trondjem*. One is Priestley's 'Faraway' which I have enjoyed re-reading. There is a lot about Papeete and the South Seas generally. We have been to the 'Circla Bougainville', a local club in Papeete – but it is duller than the written account and the native girls are just grim to look at, flat noses and thick lips. A Swiss who is settled here came on board for tea with his native mistress/housekeeper and the latter's cousin, who spoke only Tahitian. It was absolutely impossible to make any mental contact whatever; the housekeeper had a little French, but that was not much good to me either.

INDEPENDENT FREEDOM: TAHITI–MOOREA–TAHITI
AND A NEW ENGINE

Monday 15 June to Tuesday 8 September 1998. I reported to the Port Captain, where our mail was waiting, and to Immigration and Customs. I was forced to pay the bond despite Michel and I being citizens of the European Union, but I was able to do so with plastic money at the bank. We did not like the noisy, smelly traffic which ran most of the night astern of the boat. The next day we motored round inside the reef, past the airport and anchored off the hotel at Maeva beach, which we found very pleasant. The swimming was good and it was only a short dinghy ride to the reef for snorkelling.

We hoped to have the generator repaired and returned to a small marina the other side of Papeete. The mechanic electrician took one look and said it was too old to repair. When motoring back to Maeva beach we passed through some rubbish and Michel dived to remove some nylon round the shaft.

Michel completed another diving course and was now a master scuba diver. I did a tour round Tahiti and found it not much changed from my grandfather's description 'through coconut groves and the usual tropical trees', although rather more built up in places.

Papeete was no less 'jaded' and the effects of the French military reduction with their wind-down of nuclear testing were only just beginning to be felt. It was very expensive to do anything, from a taxi ride to eating out, and the night clubs charged $10 for a Coca Cola. I enjoyed visiting Stevenson's lighthouse at Pointe Venus, where there is a memorial to

Captain Cook, who was there in 1769 to observe the transit of Venus and the sun and so calculate the distance between the earth and heavenly bodies. There was a restaurant high up the mountain side with spectacular views which were well worth driving to, but the food did not match the panorama.

Knot Yet, the American yacht in Ahe to which I had sold baguettes, was in the marina close to where we were anchored. John, the owner, was crewless and he had come with us on our trip to repair the generator. We made a joint expedition to Moorea which was fun, much quieter and more relaxed than Tahiti. We took a bus round the island and enjoyed an excellent lunch at a French-run restaurant. The return was on an eighteen-year-old ex-Japanese inland sea ferry. I had a look on the bridge and found the Captain sitting with his feet on the engine console and his quartermaster steering with his toes, and that summed up the general state of the ferry!

Thursday 2 July. It blew hard all day. I obtained port clearance in Papeete for Bora Bora. The next day we slipped from our Mediterranean-style mooring at the Marina Taina where we had moved, bunkered with duty-free fuel, and motored out of the Passe de Taapuna with the swell breaking on either side. It a was pleasant sail – the short distance along the edge of the reef to Moorea. When I started the engine to enter the pass it made a funny noise. Michel dived but found nothing wrong with the propeller.

The anchorage at the head of Cook Bay (Paopao Bay in *Caplin*'s account), past an anchored passenger ship, was spectacular with its mountainous scenery. 'This is the loveliest bay in the world' wrote my grandfather, and it still is, with its fantastic mountain peaks, jungle and coconut palm foreshore. It has remained unspoiled. After buying supper at the store ashore we moved anchorage out to the reef where the water was clear and good for snorkelling.

The next day, after Michel dived and cleared the snagged anchor, we motored round to Papetoai in Opunoho Bay. I hung off while Michel went ashore in the dinghy for cigarettes and bread, and then anchored inside the reef to the west of the bay.

Oil in the bilges

In the evening Michel found oil in the bilges, and investigation found the gear-box casing broken with the teeth showing through. My heart sank. On Sunday 5 July I flew back to Tahiti, a ten-minute flight. I arranged for a berth at the marina Taina, and for the mechanic to meet us at Passe de Taapuna with his boat, to tow us in. I was lucky to find anyone on a Sunday. I asked John on *Knot Yet* to keep a VHF radio watch for us.

It was dark, but a light south-easterly breeze was blowing as we prepared for sea. The eight-foot rubber dinghy with its 5-horse-power engine was secured on the port side for towing. We beat out of the anchorage, close-tacking amongst the anchored boats in the gathering light, with the unlit beacon just visible. We bore away round the red beacon and ran out of the pass, transferring the dinghy to a long painter. It was a lovely sail close in along the reef in smooth water, until the wind started to fail off Pointe Faaupo, where there was a moderate swell running. We kept radio contact with *Knot Yet* at the marina.

Once we had resecured the dinghy on the port side, Michel climbed in and started the engine. He remained as ballast and towed *Independent Freedom* 'on the hip' the rest of the way to Tahiti, the dinghy behaving well in the swell. There was no mechanic at the pass so we continued through with breakers on both sides to the berth at the marina amongst the super yachts. It was very satisfactory to have done it without outside help.

'Mission control' had responded to my fax sent from the Maeva beach hotel, and arrangements were in hand to fly out a new gearbox. All that was needed was patience with the French Bastille holidays coming up.

Patience was a commodity we needed in large supplies. Michel fitted the gearbox when it arrived from England only to find the bilges full of oil after testing the engine. When it was taken ashore, after waiting a week for the mechanic, the engine was found to be porous and the block condemned. Perkins confirmed that internal electrolysis could have caused it, although it was unusual. A new engine was ordered from New Zealand.

Bureaucratic nightmare

Difficulties are there to be overcome, but they were manifest on this occasion – not least, the bureaucratic nightmare to extend our visas. It entailed three visits to a French lady bureaucrat, letters from the marina, from a mechanic and from myself, also translations and a fee. It took a month! The boat could have remained with no further permission but not us! The frustrations and delays caused me to seriously consider leaving for New Zealand without an engine but with no generator we could not charge the batteries and so would not have had any electronics. It was tempting, but this was 1998 not 1939!

Michel made use of the idle time with a new friend, and very nice she was too. They went off in *Knot Yet* to Bora Bora and from what I could gather had a wonderful time. The super yachts made me feel very uncomfortable and I was glad when we were able to move into the marina. The one saving grace during these months was the excellent French-run restaurant.

Caplin: Tahiti to Tonga

Rarotonga: news of war

Friday 8 September 1939. Arrived here two days ago and heard war had broken out. We knew it was imminent and got the news from some people on the quayside. Went to see the British Resident as, being ex-Navy, needed to report. He didn't know what to do and suggested we should sail on to New Zealand and report there. Lionel will have to leave us here to rejoin the Navy and we shall get down to New Zealand as soon as possible. We were six days from Tahiti, less a few hours – a distance of some 640 miles. It was fairly rough at first. Lionel was desperately seasick and the Mate run down after her flu, but gradually recovering her strength, so this was not too enjoyable a trip.

This island is a gem – six miles long, with five thousand natives and two hundred whites. The liquor is restricted, so the natives are far healthier and happier. They seem a jolly crowd, mostly with a few words of English. Everyone is very friendly;

there is a far nicer atmosphere than in Tahiti, and if it was not for the war we should be loving it. We have been to lunch with Mr Ayson, the Resident, and he motored us round the island. We saw the bay whence the natives sailed to discover New Zealand nine hundred years ago. We lie alongside the pier in a tiny harbour formed by a break in the reef. It does not seem too safe, but local people assure us that it is all right this time of the year. We are going in a few days to Tongatapu, which is on our route to New Zealand.

Tonga.

PASSAGE TO TONGA

21° 57'S 167° 25'W, Sunday 17 September 1939. We are
six days out from Rarotonga, where Lionel departed from us
in great friendliness to rejoin the Navy. The islands ahead of
us are the Tonga, or Friendly Islands. The chief island is
Tongatapu, and port Nuku'alofa. Thence a chain of islets runs
north 160 miles to Vava'u, next biggest island. They are
governed by a native Queen – old dynasty – and under British
protection, and I think with some British advisers.

All our acquaintances at Rarotonga came down to see us
off at 14.00. The harbour is only a tiny cove, so we motored
out with much waving etc. The weather is not too good; one
day was partly head winds and a very lumpy sea, then light
winds and a very heavy southerly swell; the last two days' swell
has gone down a bit and the ship is quieter. The wind has been
very fluky with squalls – not bad ones – and rain, but each
night *Caplin* has looked after herself, so we have had plenty of
sleep. For the last three days we have been ambling along with
the spinnaker making 2 or 3 knots and a strong adverse
current, so that we are nearly a hundred miles behind the
logged distance. Now about 400 (total 840) miles from
Nuku'alofa; the last three days' runs were 84, 37 and 50 miles,
but the war will not be over by the time we make port.

HIDE AND SEEK WITH REEFS

At sea, Monday 18 September 1939. As I wrote the last
words a puff of wind came from the south and the mainsail
gybed, breaking the boom guy. No harm done; it is a piece of
old rope meant to break if the mainsail gets aback. Then the
wind went altogether and we lay without steerage-way till
03.40, when a light southerly woke me up, but what a
morning at daybreak – black heavy clouds and a slight drizzle,
but a nice light breeze giving us 3 knots on our course.

There are some reefs, not too well known, between
Rarotonga and Nuku'alofa. One, Harrans Reef, is on our
course. Reported in 1842 by a schooner; it was reported again,
but position sixty miles different; sailing directions say that it is
marked on the chart in the former position P.D. (position

doubtful). We have been trying hard to keep well to southward, but an unusual current has set us north; seems determined to set us near the reef, but yesterday's sights, good ones, put us comfortably to the south of both recorded positions. If it is too cloudy for sights today, we shall heave-to at night. Sea breaks heavily on the reef so we shall see it all right, and there is now a young moon. We ought to hear it too, if awake.

Quite a lot of ships pass between the Tonga Islands and Rarotonga, and I don't understand why there are not more recent and authentic reports. Perhaps it is like Falcon Island, which has been bobbing up and down for a hundred years; it is a submarine volcano just the other side of Tonga.

INDEPENDENT FREEDOM: TAHITI TO TONGA

POORER BUT NO WISER

Tuesday 8 September to Saturday 19 September 1998.
Tahiti may be beautiful, mysterious and seductive, evocative of erotic tropical romance, but for us it is the place we left considerably poorer but no wiser! The problems of obtaining a new engine, the seven-year-old Perkins having gone porous, and the even more difficult and expensive one of having it fitted, removed the dream and force-fed the reality.

It cost as much to transport the engine from the airport the 5 miles to the marina as it did to transport it from the workshop in Auckland to Tahiti, and as much again to hire a crane and lift it on board *Independent Freedom*. The mechanic at the Marina Taina had delayed and prevaricated so much that it was now September and the hurricane season was approaching. On trials there was considerable vibration and for another US$1,000 he realigned the engine but took out the flexible coupling.

Tuesday 8 September. At 11.30 we motored out of the marina for a new sea trial. There was no vibration below 1,800 r.p.m. so, in consultation with Michel, I was prepared to gamble – to leave it as it was and have the whole thing sorted out in Auckland. In a frenzy of activity, while Michel prepared the yacht for sea, I paid all the bills, reclaimed the bond in

Papeete from Immigration, had the two-month-old port clearance endorsed, shopped at the supermarket, returned the hire car which had been damaged in the car park, and made it back to the marina in time to save our daylight out through the Passe Taapuna in a calm.

GLAD TO BE AWAY

I checked the deviation of the compass on the pass leads, as the new engine might have altered it. About 8 miles from Tahiti the engine was turned off and we sailed close-hauled in a light westerly. It was a lovely night, the lights on Tahiti bright, cascading down the mountain side like rivers of silver. We were glad to be away.

The weather was mixed with the occasional squall but a fair wind gave respectable days' runs exceeding 5 knots. Four days later we sailed close along the cliff of the north shore of Mauke Island, part of the Cook group, in heavy rain. There were people walking on the narrow surrounding reef. Once clear of the island it breezed up, the southeasterly swell increased and the tricolour masthead lantern and anchor light blew off the mast.

Sunday 13 September. The next day, Sunday, we closed Rarotonga in the rain passing close to the entrance of the harbour where there were a couple of yachts. It looked no bigger than my grandfather's description of 58 years ago. It was here they were told war had broken out in Europe and if it was not for that they would be loving it, finding the atmosphere far nicer than Tahiti. However, we had a date in Tonga with 'mission control', namely my brother Edward and his wife Philippa. It was tempting to call in but having been so delayed in Tahiti there was no time to stop, so missed this 'gem', which was a pity.

Once we were clear of the island it blew a gale for two days, and on Monday the day's run was 164 miles, with only the double-reefed foresail set. It was rough with a heavy swell but the yacht went very well and was really very comfortable, although the rolling became a little boring.

The mainsail was not hoisted until just after noon four

days later. On Saturday, we sailed in bright sunshine, for the first time in more than a week, into Nuku'alofa via the Piha Passage. The 'Pacific Guide' suggests 'should not be attempted without first class information', a challenge I had to accept! In the event the leads and buoys were in place. I had a minor panic when the GPS failed and had to use the hand bearing compass to fix the position.

CAPLIN: ARRIVAL AT NUKU'ALOFA, TONGATAPU GROUP, TONGA

Tuesday 26 September 1939. We have arrived at Nuku'alofa and have crossed the date line and skipped a day. It has been an unpleasant passage; there was big swell and bad motion all the time. We were continually reefing and unreefing, but *Caplin* did her best for us and kept some sort of course without ever being steered; every night we both turned in but taking twelve days to cover 840 miles is slow. We had a strong current against us and had actually sailed 1,060 miles through the water. Mate has been very seedy with indigestion and sick as well and is rather played out. It was worrying for me as well as grim for her, but as before she was definitely recovering by the time we got in. Now she has gone off to stay with Mr Armstrong, the Consul. He and his wife are most charming and friendly. We can wait here for a time – perhaps a month, when the weather will be better for our trip to New Zealand. This is a bad anchorage and yesterday the *Caplin* was jumping about so that I did not like to leave her till the evening; but I got the Mate ashore in a native boat – she was looking better already. I dined with the Armstrongs.

I enjoyed bacon and eggs for breakfast, having had neither of these foods for ten days. Today the wind has gone down and the ship is quieter, but it is raining steadily.

Sunday 1 October. We have been enjoying a very pleasant rest here; the Mate is staying with the Armstrongs, and I go up for dinner in the evening. I've been able to do some of the usual odd jobs aboard, mending sails and installing some new rigging. On Tuesday we propose going off to explore the Northern Islands.

ENTERTAINING ROYALTY

We have been entertaining Royalty. I had an introduction to the Prince Consort – sounds grand doesn't it? As well as being husband of the Queen, he is Prime Minister and head of the government, and a full-blooded Tongan, educated in New Zealand I think and speaks quite good English; he is a middle-aged, huge man and fairly stout. I had an interview with him at his office, and a day or two later he came to tea on board; he was much interested in the ship and a pleasant-mannered knowledgeable man. He calls himself Tungi, but I think that is his title and not his name.

Nuku'alofa is the capital town, situated on the island of Tongatapu, which is 18 miles long and 5 miles wide, flat and covered with coconut palms. It is a scattered sort of village, with an ornate wooden palace, a few European bungalows and stores, and for a mile or two round native houses of wood or thatch; all are very tidy, with the grass cut and good roads. At dinner one night we met another Tongan – one of their nobles, dressed like us in a dinner jacket, but I could not get much him to talk much. He is one of the ministers. The upper class Tongans think a good deal of themselves and have pedigrees going back for hundreds of years but, in clothes and conversation, they have a layer of English culture. I hope we may see more of the real native life in the Northern Islands.

It has been quite smooth in the anchorage the last few days, but this morning a little swell is rolling in. However, I don't think there will be any really bad weather this time of year. We are going to motor round the island today and see the flying foxes, Moraes (burial grounds) and rocks spouting water on the south shore. Tomorrow we shall be busy getting in stores and preparing for sea.

INDEPENDENT FREEDOM: NUKU'ALOFA

FLYING FOXES AND CAPTAIN COOK

Saturday 19 September to Thursday 25 September 1998. We had assistance, mooring Mediterranean-style, in the small boat and fishing harbour, and were pleased with the 5.7-

knot average speed for the 1,505 miles from Tahiti. It had been rough but the speed made up for the discomfort! We had crossed the dateline, so we advanced the clocks one hour and the date one day. There was no harbour in 1939 and *Caplin* had some uncomfortable days in the 'bad' anchorage.

I dressed up in collar and tie and called on the British High Commissioner at the pleasant Residency. I told him about my grandfather entertaining the Prince Consort and asked him if the present King would be interested. I was told "No, His Majesty operates on an International level", so I did not pursue the matter any further.

My brother Edward and his wife Philippa arrived at the airport on time. I had hired a car and we toured Tongatapu for the day, which was fun. We too saw the flying foxes, trees black with them all squeaking away, climbed over burial mounds and watched the blow-holes spouting water. We stopped at the memorial to Captain Cook, who had visited the islands in 1773, 1774 and 1777, and also at the one commemorating the visit of Queen Elizabeth II. The island is very 'Third World' and different from Tahiti – the people are more friendly for a start. There is much more evidence of the land being worked, just as Captain Cook had found. The people are very much their own people; no doubt not having been colonized helps. We dined at the Dateline, which is a rather sombre hotel, and walked back to the dinghy which we had moored at the fish dock.

CAPLIN: NORTHWARDS THROUGH THE FRIENDLY ISLES (TONGA)

NOMUKA GROUP, TONGA ISLANDS

Friday 6 October 1939. I am worried about the Mate. She consulted the doctor at Nuku'alofa and he did not think there was anything basically wrong. He gave her medicine, and the week at the Armstrongs' did her a lot of good. Mr Armstrong is about the middle fifties – small and cheerful. Mrs Armstrong is perhaps ten years younger – has been very pretty and still retains much charm of manner. I think she enjoyed having the Mate to stay. The other Europeans – New Zealanders and Australians – are very pleasant. Mate came back with me after dinner on Monday night, and we were under way at 06.30 next morning. There was a light wind and pleasant sailing for a few miles until we were clear of the reefs, and Mate got breakfast while I navigated. When clear we could just sail the course close-hauled, but the wind freshened and with a nasty chop we were battering into it uncomfortably. Mate felt the motion but she wasn't sick.

The first island, Kelefesia, is forty miles ahead and it is touch and go if we should make it by dark. This island is three-quarters of a mile long with fringing reef. At the north end on the west (lee) side, the chart marked an opening in the reef. A Tongan sailor had told me one could moor there, but the chart showed no soundings, just a small white blank with the projecting reef – awash – on each side.

At first it seemed impossible for us to make it by daylight, but the log showed we were making good progress. At 15.30 I sighted the island, a tiny speck on the horizon – probably twelve miles off. It quickly rose out of the sea as we approached. As the sun set we were close to the island and I could see the breakers on the reef on each side and the smooth-looking cove ahead. A bearing of the island kept me in the middle of the cove, but I had no idea of the depth in it nor if there might be rocks. And in these waters the coral heads are so steep that the lead-line gives no warning. With the sun high and behind, one would see the shoals clearly, but now the sun had just dipped. We dropped our sails and gave a push with the engine, stopping and starting so as to just keep steerage way. Large breakers on the reef each side thundered alarmingly. We could see the bottom under us and it looked deep.

'WOODEN SHIPS AND IRON MEN'

Just within the entrance I registered five fathoms and hastily dropped anchor. We dragged a yard or two and then brought up. What lump of coral had the anchor got round and should we ever get it up? However, I had a line to the crown of the anchor with a cork on the end, so if the fluke was hooked in a rock it might still be possible to pull it out by the line to the crown (buoy rope). The sea was quite smooth except for a long low swell coming in, to which we rolled a bit, but not too badly. However, I did not like it – at about seventy yards on one side and a hundred and fifty on the other the breakers piled up on the reef, and their thundering was alarming. We seemed reasonably safe – I did not think the wind would shift and if we dragged it would probably be out to open sea, but I felt anxious; 'wooden ships and iron men' sounds well, but I am really a bit timid. Well, we had supper comfortably enough and turned in dead tired.

I looked out during the night several times and found the ship lying safely enough. It was a lovely fine morning. We had breakfast at 06.00 and went ashore to explore this desert island. It is of coral limestone with a 120-foot ridge in the middle, all covered with trees. We landed on a lovely sandy beach. No sign of inhabitants, but tracks in the sand of what Mate said was a dog so we cut sticks from a bush; we had not brought our firearms! We started to walk round the island. A hundred yards brought us to the north tip of the island, and then we saw a stick – obviously cut with a machete – sticking upright in the sand. A few more yards and we saw through the trees a house. It was unoccupied, but contained tools and cups; big clumps of red lilies (amaryllis?) were flowering, and bananas, pawpaws etc. growing, but none were in fruit except the coconuts. The house had obviously been occupied recently and was in good repair.

We continued along the beach, but as soon as *Caplin* was out of sight I was anxious about her. Cliffs prevented us making a complete circuit and we had to return; there was *Caplin* quite happily at anchor. We climbed a little hill and had a lovely view of the tree tops to one side and the reef-strewn waters, green and blue, on the other. Then we returned to the house, pulled down some coconuts with a long harpoon we found in the house, and drank the coconut water, but what a job they are to husk when one does not know the knack. It was just lovely exploring this desert island.

We came back to the ship and got under way. There was not much room to manoeuvre so I ran up the foresail. With the mainsail set, the ship takes quite a bit of space to pay off before the wind. Clear of the cove we found the wind fresh and a big sea. The chart marks 'blind rollers' which I think means a very big swell probably caused by an uneven bottom – though possibly quite deep. Poor little *Caplin* rolled and rolled. We had to run several miles to leeward, clear of outlying reefs, before I could get the mainsail up, and it was blowing so fresh we needed four or five rolls which are awkward to put in if the sail is not hoisted right up. The wind freshened up to perhaps force 6, with driving rain – most unpleasant, but when we were well clear of the islands and past the blind rollers the sea was not too bad.

NOMUKA: A PRECARIOUS ANCHORAGE

Our next harbour was now about twelve miles away (21 miles altogether) but with the rain storms and strong wind it was not too pleasant. My anxiety was that our harbour (Nomuka) might not be tenable in the strong wind. It is formed by two islands about a mile apart. The strait between them is open to ESE winds, but for half its width it is protected by a coral reef. There is no protection from the wind, but there should be fair protection to leeward of the reef from the sea. The pilot book said the anchorage was well protected in easterly winds. In the northern island there were two little coves in the fringing reef where I had been told one could anchor; places one could feel one's way into in a light wind, but impossible when it is blowing hard. As soon as we got clear of the reefs round Kelefesia, Mate had gone to lie down. With the hard wind abeam, *Caplin* tore along and in spite of the passing showers and leaden skies I should have enjoyed the sail if we had been sure of the harbour ahead.

Another hour and Nomuka Island showed up ahead. A little later I could see the breakers on the reefs which surround it. I sailed to leeward of the two islands and then had to call out the Mate to help. First to take in the jib, because with four rolls in the mainsail (nearly close reefed) the ship would not stay (on course) with her two full headsails. It is much easier to take in the jib if one has someone at the helm to keep the ship dead before the wind. This lessens the force of the wind, so the sail rolls up quite easily. If the boat is head to wind, the sail flogs viciously and one cannot roll it up; one has to lower it. If I had been single handed I would have taken it in long before, and probably set a small one in its place. Well, now with only a reefed mainsail and a staysail we had hardly enough canvas to plug to windward. The yacht stayed without hesitation, but I was careful to plan the tack in plenty of time, so if we missed stays there would still be plenty of room to gybe round instead. However, we made very slow progress and after several tacks seemed to have made very little ground.

The island on each side had the usual fringing reef so we could not approach either of them very closely. I started the engine so that we could lie a point closer to the wind, make better progress and be sure of tacking. Running to leeward, or if the wind is abeam, the ship goes well with only a rag of a sail, but to beat to windward one must carry all the sail one possibly can – there is so much windage on the hull and sides to overcome. Mate steered while I handled the sheets and took bearings, but a 'man and girl' team is very short handed for a hard beat in such narrow waters. The larger sails of *Caplin* compared to *Emanuel* make quite a difference.

We had barely a couple of miles to go. The engine and close-reefed sails make a splendid rig for getting to windward, and between the islands the sea was fairly smooth. I could see the reef half way across the entrance and to my enormous relief the sea appeared smooth enough to anchor. Otherwise, there would have been nothing for it but to run to open sea to leeward and heave to for the night. It would have been necessary to run several miles to leeward so that one would not forereach on to the reefs in the night, and at daylight one might have been so far to leeward that it could have been dark before one got back. There are more islands to the north, but pilotage is intricate and only possible in fine weather. The only sure harbour is 120 miles away. It is the land and not the sea that is one's anxiety. In mid ocean one can always let the ship look after herself and rest when one feels like it.

The difficulty now was to find shallow enough water to anchor without getting too close to the reefs. Working by bearings of the shore I approached a spot where the chart showed three fathoms. Then lee-o, stop engine and leave staysail aback, while I get a sounding, but the yacht is rapidly forereaching away from the land and I get no bottom at about nine fathoms, and beyond this the line to which I had added a lengthening piece tangles. By the time I get it clear we are still further into mid-channel and no bottom. We gybe round, start the engine to ensure staying and try again. We really were short-handed; we needed a third person to sound continuously, while I managed sheets and engine, and Mate steered.

We try again and get a good sounding this time, but still no bottom. A little to windward the water looked greenish and that will be shallow enough to anchor, but there is a breaking shoal to leeward I must look out for, and another suspicious dark patch to windward, which – I think! – is the one marked on the chart. In we go again and into the green (as opposed to blue) water. I can see the two shoals above mentioned; one is directly to windward and the other well clear of us to shoreward and to leeward. This time I get five fathoms. Telling the Mate to haul in the lead line I jump forward and drop the anchor. I let the staysail halyards go and Mate rushes foreward to help. I can now see the bottom quite clearly. I tend the winch with one hand and help drag down the furiously flogging staysail with the other. The Mate lowers the mainsail while I let out about twenty fathoms of chain and the ship brings up. A boat anchored in shore remains in line with a tree, showing that we are not dragging.

A VICIOUS-LOOKING DARK CLOUD

We get the boom in the crutches and start making up the mainsail – everything to lessen windage and reduce strain on the cable. Then I see a vicious looking dark cloud to windward and close. Is this going to be an unprecedented squall? I get the second anchor out in case. The Mate finishes putting the ties round the mainsail and I grovel under the cockpit to get the kedge anchor; coils of rope, trammel net and various oddments are flung into the cabin. The kedge rope is on the forecastle all ready. We give the ship a push ahead with the engine and drop the kedge. The squall has broken – not too much more wind but sheets of rain. We are both pretty wet, but the ship seems safe, pitching a little but quiet enough below. Mate throws herself on the bunk, worn out. For a few minutes I finish tidying up on deck and then I come below too.

Poor child, she was desperately tired. It had been pretty rough virtually all the way from Tahiti. We had had no what I might call 'pleasant' sailing. I got her a cup of tea and made some toast. She remained on her bunk for the rest of the day, but at supper seemed better. I made an omelette and heated asparagus and she had a good meal so I am hoping she is all right. We turned in after supper and had a comfortable night.

The weather was much the same this morning, still blowing hard but I think the ship is reasonably safe, though I wish she were insured. Mate woke up at 06.30 with a bad headache. It is now 11.00; she took some aspirin an hour ago and is still in her bunk. One wants to be tough for this sort of life; I'm wondering if it is proving too much for her. There is a little more motion at the present, I think because the tide is higher – a five- or six-foot rise and fall, so that a little more sea comes over the reef to windward, but I think we are reasonably safe.

When I broke off writing, we were anchored rather precariously at Numuka. The wind moderated a little the next morning, so we sailed across the strait and were finally piloted through the reef to a tiny harbour off the main island of Nomuka. There was one white man, a rather disgruntled storekeeper from Yorkshire. Next day, the weather moderated still more and we sailed through the Huapai (Ha'apai) group, finally reaching another very exposed anchorage off Harfeeva Island.

On again the next morning, but there was still a big swell; we looked for an anchorage in Ofolanga, but were scared by a huge surf on the reef, so we sailed on through the night. It soon fell calm so we lay idly till daylight. There was a light wind the next morning; we made some progress and then used the engine for 6 hours so as to reach Neiafu. Rather fun motoring for a couple of hours through a landlocked channel in the dark, but no shoals so quite safe. Mate is gradually recovering, but still a bit weak and run down. I've had some anxious moments about her and shall be glad to reach New Zealand, where a change of climate should really set her up.

INDEPENDENT FREEDOM: NUKU'ALOFA TO OFOLANGA ISLAND

WHALES AND A RACE

Thursday 25 September to Tuesday 13 October 1998.
Port clearance is necessary to move between the different groups of islands in the Tongan Kingdom. I obtained it on Thursday morning and got rid of the car. After watering at the fish dock we motored out of the harbour and hoisted the double-reefed foresail and triple-reefed mainsail. It was smooth-water sailing inside the reefs, but once clear and out into the Pacific it was rough and hard on the wind for the next 26 hours the wind east force 7/8. It was bad luck on our new ship-mates, Edward and Philippa, who were still suffering from jet lag. No one felt like any dinner! The weather was even worse than in 1939, when the Mate on *Caplin* was so exhausted.

Michel cooked a huge scrambled egg supper when we anchored the next evening off Kapa Island. I tried to get clearance the next day at Neiafu, the town on Vava'u, but the Customs were away for the weekend. We sailed round to the sheltered anchorage on the other side of Kapa Island in a near gale, but the waters were sheltered and smooth so it was great sailing. The snorkelling was quite good and the water clear. A man and a young boy were selling black coral and shells from a dugout canoe. We attended a Tongan feast with dancing in the evening; it was interesting, although one of the European 'guests' had rather too much to drink and made a play for the ladies, which was not much fun for them. The older gentlemen found it difficult sitting crossed legged on the hard ground, and there was insufficient light to see what one was eating!

The next few days were spent sailing amongst the islands, which was great fun in the sheltered waters, using a different anchorage each night. Michel dived with the *Mango* people – we had last seen them in the Galapagos, and we snorkelled in the clear waters. We sighted whales on two occasions – very exciting, especially when a mother and calf came close to the yacht. We dined ashore at some pretty basic and rustic places, including an eco-friendly one spoilt by electric light. Some of the landing places required considerable agility but it was all interesting and fun. On Friday we raced in the local charter company Moorings race and came first of the cruising yachts; the race was followed by a jolly evening ashore with Tongan dancing.

Monday 5 October. I obtained clearance out of Neiafu, and we had a fine-weather sail in bright sunshine to the Ha'apai group with just a single reef. *Independent Freedom* sailed so fast that we crept into the lee of the reef of Ofolanga Island at 01.00; that was where *Caplin* had been scared of the surf. In 1898, *HMS Penguin* found the anchorage sheltered from winds north through east, and so it proved again. The reef and sand on the cay were visible in the bright moonlight and we let go the anchor in nine metres.

It was a beautiful morning and the swell was breaking on the reef close by. Whales were seen thrashing the water with their tails as we beat through the reefs to the little harbour at Pangai. It was built with Australian aid. There was just room to anchor inside, clear of the small Naval base and the swinging basin for the supply ships.

We hired a very ramshackle taxi for a tour of the island, crossing the airstrip and the causeway to the next island north, all palm-tree plantations. The village was very poor and dusty. We dined at an extremely rustic resort with a plastic table cloth on the communal table. Two agricultural aid workers from New Zealand and an old 'rustic' European, together with the Tongan owner's family, making up the company. It was interesting and fun, and for Edward and Philippa as different from England as it possibly could be.

CAPLIN: VAVA'U, TONGA

JUST LIKE THE STORY BOOKS

Thursday 12 October 1939. We have at last been seeing some native life, just like the story books. Vava'u is the most northern of the Tonga group, several biggish islands a few miles long, and one winds among them to the perfect landlocked harbour of Neiafu, surrounded by hills up to 600 feet. We carried a letter to Mrs Cecilia Akauola, wife of a Tongan minister for police we had met at Nuku'alofa. We heard she was staying on her island of Taunga (or Taonga?), several miles away, so yesterday we sailed down from Neiafu to see her. Her husband is a full-blooded Tongan; she is rather a pretty woman of twenty-four, with white blood, but it doesn't show. She was educated for five years in New Zealand and has travelled there and in Australia, so that she is a comparatively cultivated woman. Being nobles, they are entertained by the Governor when in New Zealand.

We anchored off her island, a strip perhaps two miles long, covered with the usual coconut palms and surrounded by a gleaming white beach. There is a fringing reef which sticks out three-quarters of a mile, but a break in this on the lee side makes quite a good anchorage. We arrived about noon and were in the middle of lunch when we received a message from Cecilia asking us ashore, but the boy's English was not too good, and there seemed no reason to hurry. After half an hour a second message came so we went ashore.

First we sat in her verandah and were introduced to various relatives or retainers – no English spoken except by Cecilia. Then we walked a quarter of a mile to where a shelter of tapa (native cloth) had been erected near the beach; there were mats beneath the shelter for us to sit on. Presently two men appeared carrying a huge basket of woven leaves, a long narrow affair, one man at each end. This was put down in front of us and we ate what we could. Fish, chicken, breadfruit and yams, coconuts to drink, and a sort of sweet of breadfruit in syrup. We ate with our fingers plus a stray knife or two. Cecilia, ourselves and a few more elite sat in the shelter. Perhaps it is not fair to say I would have preferred yacht food, as we were not really hungry. Most of the remaining islanders, who are Akauola's retainers or tenants, sat outside.

They finished what we left, then a troupe of young men and girls, and children – eight or twelve – paraded round dancing. Music was provided by drumming on a kerosene tin. There was an interesting war dance, which involved twisting wooden spears and posturing. Dress singlets, pareus (loin cloths) and garlands of flowers. Then two young girls dressed in raffia skirts, with garlands round their heads and leaves on their wrists, danced – really very pretty and rather seductive; between dances they sang Tongan songs. A shame we had no cine camera – words alone are not enough.

There are no whites on Taunga and the natives have kept their old customs to some extent, except they are all Christianized and much under the thumb of their clergy. Taunga has a Tongan minister.

Today we took Cecilia and several Tongans for a sail and picnic on another island several miles away. I think she has enjoyed our company. Tomorrow we go back to Neiafu for a few days, and then work our way back through the Ha'apai group to Nuku'alofa. We expect to reach Auckland about mid-November.

HA'ANO, HA'APAI GROUP

Friday 20 October 1939. Vavaa (or Vava'u) was delightful. We were taken for a walk and a motor drive round the island. At five hundred feet high one gets wonderful views. The doctor had to visit an outlying island, and took us, his wife and another woman, and we made a picnic of it. Various natives gave us presents – mats and fruit, and rings which they make out of coconut or a toothbrush handle, and inlay a tiny fragment of silver – no intrinsic value but rather pretty and pleasing for the Mate. We left Neiafu at 04.00 – rather an effort, turning out at 03.15. Some ten or twelve miles to the open sea, with a strong trade wind from the SE. We could barely steer the course, through the rain and a big sea, so we turned back and found a very pleasant anchorage a few miles short of Neiafu.

Next morning we tried again and had a lovely sail, some sixty miles with a light beam wind to this island (Ha'ano). It is the first in the Ha'apai group; Lifuka, the main island, is ten miles further. We only made the anchorage just as it was getting dark; a break in the fringing reef and the colour of the water were all we had to avoid shoals, but I got a sounding of eight fathoms and dropped the anchor. The difficulty with all these anchorages is to get shallow enough water to anchor, and for this we have to go fairly close in, steering by the breakers and the colour of the water. Then, when we find the bottom with the lead-line, the anchor must go down quickly before one drifts off into deep water – as we did with Cecilia on our picnic. The anchor then hung at the end of twenty fathoms of chain, which is quite an extra weight to heave back in, but the Tongan boys helped us with it.

MATE'S FATAL BEAUTY

This island is two or three miles long and half a mile wide, with two hundred natives. Several canoes visited last night, but only a few words of English; they are well-mannered folk and go quite readily when we make signs. One likes to be civil and not hurt their feelings, but Mate's fatal beauty has just brought a canoe back this morning with baskets to give 'Magalita' and he wants to wait till she wakes up, like Pointe à Pierre in Trinidad, except that, there, they used to swim off after work.

INDEPENDENT FREEDOM: HA'APAI GROUP, TONGA

Thursday 13 October 1998. How my grandfather would have loved to have had an echo sounder, to just sit there and look at a machine giving one the depth instead of having to physically heave the lead – worth an extra crew when coming in to these reef anchorages.

Voleval Island, the next one south, has a fantastically beautiful sandy beach – clean, white and empty, backed by green palm trees. It was perfectly sheltered from the prevailing winds. We only spent one night there before returning to Pangai. Alongside the jetty we saw *Opa*, an open boat with a cuddy forward. Inside was a parrot in a cage looking very bedraggled. Sitting amongst the forty-gallon drums of petrol was a large dog which looked as though it had suffered a heart attack. The two Europeans asked us if we would maintain a radio watch with them the next day, while they continued their voyage to Vava'u. I personally would not have crossed the Serpentine in it and they admitted they had almost been swamped on the way from Nuku'alofa, hence the requirement for a radio watch!

When we set off with two reefs in each sail, there was

more south in the wind, and that gave us a reach back to Vava'u. The purple-painted *Opa*, with the parrot and dog, set off at the same time. Once we were clear of the island, it was rough and the wind increased to force 7, although the bright sun was warm. *Opa* had an electrical problem and 13.00 was the last time she was heard on the radio. We debated whether to raise the alarm but decided to wait. We picked up a mooring in the lagoon at Hunga after averaging 6.9 knots for the 74 miles from Pangai – a fast sail. *Opa* had arrived safely in Neiafu with the parrot and dog; one of her engines had been knocked out by a wave.

On Saturday, once we had sailed clear of Hunga, it was still blowing a near gale. We anchored in the pretty anchorage close to the shore of Tapana Island. This was the island owned by Cecilia who entertained my grandfather and his Mate to a feast. Having no introduction, we did not go ashore.

Kenetu Island, reached by an intricate passage through reefs and shoals, whose eastern coast faces the Pacific, has a bar but it was shut. The German woman who owned it said she was taking a year off! However, the visit was still worthwhile for the quite spectacular scene on the windward coast. There was no beach, just a cliff with a series of coves. The great Pacific rollers curled straight into the bays creating a maelstrom of hissing seething water, flinging spray high into the air, the backwash hurling itself onto the next wave. It was a truly amazing sight.

Today we went alongside the wharf at Paradise Hotel for a farewell breakfast, on the verandah overlooking the harbour. It was with much regret that Edward and Philippa set off on the long journey back to England. They had visited 21 anchorages and sailed 518 miles.

Caplin: Ha'apai Group, Tonga

Yachting the proper way

Saturday 21 October 1939. Lifuka, three or four miles long and half a mile wide, is one of a chain of islands of the Ha'apai Group running north and south. They are joined by reefs to windward, so there is a good lee on the west side, off which is a regular maze of reefs but, with a good chart and some of the reefs beaconed, it is fairly easy to find one's way in. There is a narrow channel through the fringing reef which leads into a little harbour half a mile long and 150 yards wide. The sandy beach is only 50 yards from us. Outside, the fringing reef is just awash with a gentle murmur of breakers – soothing and better than the frightening angry roar which we endured at Kelefesia. There is a wharf and various houses and sheds, quite a big village and three or four whites.

The island is quite flat and covered with the usual palms, but the village is on open grass. We had taken most of the day drifting the ten miles from Ha'ano. Gas is nearly three shillings per gallon so I did not want to motor, but a few hundred yards from the crack in the reef we lost steerage way and had to motor. In spite of all the beacons and buoys we touched the bottom because we did not keep close enough to one of the buoys, but we slid off without losing way. As usual, a crowd of natives came aboard when we anchored.

We went ashore and presented our letter of introduction to the chief trader, who had a very polished wife. After tea we came aboard and played the Mozart sonata. Mate had a bad headache earlier in the day but has recovered. I am anxious to get her down to New Zealand for a change of climate. She does not look well, and her face has a pinched look.

Dopey (having turned out to be male not female) has twice fallen overboard while we have been shore. He swam to the bows and clung to the bobstay, where we found him shrieking on our return. The sun is moving south and the days are getting hot. We have a Tongan flag which we fly as a courtesy gesture, though we forgot it yesterday. This is the first group of South Sea Islands which we have really explored. Quite a lot of sailing, and anchorage every night (except one), which is the proper way to yacht. There is a quite amusing history of the islands, 'Diversions of a Prime Minister' by Basil Thompson, and we have a small book on the islands given us by Tongi, with maps.

A crowd of children swam out to us yesterday – jolly smiling little brown creatures. There is quite a lot of visiting between the islands, and all the men are used to boats so that they are very interested in *Caplin*. So far we have found them pleasantly mannered, but we have to tell them when to go! We have learnt Tongan for 'good morning' and 'thank you'. It is a quaint language, and to me sounds just a jumble of vowels, but Mate would soon pick it up with her keen ear.

Monday 23 October. The last day or two has been the usual social round, tea party on board etc. No one very exciting, but it was interesting meeting a Miss Baker — an elderly lady, looking as if she had just stepped out of an English home. Her father was a notorious Reverend Baker who came to the islands as a missionary in 1860, gradually became powerful and was made Prime Minister, then apparently went to seed and was deported by the High Commissioner in 1890. We have also met the Governor, an educated Tongan. He is building a boat and wants to sail around the Pacific, but cannot navigate and there is no-one in the islands to teach him. He and another Tongan have been having lessons from me, but one cannot do much in a few lessons.

KAVA DRINKING CEREMONY

Thursday 26 October 1939. We have seen another interesting bit of native life. From Lifuka we sailed to Vika Island, some ten miles. We took a Tongan we had met, actually mate of a trading cutter. Vika has some seven hundred natives, no whites. When we landed all the children followed us — probably had never seen a white woman before. The chief sights are some cannon taken a hundred years ago from a European ship, and the burial mounds. We had a letter for the chief, or noble, but did not find him. However, later he came out to the ship, rather a fine-looking middle-aged man, but no English, so conversation through our interpreter was rather formal. We gathered we were to go ashore next morning at 07.30.

We were taken up to the Chief's house, quite a fine example of native building. Inside was a framework of polished palm trunks, joined by rather ornamental lashings of native fibre; the roof was made of very carefully plaited coconut leaves. It made a biggish and tall room. One end was screened with a curtain of tapa; the floor covered with native mats – all very clean and airy. A group of men were sitting in an oval ring, cross-legged on the ground. Malubo (the noble) at the head. At the opposite end were some women and a big wooden bowl. We were instructed to sit down in a space in the ring that had been left for us. We had been invited to a Kava Drinking.

Kava is a pounded root mixed with water. I don't think it is alcoholic, but it probably contains some drug – quite innocuous. There is a very elaborate ceremonial. On the Chief's left sits his attendant, who acts as a sort of Master of Ceremonies. The attendant called out some formula, and a woman from the other end walked across the ring and picked up a bunch of withered-looking roots. These she pounded between two stones before putting them into the bowl. Then water was put in and mixed up. Each operation was done to the intoned command of the attendant. Our Tongan friend gave us a rough translation of the formula. Finally the attendant said 'Kava is made'.

With a bundle of raffia used as a sponge, the Kava maker transferred some of the drink to a polished coconut shell. A rather pretty girl took the shell and, holding it in front of her, stood up at the foot of the ring. A man in the ring near her sang a few words – 'Here is Kava and who for'. The attendant answered 'The Kava is for . . .', mentioning some name. The person named then clapped his hands and the girl walked across the ring and gave him the coconut shell and he drank. The order of drinking is formal.

Apparently the attendant drinks first to see if it is poisoned, and the same ritual follows for each person. The Chief drinks second. Then, as far as I can remember, one or two natives and then Marguerite, some more natives and then me. They had only given me very little; it tasted rather like soapy water and we felt no effect from it.

We talked a little – mostly direct personal questions – 'How old are you?', 'Have you many children?' etc. Then another round of drinks as before. Then native food was brought in for Marguerite and me, in the usual long coconut-leaf basket, covered with banana leaves. Before we ate they said a Christian grace (in Tongan). Chicken, yam and sweet potatoes, and coconuts to drink. A woman sat in front of us fanning the basket to keep off the flies. I was pretty hungry – we had purposely not eaten breakfast so we could put up a fair show – but I actually prefer using knife and fork to my fingers. A little more talk; the Chief regretted he had nothing to give us and then presented a huge roll of tapa. Mate had already been draped in a native skirt.

We sat a little longer and then the Chief said, through our interpreter, that if we wanted to go, we should please ourselves. We took the hint and departed with much smiling and shaking hands. This Kava drinking ceremony goes back hundreds of years. Basil Thompson describes it, and it was most interesting to have seen it; I don't suppose many white women have. They all know their part in the ceremony, and go through with it without any trace of self consciousness. They are all used to boats, and know about sailing, so I think we have considerable prestige on account of our voyage.

Back to Nuku'alofa

Saturday 4 November 1939. We stopped at two or three more islands, working south, and then made a night passage back here to the capital. We are getting ready for our trip to New Zealand, planning to sail on 6 November. I expect it will take about eighteen days, but it might be anything, as for the last few hundred miles we will be south of the trades into the westerlies. I shall take a westward course till about north of New Zealand and then work south.

Tongan agricultural show

The chief interest here has been an agricultural show; very well run little affair, for two days. I've been to lots of them in England; it is rather funny to see coconuts, bananas, yams etc. on show instead of apples. The competitions were amusing. Making a light by rubbing two sticks together; the winner took about ten seconds. There was also jumping, log cutting and copra cutting. The natives were excited, just like children. Every boy, when sixteen, gets an allotment of eight acres: yams, bananas etc. grow with little labour so there is ample food for everyone. If he wants a house, his friends assemble and help to build one of coconut leaves, so naturally everyone is smiling and happy-go-lucky.

Some of the native basket work is lovely. We have acquired several as presents, as well as native cloth, a turtle shell, rings and so on. We have got involved in the usual social round but no one is very interesting except the Armstrongs, who are charming. The Mate's health is better and she seems to have recovered her strength. I was quite worried about her.

INDEPENDENT FREEDOM: BACK SOUTH TO NUKU'ALOFA

Thursday 29 October 1998. It was time to think of the voyage south. I intended, like *Caplin*, to make Nuku'alofa the departure port for New Zealand. Some minor repairs were done on the bimini and mainsail. I went on an enjoyable day tour although, much to my embarrassment, I suffered an attack of vertigo on the hill and had difficulty getting down again. The view had been magnificent over the 'land locked entrance' to the harbour. Faith, an eco expert with whom I had some interesting arguments about the new environmental elite, joined us on *Independent Freedom* for the passage south through the islands. We completed the Friday evening race but did not do so well this time! The Tongan dancing was very much as my grandfather had described it although the music was provided by a band, not a tin can.

Saturday 17 October. After clearing out and returning the dinghy lent us while our own was repaired (after it had been punctured by a nail in the Moorings dock), we set sail. I noticed an RCC burgee in the rigging of a yacht and had a quick chat with David Mitchell on board *Ondarina* as we sailed past. Michel dived into Mariners cave, subject of a Tongan love tale, while I hung off, and the night was spent at anchor off Langito Island. Full sail was hoisted early next morning for a very pleasant run down to Pangai and dinner at the Sandy Beach resort.

The snorkelling was good off the reef at Voleval. We motored in bright sunshine across the pass to Uia Island, where the anchor was let go near the village. It was very poor, although there were two churches; the Tongans are still under the thumb of their clergy, as noted by my grandfather. There were many pigs but nothing moved in the afternoon heat. Faith was in her element, and struck up a conversation with a woman taking her ease in front of her house.

SWIMMING WITH WHALES

On the way to Oau Island whales were sighted close to. Suddenly the boat was devoid of crew: Michel and Faith had jumped overboard and swam with the whale and her calf. Half an hour later they were back on board bubbling with excitement. I tried to do the same, but the whales had fled! It was a beautiful sunny day with good visibility and the volcano on Kao Island was erupting. It was a beat into the anchorage which was surrounded by reefs and we anchored under sail. The sun set with a green flash and there was a new moon.

KELEFESIA'S BLIND ROLLERS

It was a lovely day making Kelefesia Island where *Caplin* visited bound north and were disturbed by the thunder of the surf on the reef. The white (guano) rock on Kefukana reef was left to starboard and we sailed inside the breakers on the rock off Nuku Island, thence through the 'blind rollers' to the anchorage only to find three other yachts at anchor. Oh the joys of GPS! *Caplin* had only just saved their daylight and it must have been very tense. The 'blind rollers' are sudden breaking swells which appeared and disappeared for no apparent reason.

Early next morning the 'rollers' were even bigger as we sailed past and made a fast passage to Nuku'alofa. Kelefesia Island from the south looked like a battleship with breakers as the bow wave, the hill climbed by my grandfather and my aunt in the middle as the bridge, the cliff at the north end as stern, and the last tree as the flagstaff. Faith had a date back in Neiafu and left on arrival.

CAPLIN: THE PASSAGE TO NEW ZEALAND

26°22'S 177°49'E, Friday 10 November 1939. We crossed
the 180° meridian a couple of days ago and so are really now
more than half way round the world! We left Nuku'alofa last
Monday 6 November at 12.30, and had a pleasant sail for ten
miles protected by reefs. We then emerged on to open sea
through a channel a quarter of a mile wide in the reef – big
breakers thundering on each side; the sea was smooth and
there was a light southerly wind, but next day it freshened a
bit and there was a big swell on the bow. Mate was seasick,
poor child; she is getting a worse sailor instead of a better one.
She stayed in her bunk for three days – very sorry for herself,
but is up and eating today, looking a wreck, with big inky
splashes under her eyes. And it's not even been seriously
rough. *Caplin* has stayed glued to her course and I've slept all
of each night, while she makes just over a hundred miles each
day. Today the wind has gone round to the north and I've had
the big spinnaker out since 05.00, and *Caplin* is still steering
herself. The sea is now pretty smooth, though there is still a
biggish swell.

Six hundred miles from New Zealand at noon – about
half way. I've kept a hundred miles or so to the westward of
the direct line, so as to make plenty of westing before we get
into the westerly belt near New Zealand. The odds against a
gale are about five to one according to the Pilot chart. It's
much colder; I have started wearing a vest and sometimes
trousers instead of shorts. Our single oilskin (only one left) has
been dressed with linseed oil to make it a bit more watertight;
and why, oh why, did we send our sea boots home from
Panama?

There has really been little to do so far on this voyage, and
we spend most of the day reading. 'The Prince who Hiccuped'
remains for me to read aloud after tea; the volume of
Blackwood's 'Sea Stories' is all about shipwrecks and really not
suitable to read to a seasick Mate. I suppose they are getting on
nicely with the war in spite of our lack of news of it.

Heroes in the Gale

29°28'S 177°21'E, Wednesday 15 November 1939. We heroes! My God! Grim! Grim!?? The wind has increased to a northerly gale; we are now reduced to running under reefed staysail sheeted amidships, and we are rolling horribly; cockpit nearly filled several times and needed some pumping – up to about six hundred strokes at a time. Then in the night the wind went to SW. I don't know when it turned, but when I looked out in the night we were heading ENE instead of south.

At daylight I got the mainsail on her, seven rolls, gaff jaws about five feet above boom, and hove her to. Mate was desperately seasick again after beginning to recover. It blew like blazes for twenty-four hours and there was a horrible sea, but *Caplin* made pretty good weather of it.

I'm getting too old and losing my nerves; it is just horrible wondering if we are going to spring a leak and seeing ourselves struggling and choking in the black water. I'm not really brave at all, and a thousand times worse than if single handed. Mate is quite uncomplaining, but continually trying to vomit on an empty stomach.

Incidentally I had a bad headache one night; the cabin roof was leaking badly, quite a bit coming through the skylight, and I hoped it would be all right; it was cold, two-jersey weather and I was scared I had a chill. However, I woke up feeling better. Poor little *Caplin*, being flung about; there were some terrific crashes too – one upset lamp glass in fore cabin and glass shattered on floor. It seemed an age, but the worst of the gale only lasted about twenty-four hours! The wind gradually moderated, but still remained SW, and we could make practically no progress. Minor casualties – the staysail tore near the head, through a patch being too tight, but the hem kept the sail from tearing right across. I got it down into the cabin and put on a bigger patch yesterday. The peak earring of the mainsail was chafed through, but the gaff robands held yesterday, when the wind was moderate, so I got the sail down easily enough and refitted it. The luff wire of the jib was broken, but that does not matter much as I have two smaller ones. Now the wind is light, still SW but it has backed a little, so we are slowly sailing west, on port tack. Our proper course is south by west, but I want to make all the westing I can against prevailing westerly wind.

STILL AFLOAT AND RECOVERING COURAGE

30°30'S 173°32'E, Sunday 19 November 1939. *Caplin* is still afloat; I am recovering my courage – have to store it up for the next gale – and Mate has recovered from seasickness, is eating well and seems all right. However, we have not made much progress, perhaps a hundred miles in the last four days. We have had very light head winds and now a couple of days of calm. We had thirty to forty miles of an adverse current for two days, so we've hardly made anything in the last week; but the swell has eased out – the bottle of ink from which I have just filled my pen stands on the table without fiddles. It's not unpleasant – we read a lot, but we have nearly finished all our books and too much reading makes my eyes ache.

We are not much more than two hundred miles from New Zealand now, and it's only about a hundred more to Auckland. We finished the last of the bread yesterday – no sign of mould which is rather miraculous, but the climate is much cooler. Mate has taken over the cooking again, so we have more interesting meals. Ham patties and chipped potatoes for lunch yesterday, and fish cakes and peas today. When alone, I have a tin of cold meat or fish and bread and butter. We are gradually getting things dry again – lovely bright sun since the gale. Tins in the bunk lockers got damp, but not too bad and no irremediable damage as far as we have found so far.

ONE THINKS A CALM WILL GO ON FOR EVER

31°17'S 173 43'E, Monday 20 November 1939. One thinks a calm will go on for ever. One continuously looks round the horizon and at the clouds and at the barometer, and nothing happens; but in the end it does. Last night, at about 18.00, a draught, not actually a wind, made itself felt on the beam, and we just ghosted ahead. It failed during the night but came again, from the NE, and all day we have ghosted SSE with spinnaker and topsail – no helm but *Caplin* wants to get in and runs SSE as if in a groove. We had made good 47 miles at 12.00 and were 190 miles from North Cape; it is so smooth we might almost be in harbour. I suppose we made under 200 miles in the last week, but in *Emanuel* I once made no progress for ten days. Our departure, with expected date of arrival, November 24, has been radioed to New Zealand. If this wind holds it looks as if we will hit the day exactly. A week ago Mate was saying I had given too long an estimate.

AUCKLAND, NEW ZEALAND: SAFE ARRIVAL

Sunday 26 November 1939. We arrived safely on the 24th, exactly eighteen days from Tonga, as I said. There had been no further adventures. We made Cape Brett Light, 100 miles north of Auckland, just after dark. The weather looked threatening with some rain, and it breezed up a bit, but it came to nothing and we had a bit of a calm. We got past Cape Brett and then hove to for a few hours rest; at daylight were off some islands twenty miles south of the Cape. *Caplin* ghosted all day with varying winds. We saw several lighthouses; it is so lovely to be in civilized waters again. By night we were thirty miles from Auckland and made the harbour at daylight. We spoke to the Boarding Steamer in the entrance and were told to proceed, finally motoring up to the anchorage. The officials very courteous and later a harbour launch towed us up to a snug berth alongside a shipyard.

INDEPENDENT FREEDOM: TONGA TO AUCKLAND

MAKING USE OF MODERN TECHNOLOGY

My grandfather had reported for war duty on making landfall in Auckland and was ordered to return to England as soon as possible. This was the end of their plan to sail around the world, and must have been a bitter disappointment, though one they had been growing used to for some time. However, it was months before he could get a passage home and they decided to sail down to Nelson, the home of Dr and Mrs Washbourne, the parents of Dick who had sailed with them as far as the south coast of Ireland.

From Nuku'alofa harbour I watched the weather down south on the weather maps from the boat next door and listened to the New Zealand forecasts. It became apparent a weather window was opening up. My grandfather did not have such luxuries. *Caplin* was hove to 'while it blew like blazes for twenty-four hours and there was a horrible sea'. He had bad visions of springing a leak. It all seemed to me a strong incentive to make use of modern technology and avoid bad weather if possible, especially as I was eight years older than he was in 1939!

We left Nuku'alofa on Friday 30 October 1998, a week earlier than *Caplin* had in 1939, with fine weather. It was a gentle sail in light airs out through the Piha passage, and then the wind failed. The wind, what there was of it, boxed the compass for the next three days, and we were exceedingly glad to have the new engine. We only ran it under 1,800 r.p.m. At one time I had considered leaving Tahiti without one! There were some magnificent sunsets as we progressed southwards.

Five days out, and some 500 miles from Nuku'alofa, we crossed the 180 degree meridian and changed hemisphere. The weather was fine and the yacht was sailing well with a fair wind, a moderate sea and swell. There had been mare's tails during the day and the forecast suggested a front with 30 knot winds ahead of us. There were gales in New Zealand. We sailed on for the next 36 hours making over 5 knots, sometimes close-hauled, sometimes reaching.

A PASSING FRONT AND A TORN SAIL

Friday 6 November 1998. It was overcast and dark at 02.00 when we reefed right down as the front passed over, the wind E force 6–8. By 08.00, the reefs had been shaken out and the motor was running. During the morning the wind increased from the east and the foresail tore from luff to leach, which was a blow. We took in three reefs and hoped for the best. I was glad I had the trysail on board, sent from New Zealand. It was a foul day, overcast, rain and drizzle, with a confused sea and a south-easterly swell, but at least we had decent oilskins. The one on *Caplin* had to be coated with linseed oil to make it more watertight prior to the passage.

The next day was fine but there was a low-pressure system to the north of us and one to the south. However, the barometer remained high. The day's run was only 80 miles. It was a moonlit night with bright phosphorescence, and the forecast said a high was moving in towards New Zealand. Maybe we would make it without a gale.

Monday 9 November. Although there was a good sailing breeze on Sunday, the day's run was only 87 miles; the three reefs in the foresail did not help. Monday dawned fine and clear, and it was a beautiful morning with the barometer sky high at 1040 mb. Michel made use of the calmer sea to refuel from the cans on deck. At 23.30 Mukohinau Island light was sighted: New Zealand at last.

It was a lot colder; we wore sweaters and long trousers for the first time in almost a year and, unlike my grandfather, I had not sent the sea boots home from Panama! On November 10 there was a fiery dawn to port and Great Barrier Island to starboard. The coloured cliffs of Rakitu Island were tinged pink by the rising sun out at sea, the grass green on top. Oh the green grass of a temperate climate! It was motor-sailing through the Colville channel and the rest of the way to Auckland, with an increasing head wind.

Instructions were received over the VHF to anchor for the night off the Compass dolphin (a structure in the harbour used for taking bearings when swinging a compass; it subsequently blew down in a storm). We anchored just before midnight, thankful to have made New Zealand without bad weather. It blew hard the next few days and a yacht which left after us from Tonga was lost: we had dined with them in Vava'u.

The passage had taken eleven days and ten hours, an average speed of 4.2 knots. Under much more difficult weather conditions, *Caplin* had taken eighteen days, with an average speed of only 2.7 knots.

CAPLIN: SOUTH ON THE EAST COAST
OF NEW ZEALAND

(FROM A ROUGH LOG – AUCKLAND TO NELSON, 1939–1940)

Thursday 7 December 1939. Just a lovely sail yesterday. Up at daylight getting ready; we had an early breakfast and slipped from the jetty at 08.30. Bright sun and warm but no wind, so we motored. We passed a man-of-war, with friends on board, so we signalled. Then a light air and we made sail, nearly a head wind, long and short leg through Motukorcho Channel. Off Browns Island wind freed a little and setting the topsail we reached fast through Tamaki Strait. There is land all round us and perfectly smooth water; what a relief after thousands of miles of ocean.

We have been told – till we are rather tired of it – that the Hauraki Gulf and adjacent waters are the best yachting grounds in the world. So far they are good – very good – but the 'English' scenery is tame; rolling hills and green fields; there are many villas near Auckland and then plenty of detached houses or villages. Tamaki Strait is about three miles wide and reminds me a little of the Solent. The scenery not a patch on, say, the west coast of Scotland. Then we had to beat three or four miles to a little bay, nearly landlocked, in Rotaro Island. Mate had a rest while I tacked back and forth from shore to shore just loving it, and forgetting the war.

INEBRIATES ISLAND

We anchored about 15.00, had a cup of tea and were taking a little rest when a launch came alongside with three men, one dressed in Salvation Army uniform. There was a big building on shore, perhaps a hotel, but it looked rather institutional. We found we had come to the 'Inebriates Island'. Poor *Caplin*, but the Manager was very friendly, and had read of us! He took us round the place. Finally, we came back with a gift sack of vegetables.

A small motor fishing vessel had come in. The skipper visited us with a gift of lovely dabs (all cleaned) but really to tell us we should shift berth. He stopped talking while Mate cooked the fish (baked in oven in milk and butter); as he made no move to go, we asked him to stop for our meal. He was the captain, an ordinary working fisherman, but such a nice man – about thirty-five, good looking, good table manners and most interesting about his life and fishing. That's one of the advantages of this life – all the different sorts of people one meets.

Today is not so good; wind strongish, dead head wind and open sea. It means a hard beat for twenty miles in the open. We shall probably go out and look at it and then find shelter again. We want to make this a pleasant yachting trip.

Friday 8 December. Well, we sailed away from the Drunkards' Island; a fresh breeze and dead ahead though not much sea; occasional drizzle and pretty grim, but ten miles ahead of us lay Coramandel, and just south of that Tekouma Harbour. The chart now was three miles to an inch – rather a small scale – and Tekouma was only a tiny slit, but it looked all right; the sailing directions mentioned 3 fathoms at the entrance. The entrance was protected and the tide rising; tides here rise up to nine or ten feet. As the entrance opened up we saw a delightful little sound ahead, but only dimly as a shower passed. Rolling green hills round us, and a land-locked sheet of water about two miles long. No sign of humans, but plenty of sheep.

Went for a little walk after tea; jolly on the springy turf and some very good views from the hill top, but it rained and we both got soaked. If we did not want to get on, this would be a jolly place to stop for a few days. There were too many people in Auckland. The weather changed suddenly last night; the wind dropped, there was a terrific downpour and then it cleared. Now bright sun and no wind.

THIS VILE CLIMATE!

Kennedy Bay, Sunday 10 December 1939. This vile climate! Mate says she cannot tell the difference between December in England and December in New Zealand. Windy, blowing, rain and cold, though not really of course as cold as English winter, and in these latitudes this is the summer! We left our last bay on a fine day; we drifted out, no wind, or just the suspicion from dead ahead, so after a time we motored for some four hours. Broken Heart began to run badly, so I stopped it, but then it would not start again and finally the starting handle broke. Well, I sailed *Emanuel* a good many thousand miles without an engine, but it is annoying when one has come to rely on it; I hope it is nothing serious.

We drifted all night, having just rounded Cape Colville at end of Moehau Peninsula. With malignant hatred, the wind – after a calm spell – went round dead ahead again; we beat tediously against it all day, with occasional showers. We looked at the river mouth but could see no gap in the breakers, so then came back a few miles to this bay; it is a good shelter from every wind except due East, and that's where it had gone round. However, I don't think it's really going to blow. The hill tops are all covered in woolly clouds, and a few minutes ago it was really dark in the cabin, although long past sunrise. This is a big bay, three quarters of a mile across entrance and a mile or so long, about square in shape, surrounded by rather wild tree-clad hills. There is no sign of cultivation except a fair amount of grass on the slopes and a few houses at the end of the bay; otherwise it just looks wild.

A little boat was sailing in the bay as we came in; the owner showed us where to anchor, and then came on board – young school teacher, very pleasant and like nearly all New Zealanders mad on yachting. Our fame had preceded us of course, and he recognized *Caplin* from accounts in the press. Ashore was a Maori settlement, a hundred or so people, apparently mostly living on a Government pension – why? – perhaps compensation for land? Would quite like to spend a few days here – in fine weather. We probably shall anyway, as it does not look too good today. We have only made good 60 miles in four days and Nelson is 600 miles off; we may not get there for Christmas but it doesn't really matter.

Same day – 18.00. Furious gale, glass dropping as I've only seen for a hurricane. We are fairly well sheltered, but a little swell comes in the bay. We are about a mile from the shore, biggish hills. Outside, the wind must be blowing across the mouth of the bay, but furious squalls blow round the point and straight in from seaward. *Caplin* sheers about a good deal and occasionally a squall hits us on the bow and we heel over quite a bit. The howling of the wind is wearisome. I've got down three anchors (one is only a little one). We should be all right; as long as she does not snub at the cable, it should hold against any wind that blows. However, I am very anxious; I don't think there is any danger to life, but if the cable parted or dragged, we could be blown ashore and I don't know what would happen to the ship. The barograph is dropping steadily; when will it go up? We shall then get a change of wind. If it backs as I think it will (anticlockwise) we should be all right. If it veers, quite a heavy sea might come into the bay; just don't know yet. There are islands ten miles off which should break some of it and there is only a very small area open to seaward.

I have just been on deck getting the other anchors down, and came down shivering, part cold – and perhaps part fright. There's so much waiting for things to happen at sea – which tells in one. Mate is very good and does not complain. It's not actually too bad on board; there is the dry warm cabin and not sufficient motion to be uncomfortable. But that horrible howling of the wind! I wrote once before that I thought I was getting too old for yachting. This morning I bored ventilator holes – at last – in the cabin lockers and did odd jobs. After dinner I struggled with the blasted engine. Everything seems in perfect order, spark, petrol, compression, but the Broken Heart just won't beat. That's another, smaller anxiety, though now in this gale it would not have power enough to help us, if we did part.

Continual rain and we have lit the lamp though it's not yet sunset; thank heaven for short nights, only eight hours of darkness. The glass is still falling, but as it is already blowing a gale, it probably won't last long; there should be a change in the night or tomorrow.

Thursday 14 December. Our anchors held very nicely, in spite of the furious squalls; not much sea came in. A fishing boat (motor) had come in for shelter too. Next morning I went over to them, found two Englishmen, crayfishers. They were short of food so we fed them. The wind had taken off, but there was more to come so we stayed at anchor. Brains and

Keeling, the two men, took us ashore – a small village, mostly Maori, but there were no stores nor supplies. We managed to get a pound of butter and a little tea, but no bread. Then our two friends worked on my engine; magneto, carburettor etc. – all the things I had done. No result. At last, by chance, we thought the petrol funny, and on examining it closer it was kerosene! Must have been Lionel's last effort, because the two tins I filled the tank with had not been touched since Tahiti. Got two gallons of petrol ashore and off she went! Played bridge in the evening.

Next day the 'more to come' was there – blowing hard from west but out of bay and so safe. Played more bridge; went ashore with Keeling and shot a wild – feral – turkey. Mate spent all afternoon cooking it; it was big, and had to be hammered into our oven. Just a lovely supper, the turkey was very fat and no basting necessary.

Yesterday the glass had risen and there was really an improvement in the weather. There was a tangle of my three anchors, but they came clear quite easily and we had a jolly sail here – Whitianga I think the name is – the head of Mercury Bay. First, there was a nice fair wind; then calm – so disappointing and we envisaged another night at sea. It took several hours rounding the first headland – inside all sorts of rocks and islets. Then a very jolly beat three hours up Mercury Bay – a nice breeze, smooth water and *Caplin* sailing her best and tacking within eight points. The sun set in a long rosy glow over the hills ahead. We have only a small-scale chart but Brains had told us about the approach, and we made out the river mouth before just dark. Just lovely tacking back and forth across the Bay, between lovely cliffs and hills, and beaches. There was a very narrow entrance and we just flashed in with a sluicing tide, nearly dark.

Great fun looking out at daybreak to see what sort of place one has got into during the night. The river is 200 yards wide – cliffs with bushes on one side and the village on a flat on the other. The patches of bush – very small – I've seen so far are fascinating. Great tree ferns and now a Christmas tree is about to flower (Netrosideros Tormentosa) in great splodges of dull red and so funny, for the petals are minute and the effect of colour comes from large bundles of long red stamens.

It would be fun to stop here a few days and explore up the river but we must get on, though our chance of reaching Nelson by Christmas is slender, but it does not really matter. Such a jolly scene here – the smooth water gurgling past, and the mountains behind the village.

Whitianga, Friday 15 December. Orgy of shopping yesterday, then a little maddening job on the engine – joining a new starting chain, but link would not fit. Fiddled for an hour or so, then went ashore to a garage – no good, finally wired it. Will serve, but the chain will break from time to time – easily repaired – and by this time in such a temper. We had roast mutton for dinner and were then under way.

Lovely sunny afternoon, hot, light fair wind, but a big swell is coming into the bay – booming on the rocks and the glass is falling sharply; getting us scared. I'm feeling anxious; if it did blow, it would probably be from north and we would have nearly 150 miles of lee shore. We beat back for a couple of hours and then it was almost calm, so we motored in.

PROPERLY SCARED

About an hour after we turned in, the glass started rising! The fall had been nothing but the diurnal inequality prolonged for an hour or so, and it has been a lovely night; if we had gone on we would be nearly across the Bay of Plenty by now. Never mind, one must back one's judgement and I'm properly scared of this coast. Although the sun is hot, nights and bad weather are bitterly cold and I don't know either the coast or the weather. There are a few paragraphs on the latter in the 'Sailing Directions'.

THIRTY MILES SOUTH OF EAST CAPE

Monday 18 December 1939. We got out of Whitianga next morning at 08.00 and had a fine sail across the Bay of Plenty; light fair wind, and averaging 5 knots with the spinnaker; first decent sail in New Zealand waters. Made land next morning at Cape Runaway and lost the wind; idled and drifted forty miles in the next twenty-four hours. Think I've got my dates wrong; this is December 18 and so we must have sailed on the 15th; a.m. on 17th off East Cape; some drenching rain and cabin roof leaking again – must get it re-caulked, but no opportunity yet. Occasional puffs from dead ahead and a horrible swell off the Cape; most depressing day. Now we are about 30 miles south of East Cape and just steerage way, but she will only make about six points from the wind and we make practically no progress. This is a simply beastly coast – 300 miles to Cape Palliser and no harbour of refuge. There are one or two places we could go to in fine weather. If it blows hard from the east we are in a mess, but the prevailing wind should be west and the glass is high and steady. Today is warm and sunny and the swell has abated, so it is comfortable enough.

Gisborne, Thursday 21 December. We drifted and drifted, either oily calm or just steerage way to a head wind, tacking offshore for a few hours and then back again to find we had only made good a mile or two. At last we got round Gable End Foreland – called that by Cook because the cliffs look like it; and then we motored the dozen miles on here. Jolly little town, with 17,000 inhabitants, which is big for New Zealand; it has an artificial harbour with a little basin, entered through two projecting breakwaters. Yesterday, the weather report spoke of a depression to the south so we stayed put, but expect we shall get on today.

Thirty miles East of Cape Kidnappers, Friday 22 December. We got off yesterday about midday; there was a fresh breeze behind us and we reeled off the knots, counting the miles to go, to see if we had a chance of making our date, but when I relieved the Mate an hour ago I found the wind had fallen to a mere draught. We exchanged the spinnakers, putting up the big one, and we are still ghosting, but not fast enough to make Nelson by Christmas. *Caplin* is steering herself goose-winged. What a joy to have a fair wind after the days off East Cape. Even with this draught we can hardly expect to make fifty or sixty miles a day. It was hot at Gisborne, nearly as hot as we have had it in the tropics, but it was cold at night. I now wear two jerseys and a coat.

OFF COOK STRAIT, MONDAY CHRISTMAS DAY
1939: PRETTY GRIM!

What a way to spend Christmas. We got off from Gisborne and had a good run down the coast, with a fair wind and smooth sea – well offshore and out of sight of land, but fifty miles short of Palliser Cape – two days out, we lost the wind, and hardly made any progress. The weather report spoke of a NNW gale in Cook Strait, and then radio died again. By 02.00 we were within ten miles of the Cape, so motored round but when Mate relieved me at 05.00 the wind was freshening so we reefed down. (Horrible swell all the previous day). By 08.30 it was blowing hard. Plugging to windward at the entrance to Cook Strait, close reefed, we made little progress.

We later hove to. Then, at 16.00, the peak lacing chafed through and we had to get the sail down. Mate felt sick but was not actually sick. It was blowing so hard, we did not hoist the mainsail again and lay all night a-try. Pretty grim! The decks and skylight are leaking and the cabin a swamp. *Caplin* is too long used to the fine weather of tropics. The after-mizzen shroud parted, so got that temporarily repaired today. We drifted miles and miles to leeward during the night and the glass is falling slowly; but not as much as I expected, though it blew gale force.

The wind moderated a little this morning and I made sail at 05.00; all day we have been gradually making towards Cape Campbell in South Island, with snow-capped peaks. The close-reefed mainsail with a reefed staysail just gives 2 knots. Land is now 10–15 miles off, and looks closer than it did this morning, but I doubt we have made much to windward. At times the wind has moderated still more, and cabin is getting drier, but skylights still let water pour through when she takes a big one aboard.

At the moment, we could carry more sail, but it makes the motion excruciating, plunging and bumping into the waves – now going slower so she rides them easily. It is bitterly cold, and we only have one ragged oilskin between us, so I keep Mate below. When I go on deck I take most of my clothes off, so they shan't get wet. The wind is cold and piercing, but wrapped in a blanket we keep warm below.

THESE GALES ARE SO FRIGHTENING

As well as uncomfortable, these gales are so frightening. The ship plunges and waves crash against the hull, so that she shudders all over; if a plank started we would be under in two minutes. Also, sails and rigging may carry away and I'm practically single handed. Mate is very plucky and does not grumble. I watch the barograph – still falling but I think the curve is flattening out. Probably with the rising glass, it will blow harder than ever tomorrow.

Same day, 16.30. We are getting near land – run after run of mountains – hoping soon to identify Cape Campbell, then I shall know if we have made any progress. One of the dangers is that the wind may shift suddenly and put us on a lee shore. If we know where we are, there are harbours we could run for. Dopey is the only one of us in good spirits, jumping about after flies, but he is scared when a cloud of spray dashes over the cockpit or comes down the hatch. The sails are a bit worn and staysail very bad, but reefed it is holding on so far. Thank heaven the nights are short and that there are good lights on the salient points. Shall go about at 02.00; thirty or forty miles to the North Island shore, so we have plenty of room. I shan't keep watch, nor can we carry lights, but there is a full moon and not much traffic. Now blowing force 5, with short sharp seas.

Fangyn Bay, Thursday 28 December 1939. This climate! It is so cold. I am sitting in my sleeping bag, wearing a jersey and with a blanket over my shoulders. On the floor, fore side of table, is the primus; over it is a string of washed handkies and drying clothes. I think I was last writing off Cape Campbell. At dark the light showed up where I thought it would. We had made a little progress – ten or fifteen miles – during the day, but what a desperate fight each mile to windward is. The wind backed to westward and went light, so from 20.00 to 04.00, still more progress passing Cape Campbell. Then the wind went almost completely; it remained overcast and has been drizzling almost continuously ever since.

Started motor at 08.00, anxious to get in, but slow, slow progress. We closed the west side of the strait at 13.00, with a strong tide against us and we barely held our own by the shore.

With petrol 2/7d per gallon (and not much of it), I just could not bear having the engine at full speed and no progress, so I stopped it. We were making just enough way to keep the ship headed, but in a couple of hours when the tide eased we had naturally drifted back several miles. Had a great tussle with the engine – trouble eventually traced to a clogged strainer in the petrol pipe; but the shortage of petrol in the carburettor affected one cylinder more than the other, so I thought trouble to be plugs for a long time. I could not get the starting chain properly repaired, so I keep copper wire etc. handy. Also, I have learned how to start to crank without the weak link taking the strain.

About 15.30, started engine again – good progress; 17.30 in Tory Pass, a narrow passage with a furious tide leading between high cliffs into the Sounds (leading to Picton). Rocks on both sides and the tide rips, almost with the appearance of breakers right across entrance, but I know tides well enough and what it would be like. No suspicion of wind. Then, just as we felt the tide take hold of us to swirl us through, the engine stopped. I was not seriously alarmed because it was all clear water in the middle of the pass and a tide generally keeps one in the deepest water. Tide ripped nothing to speak of and did not splash over the cockpit.

OYSTER BAY: BLESSED RELIEF TO BE STILL

After half a minute, engine started again; still have no idea why it failed; can't help thinking it is just a gesture on part of the Broken Heart. Gave it a rest for a little while as we swept up the sound. High rocky hills and grass covered with bits of forest in glens. All going for miles and no sign of man – no, there were one or two houses and a lighthouse at Tony Entrance. Three-and-a-half miles inside was a sheltered bay off the side of the Sound, Oyster Bay, so we poked our bow in and anchored. Blessed relief to be still; five days at sea and desperately unpleasant drizzle and cold.

We had supper, and had just launched dinghy when two men came over in a boat – the farmer and his son; they asked us ashore so off we went. He had a wife and several adult children of both sexes; it was lovely sitting by the stove in the kitchen. Mr Emily has a sheep run of 30,000 acres, and runs his farm house as a guest house – thirty visitors at the moment. Mrs Emily had seen our photo in the papers and was very pleased to meet us; we were given masses of food – two joints, bread, butter, milk and vegetables, and all payment refused. Also, six gallons of petrol, but that I was allowed to pay for. They asked us to come back and stay with them.

Next morning (yesterday) was an early start to catch tide; we motored five miles up and then into another branch of inlet, and down towards the sea with a faint air. Mate was cooking a leg of lamb so we tried to get anchorage for noon. The first bay was too deep, so we went on to Resolution Bay (shade of Cook), Mate thinking dinner would be spoiled. We had the mainsail up and down several times, but got an anchorage in a cove just in time, and had a lovely dinner.

There is a holiday camp for Boy Scouts ashore, but no contact. Everything seems lovely; we rest after lunch, and then find the wind has changed right round and is blowing fresh. So, we are on a dead lee shore with a fetch of several miles, and within stone's throw of shore too. We quickly set the mizzen, start the engine slowly; there is a rattle in the cable as she forges ahead and breaks the anchor out; signal full speed to Mate; and full speed on windlass to get the anchor up. *Caplin* gathers way gallantly, the wind light between squalls. We are soon clear of the cove, set the staysail and look at the next cove, but the wind is not too good for that, so up mainsail – reefed, stop engine and plug to windward. There is a strong wind and a smooth sea and *Caplin* is sailing grandly. We can see that the water looks strange on the far side of the sound; as we approach, squalls develop – fiercer and fiercer; but we are making good progress to a weather shore, towards high hills, low clouds and drizzle. In with the staysail and more of the mainsail is rolled up; the squalls are really fierce now; here and there on the water one can see clouds of spray torn off the surface and scurrying in different directions like white clouds.

I had realized from afar something funny was going on. *Caplin* felt almost as if she was being struck by blows and heeled over far – back and forth, squalls first on one bow and then on the other and calms between. So within a mile of the head of the bay, where I had hoped to find anchorage, I was glad to see a boat at anchor there; nothing in 'Sailing Directions'. We were making slow progress and Mate was thinking of the pork to cook for supper, so we motored and got anchorage in five fathoms near the boat at the head of cove.

We think we are pretty safe for any kind of wind, and fine for present one. The sea is quite smooth, shore 100 yards – all grassy hills, but there is a house. Squalls still strike and *Caplin* heels quite a bit, even at anchor. Got a second anchor down while Mate produced supper. Had a very pleasant evening and very snug; good night's rest and weather looks like improving this morning.

CATHERINE COVE, ADMIRALTY BAY

Friday 29 December 1939. Here we are in a fine pickle, high and dry on the beach! That's what the Mate calls my picturesque writing. A very mild pickle, but when I woke at 05.00, *Caplin* had tailed in towards the beach and grounded, taking a slight list at low water; the tide is now rising and she is upright, but still aground aft. The bay is sheltered, the weather calm and the sea like a pond, so there is no danger whatever. These sounds on the northern end of South Island are lovely fjords running twenty miles inland, with wild mountains some thousands of feet straight up from the sea, covered with grass and forest, and hardly a sign of man. Just an odd house here and there in a bay. We had a lovely sail yesterday. Got under way after breakfast, still very squally, but there is a clear blue sky and at last we can see the sun again. The water in the bay was whipped white with squalls; we dodged about for twenty minutes making up our minds whether to go on. The wind is probably right and may only be fresh in the open. However, if we run to leeward it may be difficult to get back if it really blows hard.

At last Mate said 'Let's go on' so we bore up and ran down the bay. The squalls were less vicious and as we reached the more open sound only a fresh breeze. *Caplin* was sailing fine and loving the fresh fair wind in smooth water. Got out to Cape Jackson where there was a nasty tide race – curling waves breaking in all directions, just tumbling over each other, but no real sea and the wavelets were too small to be any danger; we did not actually get splashed. Then southwest, passing headland after headland, gradually putting on more sail as the wind eased. Two yachts passed, the first we have seen cruising here, but not close enough to hail.

At 18.00 calm, slight progress with the tide; at 20.00 started the engine, but not too much gas left; motored across Admiralty Bay and got to this cove at dark; spectacular moon rising at 21.00. Cove very deep, groped our way, stopping and starting very close to beach, pretty dark as moon was low and hidden by mountains. At last got thirteen fathoms – deep but not too deep, so I let go. Chart is too small scale for detail and Pilot Book rotten, very sketchy; so we are almost like explorers. Had to let out a lot of chain as water so deep; during the night slight breeze onshore so tailed in and grounded at low water. Now we are actually only thirty-five miles from Nelson; perhaps we shall actually get there.

Voyage's end: Nelson

Sunday 31 December 1939. We have at last got to Nelson. Went through French Pass, which is a passage a hundred yards wide connecting two bays and with a tide like a waterfall, but we took it near slack water, with a fair breeze and all quite easy. Five miles further on we called at a bay where we were told a farmer could let us have some petrol, of which we were short. Sailed on well along the coast for a few hours – then almost calm, but ghosted through the night and finally motored the last few miles and got here at 09.00 yesterday.

We stayed some months at Nelson, living on board but frequent guests of Dr and Mrs Washbourne, the parents of Dick who had sailed with us to Bantry Bay. We then sailed across to Wellington where the yacht was laid up for the winter. I subsequently sold her and returned to England. My Mate preferred to remain in New Zealand.

INDEPENDENT FREEDOM

HAULED OUT AT THE HALF MOON BAY MARINA

Independent Freedom spent the next two-and-a-half months out of the water at the Half Moon Bay Marina, undergoing an extensive and expensive refit; more work was done than otherwise would have been, because of the low New Zealand dollar. We hired a car to explore the North Island by land; it is a beautiful country. Michel spent Christmas with his uncle and aunt in Melbourne and I spent it with some cousins (also grandchildren of Commander Graham) in Hamilton, a hundred miles south of Auckland

FROM A LETTER TO MY AUNT

It was my aunt who had been my grandfather's Mate on board the *Caplin*, and it was from her I had obtained the above account of the Pacific crossing. The main purpose of my crossing of the Pacific was to meet up with *Caplin* in my own boat, and the following is from the letter I sent her.

Port Tauranga, New Zealand,
Tuesday 23 March 1999

Mission accomplished! I spent a fortune on the yacht in the Half Moon Bay Marina: new sails, radar, VHF and, most importantly for these waters, a weather fax – how your father would have loved a daily map with the weather pattern for the whole of the Tasman Sea – a new engine fitted in Tahiti realigned and remounted, new halyards, a new windlass, anchor and chain, a stowage platform built on the stern, a new fridge, new electric wiring and a clean bottom and hull!

We sailed in rough weather to the Bay of Islands, the new sails much enhancing *Independent Freedom*'s performance. Cape Brett lighthouse, the first New Zealand one you saw, was passed close to. The Cape was named by Captain Cook in honour of Rear Admiral Sir Piercy Brett and if you had passed in the day you would have seen the cathedral-like arch in Piercy Island just off the Cape through which we saw tourist launches speeding, 'thrilling' their passengers.

The weather we experienced was not much better than yours, and we were storm-bound for a week with easterlies making the coast a dead lee shore. When the weather finally relented the engine had a problem and we had to return to Auckland and have the fuel system renewed. Luckily Brian MacNurty of Whiting Power, who had sent us the engine in Tahiti and refitted it in Auckland, took pity on us and the work was done in record time. I am not superstitious – well may be a little – but this is second time we have had a serious problem sailing on a Friday!

You of course sailed to Nelson down the east coast, but the perceived wisdom circumnavigating North Island is to sail south down the west coast and north up the east coast. We again left Auckland, this time on a Monday and in fine weather, passing America Cup yachts practising in the Haruaki Gulf. We had a good sail to Bon Accord harbour where I had a swim, having anchored off Swansea Bay.

The next day it blew hard from the east, force 6/7, making the coast a lee shore. It was a dead beat out of the North Channel with its tide rips into the Pacific. We had a fast reach in rough seas north to Whangaruru where we were storm-bound for four days, moving round the harbour as required to obtain the best shelter. It was wet and cold just like England! You remarked that December in New Zealand was like December in England, although this was February.

It was rough rounding Cape Brett and the wind then died. We motored on to Whangaroa, where we dined ashore at the excellent restaurant near the entrance to this fine natural harbour, spending the night on one of their moorings.

There were storm warnings for the south of North Island when we set sail on Sunday 28 February 1999 bound for Picton, South Island, home port of *Caplin*. It was calm as we motored in anticyclonic gloom round North Cape that evening. The wind got up enough to sail round Cape

Reinga in bright moonlight, the yacht pitching in the heavy southwesterly swell. The Cape has a fearsome reputation and, according to the forecasts, which we listened to on a regular basis, it certainly lives up to its reputation. We were glad to be round.

The west coast, which we were now off, has no safe port, except New Plymouth, for its entire 400-mile coastline, and the prevailing winds are westerlies blowing across the Tasman Sea. Once round Cape Reinga there was too much south in the wind to quite make the course, so it was hard on the wind for the next four days. There was a heavy swell, plenty of wind, too much at times. We had a few hours of full gale and twenty-four hours of force 6/7. *Independent Freedom* went well, reefed right down, although it was pretty wet and cold! Unlike *Caplin*'s gaff, the Bermudan rig and a modern wing keel certainly makes windward work a lot more rewarding in terms of progress made good.

I hand steered quite a lot during the day because I like it, not because I had to; the autohelm worked perfectly. Michel spent quite a lot of time in his bunk, but he did spend a good few hours with the floorboards up, tracing a leak, and he is always on deck for reefing! He can also cook in most weathers which is an absolute boon; I don't like cooking at the best of times.

Mount Egmont was first seen in the evening, stark and beautiful in an azure sky. Named after the Earl of Egmont, First Lord of the Admiralty from 1763 to 1766, by Captain Cook when he sailed down the coast in *Endeavour*. The conically shaped mountain was in sight for twenty-four hours and, when it dipped, South Island was sighted.

Cape Jackson, where you experienced a 'nasty tide race curling waves breaking in all directions' was passed early on Friday March 5. When motoring up Queen Charlotte Sound, very eerie in the cloud-muted moonlight, I phoned my brother Edward in England. He was getting ready to go to London with my mother and his wife Philippa, picking up Donald, another brother, and his wife Lucy on their way, meeting James, another brother and his wife Emma at *HQS Wellington*, moored on the Thames

Embankment for the Annual Royal Cruising Club Dinner, where Edward was due to receive the Founders Cup on my behalf.

I suggested he inform the Commodore that we would be making the rendezvous with *Caplin* in Picton some sixty years after grandfather, a prominent member of the RCC, and you arrived in Nelson. I am eight years older than he was in 1939, it would be an historic moment for the Club. Not many grandsons have followed their grandfathers across the Pacific, let alone gone on board the yacht he had sailed in, and been members of the RCC.

Caplin was moored in the Waikawa Marina. It does not have a VHF, but I was able to obtain the telephone number from Marlborough Radio and spoke to the Marina Supervisor. He told me in no uncertain terms that there was no berth for us and I should proceed to the public jetty in Picton. Luckily the Marina berth holders were much more helpful and civil and, within the hour, *Independent Freedom* was tied up snug and secure in berth number 18.

In the early evening, a soft Scots burr heralded the arrival of ebullient Hamish Fraser, the enthusiastic owner of *Caplin*. He took us off for the historic meeting with the yacht which had brought you across the Pacific. I had lived with her through your father's account during our voyage, reading the passages relating to our position, reliving your voyage of 59 years ago.

Now I sat in the cockpit holding the tiller which Anderson the builder had carved for you, so different from *Independent Freedom*, where the cockpit is much bigger and steering is by a steel wheel. The cabin below is just as your father described – from drying his clothes on the primus moved forward for the purpose, beating into Cook Strait, to you cooking dinner in the galley. In particular, your beat into Kelefesia Island, Tonga, through the 'blind rollers' to the anchorage inside the reef which we faithfully followed. It was a poignant moment for me. We had followed you for many months across thousands of miles of ocean, in fine weather and in bad, feeling for you when it was rough and you were not feeling well – discovering the South Pacific is not all blue skies and gentle seas!

The journey that started on that cold misty November day in your sitting room one-and-a-half years ago, when you gave me your father's account, typed by you, was over, half-way round the world in a different hemisphere almost as far from England as it is possible to sail. The final words of the account written in your father's hand 'then sailed across to Wellington where the yacht was laid up for the winter. I subsequently sold her and returned to England'. 'My Mate preferred to remain in New Zealand' hints at the bitter disappointment of not being able to complete your voyage around the world due to the war.

Hamish and Jane were most hospitable – opening their large house outside Blenheim to us, lending us a car and feeding us. Sunday was a fine day and David Gillies, grandson of the original buyer of *Caplin* in New Zealand, came out for a sail in her. Hamish has done a lot of work on the yacht, keeping faithfully to the original. He says he can hear 'the Commander' telling him when something is not done correctly.

Well that is about it. When we left, David's parents, George and Mrs Gillies, were on the pontoon. We are on our way back up to Auckland sailing north where you sailed south on the east coast. We had mixed weather, some fine with great sailing and good visibility. Dolphins played under the bow, a wonderful and beautiful sight as they wheeled and dived, twisted and turned in perfect harmony with themselves and their element.

Off Cape Turnaway there was a marine distress signal, but we reported on the VHF that we had seen and heard nothing. It had been blowing a full gale for most of the day and was very rough before we closed the land. It was a dead beat between East Cape with its turbulent waters and Cape Runaway in force 6/7. However, it was daylight and I close-tacked, rock-dodging all the way along the coast, and kept out of the worst of the sea. This coast is most inhospitable and not for the faint hearted, which is no doubt the reason we have only seen one other yacht at sea from the North Cape all the way round North Island to here at Tauranga.

I posted the letter from Tauranga. The Marina Manager sat his RYA courses in Lymington, my home town! We washed off the volcanic ash covering the yacht – I had stupidly gone to leeward of an erupting volcanic island. Tauranga was a good mixture of working port and tourism with a fine beach facing the Pacific.

It was a fast sail to White Bay, Great Mercury Island, averaging a fraction under 7 knots for the 70 miles, although it was overcast and rained most of the way. On to Putaki Bay, Waiheke Island, passing Rotoroa Island where my grandfather had landed only to find it was a treatment and rehabilitation centre for alcoholics, which it is to this day. Michel managed to puncture the dinghy on an expedition ashore and I had to save him in the dark!

We completed the circumnavigation of North Island on Sunday 28 March when we returned to Westahaven Marina, Auckland.

INDEPENDENT FREEDOM ALONE: NEW ZEALAND TO THE CANARIES

BACK TO THE TROPICS

A LTHOUGH IT WAS early in the season it was time to move on. I got round the problem of starting the voyage on a Friday by saying we were going for a day sail! The electrics had been rewired and at long last worked properly. A new GPS had been installed and, at the First Mate's insistence, interfaced with the radar, amazing. We left Auckland for the last time on 9 April 1999, passing a car carrier named *Americup* inward bound. Our day sail ended at Whangerei where the night was spent in Urquart Bay, after another fast sail. It was a fair wind up the coast and the weekend was spent anchored in Omakiwi.

I had been watching the weather maps and a weather window appeared so on Monday 12 April we motored into Opua. We did our last-minute shopping, posted the mobile phone back to Auckland, and *Independent Freedom* was watered and bunkered.

Monday 4 April 1999. After clearing customs we departed from the Opua Cruising Club wharf at 14.36, commencing the long voyage back. It was with considerable feeling that this new voyage began, for we were on our own; it was our voyage and we were following no one. *Caplin* and her spirits were left behind, for the time being at least. We still had to complete our own circumnavigation and, in so doing, were hoping to complete what *Caplin* and her crew had been denied. Finally, we had the Atlantic to cross and would, at the end of our voyage, be back with *Caplin* at the beginning of hers.

The single-reefed sails were hoisted off Russel and we sailed out through the Ninepin rocks. The forecast was good. There was a glorious sunset over the Cavelli Islands, our last sight of land. The wind was SSE force 4 and *Independent*

Freedom was running fast away from the New Zealand winter towards the Tropics.

In the early hours of the next morning, after we had altered course mistaking a fixed red light for a ship, and were running fast in a strong breeze, an inadvertent gybe removed the stowed bimini and consigned it to the deep.

The wind failed at noon and the next few days required a lot more motoring, although the sea remained confused with a moderate swell. At times the sails were lowered to prevent them slatting.

On the fourth day out, some 500 miles from Opua, the wind filled in from the south and we had a fine sail in bright and sunny weather. At the time of the evening forecast *Independent Freedom* had averaged 7 knots from noon and it was quite rough. A tropical depression had formed which was to the east of New Caledonia, only 400 miles ahead of us. I immediately read my 'Mariners Handbook' to refresh my memory on tropical storms and studied the Pilot Chart for April with the tracks of old storms and read the Admiralty Pilot again. Only the previous month a yacht had been lost in a cyclone south of New Caledonia. I did not want to be caught. At midnight we had averaged 7.3 knots from noon and I was contemplating slowing down, but there did not seem much point until I knew in which direction the tropical depression was moving.

On Saturday morning I had a very weak contact with Russel Radio who said there was no tropical depression and this was confirmed by the forecast. It was a relief, although the Intertropical Convergency Zone was almost over New Caledonia. I have been at sea in a yacht in storm force 11, but not a tropical revolving storm, and once is enough! The day's run was 164 miles with an average of 6.8 knots, which was very satisfactory.

The wind died early next morning. At noon we had to luff up to pass astern of a tug towing a ship registered in Sebastopol. The odd thing was that the hatches were open, the derricks were flying and she was being towed on a single wire bridle. She was rolling heavily in the swell. The tow in that state could not be insured at Lloyds; I thought it was almost as though she had been 'cut out' – or perhaps I had been reading too much Patrick O'Brian!

Monday 19 April. We sighted the reef on which the heavy southerly swell was breaking. We sighted Amedee lighthouse, which I later discovered was an exact replica of the Roche Douvres one, between the Channel Islands and France. It had been built in Paris and assembled, dismantled, shipped out and re-built on the reef. It was designed so that it could be erected without scaffolding. This was in 1865, when there were no nice floating cranes around! There is a magnificent view from the balcony at the top, reached via a spiral staircase. We sailed close in along the reef and luffed up onto the leads. There were huge breaking rollers on the reef to starboard, the wind blowing the tops back out to sea, the water droplets of the spray, like diamonds in the air, sparkling in the sunlight. Once in through the pass we had a lovely sail to Noumea with no swell. The marina made us welcome and we were cleared in expeditiously.

We were back in the tropics with blue seas and white surf on the reefs, and the incredible green of the tropic vegetation. The engine had been used for less than a third of the time it had taken from Opua; the average speed was 5.5 knots for the 923 miles.

Noumea: heralds of the season!

As we were the first yacht to arrive this season, the local newspaper interviewed and photographed us; the article appeared the next day heralding the end of the cyclone season.

Unusually for this time of year, the wind went round to the SW, so we waited until the normal southeasterlies resumed. Noumea is the capital of a French Colony and it is quite clear who is in charge. As usual, wherever the French are involved the food is good. Also, the climate was pleasant so the time passed quickly enough.

To Australia

Saturday 1 May 1999. It was overcast when we let the lines go and motored out of the marina, hoisting the sails once we were out of the Petite Passe. At 07.25 on Saturday 1st May we bore away for the Passe Dumbea, sailing gently in the smooth waters. The swell was breaking on the reef to port and starboard when *Independent Freedom* ran out of the pass into the Coral Sea. It was drizzling, but it had not deterred the surf boarders surfing, and this was some fifteen miles from Noumea! It was fast sailing until just after midnight when the wind died for a few hours, but it increased again in the morning. It brightened up and by noon was hot. I was pleased with the day's run of 143 miles.

The weather map showed huge lows over the Australian Bight. The evening forecast from Taupo Radio in New Zealand indicated a low one-and-a-half days south west of our position and heading towards us. Townsville Radio broadcast a Pan Pan Pan saying a rescue was in progress but they gave no further information. A trough extended from New Zealand to New Caledonia. The sky was changing quickly, with the clouds moving east against the wind. *Independent Freedom* was sailing fast in the bright moonlight.

A strong wind warning was issued by Townsville Radio – SSE 25–30 knots for the whole Queensland coast. It was lovely sailing all day, with the wind increasing at dusk, so we took the first reef in. The log at 22.00 read 'Sea very rough. We have three reefs foresail, three reefs mainsail. Going like a bat out of hell'. The wind was SE force 6/7 and the yacht was shipping water overall.

02.00, Tuesday 4 May. 'Very rough, heavy swell, breaking crests, squall rain, vessel sailing fast, rolling heavily at times. Shipping water o'all (8 knots last six hours)' The wind moderated a little in the morning and the day's run was 168 miles – an average of 7 knots! At 18.00 the mainsail was lowered and it blew hard the rest of the way to Bundaberg, with the yacht reaching fast under only a triple-reefed foresail. On Wednesday, the day's run was 157 miles, and the same again on Thursday (6 May) when at noon Breaksea Light vessel was visible 2.4 miles to the NW 'bouncing around' in the rough sea. The triple-reefed mainsail was hoisted once the sea and swell started to reduce, as the yacht came in the lee of the sands marked by the light vessel. We had a very fast sail the rest of the way, not quite saving our daylight. However, the beacons in the channel leading into the Burnett River were synchronised so they all came on at the same time, which made the approach very easy. Our instructions were to anchor off beacons 12 and 14, which we did after sailing past and dropping the sails.

TRIGGER-HAPPY IN BUNDABERG

Friday 7 May. In the morning we cleared Customs at the Port Marina but were restricted to Bundaberg because Pratique was not granted. The Quarantine Officer was away but it did not stop our French butter, eggs and bacon being confiscated! It rained all day.

On our trip up the river to the town on Saturday we were shot at by a group of teenagers. I reported it on the VHF to Marine Safety and spoke to the police who said they would meet us at the marina but they did not turn up. A yacht that had preceded us by half an hour had a very shaken skipper; he also had been shot at and the bullet just missed his stern. It made for an exciting entry to the sugar cane town!

INSIDE THE GREAT BARRIER REEF

Six weeks later, after Michel had completed a Divemaster course, we departed without incident for Lady Musgrave Island, a true coral lagoon in the Great Barrier Reef, that great natural wonder of the world. I was particularly glad to get away – Bundaberg is not the most exciting town in Australia. It had taken six weeks to have a wind generator fitted after the diesel generator was condemned as being beyond repair.

It was just over 2,000 miles from Bundie to Darwin, and it us took seven weeks, visiting thirty-one ports and anchorages. The SE trade wind blew strong and true, often force 6/7 and not always with the sun shining, but this is a most marvellous cruising ground. The steep Barrier reef sea was always behind us! It made me realize just what a huge country Australia is, 2,000 miles on and we were not even half way round the coast!

The marinas at the ports of Gladstone, Airlie Beach, Cairns and Port Douglas were very welcome for easy replenishment. Many of the anchorages were in the wilderness, or in the lee of uninhabited islands, and often *Independent Freedom* was the only yacht. At Curlew Island it blew force 8 with gusts of force 9, and a sand bank astern with breakers made an anxious night. The main anchor and kedge were at full stretch.

The coast is varied, from being surrounded by green mangroves, reminiscent of Cuba at Mourilyan harbour, to the reef-encumbered Low Islets off Port Douglas, from the rain

Through Indonesia to Thailand.

forests north of Cairns to the gleaming silica sands of Cape York. All along the coast the ghost of that brave, intrepid and industrious explorer, James Cook – Bustard Head where they enjoyed a seventeen-pound bird for dinner, Cape Tribulation which speaks for itself, Cooktown where they repaired *Endeavour* after running aground on the reef of that name, to Possession Island in the Torres Straits where he hoisted the flag.

I could not but compare my use of GPS and up-to-date

Admiralty charts to his sailing blind, discovering the reefs and shallows, sounding all the way while charting the coast. The thousand miles inside the reef was fascinating and fun; although the wind was a little fresh we enjoyed an anchorage or marina most nights. Michel climbed the uninhabited Flinders Island and visited the monument on Possession Island while we waited for strong winds to pass.

Even the Coast Watch which buzzed the yacht in the Gulf of Carpentaria said on the VHF it looked rough. It certainly was, and we had a fast sail across, until we were past Cape Wessel.

Approaching the Coburg Peninsula in a freshening force 6/7 and sailing fast amongst the islands where the chart advises a full survey has not been made, 'tidal' breakers were sighted ahead. *Independent Freedom* was one mile north of the cay off Lawson Island where there appeared to be plenty of water on the chart. Michel stood forward on the pulpit. The sun was high in the sky, it being 13.00, and it was bright and hot.

'Coral heads to starboard' shouted Michel and the depth rapidly shoaled on the echo sounder. To port was the cay on the fringing reef of Lawson Island a mile away, the tide was fair and we were too close to luff up into the wind. With Michel pointing out the coral heads I steered through them wondering if the end was nigh. The depth decreased to 1.9 metres under the keel as the yacht occasionally surfed in the short steep sea breaking on the coral heads and then suddenly increased and the danger was past. I heaved a sigh of relief and sat down!

We rounded Cape Don the next morning, Sunday 15th August, and had a two-reef hard beat through the Dundas Strait with a strong fair tide; it was the first head wind in 2,000 miles. We saved our tide at Clarence Strait where the wind failed, and had to motor the rest of the way to Darwin.

It cost A$200 to be inspected by divers and for the inlets to be cleaned with hot water and disinfectant before *Independent Freedom* was allowed to be locked into the marina. There had been a striped mussel infestation earlier in the year and the authorities were taking no chances! So ended our voyage from Tahiti.

Ayers Rock was an attraction that had to be seen, but to understand the vastness of Australia Michel and I drove the 1,500-odd kilometres. It was a fast drive, there being no speed limit in the outback. I re-read Neville Shute's 'A Town Like Alice' in Alice Springs. Ayers Rock was well worth the effort and we watched the colours change at sunset and sunrise. Michel climbed the rock while I returned to the hotel for breakfast.

Indonesia to Thailand

Refugees and dragons

Tuesday 7 September 1999. *Independent Freedom* was locked out of the Cullen Bay Marina. Customs cleared the yacht on the fuel pontoon outside, while we took bunkers. The forecast was good and it was a change to have force 3/4, after the strong winds, for most of the 2,000-odd miles from Bundaberg.

It was a quiet passage to Ashmore reef enabling us to try out the large light-weight spinnaker I had purchased inexpensively in Bundaberg. Entries such as '06.18 calm slight swell, dawn, ship passing', '08.12 burning sun in an azure blue sky, ripples on the sea', '16.30 buzzed by coast watch', 'wind increased, beautiful sailing' and 'wind dying, cloudless perfect sailing', and Michel's entry '11.45 After the dolphins staying with me since 11.15 they jump, they swim around the bow, and one kept rolling over and over, I think to look at me. She touched my hand as I held it down, as near to the water as possible. With that she touched my heart' sum it up. The last day was rather different. Michel had to prime the engine every minute with the filter pump, while the swell was breaking on Ashmore reef in our lee. The hot day ended after threading the coral heads to the anchorage off West Islet where we had sundowners onboard *Clemmie*.

The channel into West Islet was well marked, small white buoys with red or green triangular top marks, with the flood tide towards West Islet. The whole reef and islets are a marine park with signs ashore indicating where 'the public' can and cannot walk. A wreck on the beach is a reminder of broken dreams, and even more poignant is a little cemetery beneath a palm tree. 'Jamil Tong and Latip B' was crudely engraved on wooden markers beside an unmarked baby grave, emphasizing the lost hope. I was angered at officialdom in such a spot more than 400 miles from Australia – a minimal minority creating areas forbidden to all but an elite.

There was a boat chartered by the Australian Government, owned by a woman who was careful to show me the photocopy of the Ministerial order concerning the reef, who kept watch. They dealt with the refugees who arrived and were at that time repairing a boat to send fifty or sixty people back to Indonesia. Surplus boats are sunk. There was a ranger on board but no-one wore uniforms, and the whole operation was very sloppy. During the cyclone season the official boat is withdrawn and the indigenous fishermen turtle, fish and coral at will, making a complete nonsense of the signs ashore.

Michel repaired the engine with the help of some pieces from *Clemmie*, and we left on the 15th September. The Indonesian boat had been repaired and she, together with her human load, were escorted out of the lagoon by the tender to the guard boat. A little piece of human tragedy played out on a tropical reef miles from anywhere – were they political or economic refugees?

It was flat calm but the sun was low so it was difficult to see the coral heads and on the way out of the channel we hit one. Luckily there was no damage and we motored all the way to Seba, on Savu Island, Indonesia. There was no large-scale chart, so we skirted round Rai Jua, the west point of the island. The swell was breaking heavily on the reef where fisherman were throwing hand nets – a method of fishing unchanged for thousands of years.

The East Timor tragedy was in full flow, with West Timor full of refugees. The two entry ports for Indonesia are Kupang in West Timor and Bali. I had no intention of going anywhere near Timor and in consultation with *Clemmie*, with whom we were sailing in loose company, had decided to cruise the islands and hope for the best, clearing-in officially at Benoa, Bali.

INDONESIA: SAVU TO BALI

The anchorage off Seba was an open roadstead. There was a concrete jetty ashore with two off-lying warping bollards. A very scruffy landing-craft-bowed ferry was alongside, loading cargo and passengers. She was the outside link for the 45,000 people who live on the island, a stronghold of animist belief.

We went ashore shortly after anchoring, landing on the beach by the jetty. An official-looking gentleman waved us onto the jetty and the harbour master issued a port clearance on payment of a small honorarium. He was, however, much keener on changing my US dollars and we left his office with more than half a million rupiah exchanged for a 100-dollar note!

On 18 September we were ashore at 07.30 for a tour of the island with the family from *Clemmie* and their enchanting nine-month-old twin girls. The minibus driver evidently needed support – he had three helpers for the trip. The traditional village proved interesting together with the hand weaving. The headman was paid the usual fee and we were shown the blackened stones where animal sacrifices took place. We were driven along the coast, past numerous rice paddy fields, across bridges and past five schools. It was hot when we arrived back at Seba, a dusty single-street third-world town, and I was glad to be back onboard.

The 115 miles to Waingapu, the administrative centre of the much larger Sumba Island, was a pleasant sail. The pilot and chart were wrong but a large red beacon followed by another and a green one clearly marked the entrance through the reefs. The harbour was protected from all directions except the north. Traditional country craft were alongside the wharf loading, one a load of empty Coca Cola crates. Trimaran fishing craft were moored on the land side of the jetty. The town was comparatively bustling – hot, sunny and dusty, and full of flowers.

The next afternoon we sailed out of the harbour, with my RCC burgee at the masthead and the blue ensign streaming astern, watched by the stevedores ashore and the crews of the country craft.

It was a good sail through the night with a bright moon. The large-scale chart for Nusa Kode was dated 1909 with corrections up to 1999! *Independent Freedom* drifted through the steep-sided entrance to the anchorage in Lehok Uwada Dasam (on Rinja Island, across the Linta straits from

Komodo Island) and a whale blew just ahead. Breakfast was eaten in the cockpit with binoculars to hand. Amid much excitement, two Komodo Dragons were sighted walking along the beach. There are only about 800 left in the world so I felt it was a privilege to have seen them in the wild. I could not resist sending a postcard later in the voyage of a dragon to the headmaster of the Dragon school! We also saw a stork, a hawk, a sea eagle and monkeys. The anchorage was surrounded by high hills, some of which were sheer into the sea while others had fringe beaches.

The next day, in bright sunshine, we mainly motored through the islands to Lehok Ginggo, on the west side of Rinja, an almost land-locked bay surrounded on three sides by steep brown hills leading down to gorgeous pristine beaches. It was completely silent with no sign of humans.

Thursday 23 September. There was little wind so we motored to the Kumuau National Park entrance (in the north of Rinja), the anchorage surrounded by mangroves. On the guide-led walk we saw a large dragon, also a water buffalo, deer and monkeys.

It was perfect sailing weather to the anchorage south of Gili Lawa Darat, although black clouds were building up over Komodo to the south and thunder was heard during the day. The snorkelling in crystal-clear water was fantastic with a turquoise-coloured reef, huge manta ray, many different coloured fish and, to cap it all, a coral garden.

The tide runs very strongly off Gilli Banta (seven miles NW of Komodo) and even when the way point was reached, the inlet was almost invisible in SE bay. There were tide rips marking the boundary between the currents running in opposite directions. However, *Clemmie* was ahead of us so I happily followed her into another almost land-locked anchorage, surrounded by barren stone hills with a beach at the head of the cove.

Sunday 26 September. We parted company with *Clemmie* and, armed with a fax to send for her, we left under power bound for Bali. During the morning Pulau Sangeang was in sight – a fantastic active volcano 6,394 feet high. It was an almost perfect cone straight down to the sea, the west end levelling out in a plain, like the train of a wedding dress, verdant and fertile. During the afternoon the wind rose and we had a fast sail with a full moon during the night. The next day the sun rose in the east while the moon set in the west, with *Independent Freedom* coasting close to the northern shore of Sumbawa.

It was a beat into the bay south of Tanjong Sarahetor in smooth water. Off the resort, an Indonesian came out in a rubber boat and handed us a letter which made clear that yachts were not welcome but we could have a tent for US$750 per night! I could make no sense of the answer to my VHF call, so we bore away and had a fine reach in smooth water. An anchorage behind Tanjong Menangu just off the fringing reef gave us shelter for the night. A fisherman used a bright light under the water to make his catch.

Tuesday 28 September. Coasting along the north shore of Lombok Island in variable winds, I worked out the time of the moon's meridian passage and then the tides in the Lombok strait according to the Admiralty Pilot. The strait was not to be trifled with, the tides running at over 7 knots. We crossed that night with the wind freshening to force 6, kicking up a really filthy sea – wind and tide against each other. At dawn *Independent Freedom* was tearing south at over 10 knots under the light south-making breeze which carried the smell of rotting vegetation. Shortly afterwards the leads were seen and with fifty degrees of set on they were followed into the entrance of Benoa harbour, Bali.

The marina was a bit ramshackle but the people were friendly and helpful. I had faxed the manager from Australia; he had obtained our cruising permit, and now gave me the original. A boy was hired for a couple of days to polish up the boat under Michel's direction and I retired to an hotel. The wind vane fitted at Bundaberg was raised a couple of inches, the additional stainless steel insert into the stanchion barely visible.

Indonesia was in political turmoil and although no yachts had been molested, one Australian told me they had taken down their ensign. Australians were not the flavour of the month due to the action in East Timor. We had sailed through what to me was the most interesting part of the country and so made the decision to make a passage to Batam Island, opposite Singapore though still, of course, part of Indonesia.

BALI TO SINGAPORE: THE STRAINS OF BAGPIPES

Tuesday 6 to Saturday 19 October 1999. Michel had made friends in the marina. We left at dawn on 6 October to the strains of bagpipes from one yacht and much waving from others, including *Clemmie* who had just arrived. From the south end of Lombok Strait, the difficulty is to get north. I had picked up as much local information as I could, but did not find the reported north-going eddy. Although the stream should have been slack we were experiencing 3 knots adverse current. I altered course towards the shore and spent the day reef-dodging, watching the echo sounder, inshore of the main south-going stream.

At 11.00 we passed a grounded fishing vessel, the crew camped out on the black sands under the orange liferaft canopies, the green hills of Bali behind. Two men standing under the stern were discussing the situation; high water and a decent tug I thought!

It was fascinating coasting so close, the coves full of brightly coloured fishing catamarans. Later in the day I watched them being launched through the surf, white on the black sands, the verdant hills a backdrop with a cobalt blue sky above. Off Padang five ferries were in sight with a tall ship anchored in a cove. During the afternoon the sea was spotted with coloured sails. Some of the hulls were fibreglass but the outriggers were wooden. Tea time found *Independent Freedom* very close inshore passing the latticed light house on Pulau Gili Selang. As the wind died, so the sails were furled on the fishing fleet, and the outboard motors were started, a timeless method of fishing brought up to date.

Once clear of Bali watches were set. The wind was fair but in varying strength, not more than force 4, and the engine was used to stop the sails slatting in the lighter periods. The sea was often confused and during the day it was very hot. The next afternoon we passed an unnamed island with a large fishing village and boats, sand, trees and reef, with palm trees providing the shade from the burning sun – the stuff of dreams.

On the second and third day out, progress was good with runs of 116 miles and 138 miles under sail. There was one squall with wind force 7/8. At night there was considerable lightning, some of it spectacular but at a distance from the yacht.

Sunday 11 October. It was calm and the engine was on in the main Karimata Strait (between Borneo and Belitung Island, off Sumatra) where there was some traffic. On Monday the wind, what there was of it, came in from ahead together with an adverse current of up to 2 knots, not what the Pilot book said! After two days of motoring the wind filled from the SW and sailing was possible again under an overcast sky. The next day the wind died; it was very muggy and hot down below.

The engine had been running all night when, on Tuesday morning just after dawn, it stopped. Looking over the stern, I saw a net and my heart sank. However, Michel was soon kitted up and in five minutes diving he had cut it free and there was no damage. The next night the lights of Singapore could be seen glowing on the bottom of the clouds some ninety miles to the NW.

There is a warning in the Pilot about pirates in the Riau straits and it suggests the most likely time is between midnight and 05.00, so speed was adjusted to arrive at the entrance after daybreak (15 October). There was tug and barge traffic and the occasional high speed ferry. The Singapore strait was entered during a squall, and the tide was adverse as we motor-sailed along the north coast of Batam to the Nongsa Point marina. Berthing was made difficult when the engine stopped in reverse. Michel dived and removed another piece of netting. The 991 miles from Bali had taken just under nine-and-a-half days at an average speed of 4.4 knots with the engine in use for just over five days We were back in the northern hemisphere after eighteen months in the southern!

The marina is part of a resort, so good use was made of the facilities although the weather remained overcast and inclement. We went to Singapore by ferry and visited the Volvo agent. When I realized that Keppel Marina, where the agent was based, could lift the yacht out of the water I immediately decided to bring her over for antifouling and to raise the waterline.

Clearance from Indonesia was obtained on 19 October, and the 22 miles to Keppel were covered motor-sailing at 6.7 knots across an extremely busy main strait. A very sharp lookout was kept for the enormous amount of rubbish which could have damaged the propeller.

Singapore is yacht-unfriendly in as much as yachts are treated as big ships, and the crew are only allowed two weeks shore pass after which it must be renewed. The marina arranged to clear the yacht but I had to physically go to immigration and sign the 1,500 Singapore dollar crew bond in front of an officer! I had lived and worked in Singapore for twelve years but left after the holding company collapsed, owing me many tens of thousands of dollars including my pension fund. It was with very mixed feelings that I stayed; coincidentally, I received papers from 'mission control' for a small payout, 14 years after the bankruptcy. Sentosa Island with its many varied attractions was visited, the cable car ridden and a night spent in the Westin hotel with a magnificent view over the harbour from the 70th floor.

TO THAILAND

06.45, Thursday 28 October 1999. The port clearance obtained by the marina was picked up from the guard at the gate and *Independent Freedom* departed from Singapore. I wanted to pass the entrance to Pulau Samulun, where my former employers the salvage company Selco used to have their base, and set course to pass through Jurong fairway. It was with considerable surprise, as we got close, that I saw cars and lorries crossing the water on a causeway. I consulted my new Admiralty chart to see that under 'causeway' was written 'work in progress' but with typical efficiency it was already finished and the fairway was blocked. We reversed course and Pulau Bukom with its surrounding islands turned into a huge industrial desert was left to starboard. Western anchorage was full of ships. At 10.12 we rounded Tanjong Piai and entered the Malacca Straits. Because of the warning in the Pilot about pirates, we held the Malaysian rather than the Indonesian side.

There was much rubbish in the straits and we decided not to motor at night unless one of us was keeping a lookout in the bow. During the afternoon it started to rain and there was so much lightning close by that the electronics were all turned off. The thunder was extremely loud. The course steered kept the yacht inshore of the north-bound traffic lane.

During the night Michel kept lookout in the bow while motoring for an hour to stop the sails slatting. They are fully battened and we have suffered more damage in light winds than in heavy! We sailed whenever there was enough wind, under a permanently overcast sky, with lightning both by day and by night.

Malacca no longer looked sleepy, transformed from when I had last seen it by high-rise buildings. The tides run strongly in the straits so we anchored in the evening off Port Dickson to await the north-going stream. It had been transformed out of all recognition from when, a quarter of a century before, I had overhauled the tanker mooring system with Selco's salvage and mooring vessel. How time flies!

We sailed out at 01.00 and continued close-hauled up the strait with a lot of traffic. It remained overcast. One Fathom Bank with its new lighthouse, not yet on the chart or mentioned in the Pilot book, was passed on the inside that afternoon. The old lighthouse was still there, scene of another Selco salvage. On that occasion, the salvage master had asked for more food to be sent from Singapore, the salvage taking longer than expected, and was sent a packet of fish hooks!

Saturday night was spent beating northwards in winds varying from force 1 to 5, and Sunday motoring during the day. Off the Sembilan Islands there were numerous fishing boats which had a viewing bridge above the monkey island, making them look top-heavy. On Monday night a long bamboo became entangled with the rudder. At daylight Michel dived to check there was no damage, and the engine was started to motor most of the day in calm seas under an overcast sky. At tea time we had a pleasant beat through Alert passage between the Thai islands of Ko Adang and Ko Rawi. That evening the weather was much finer and the wind set in from the NW making it a beat. There were numerous Thai fishing boats which all disappeared at daybreak.

On Tuesday afternoon *Independent Freedom* was beating up the coast of the Ko Lanta Yai peninsula, and that evening was hit by a very strong squall. We lowered the sails and lay a-hull until it blew over. The rain reduced visibility to almost nil, so we had to wear goggles in an attempt to keep a lookout. The night was spent beating past Phi Phi Island and the next day we entered the narrow channel into the Boat Lagoon Marina, Phuket, which proved to be a very pleasant place to stay.

The weather was foul with heavy rain, which was unseasonal because the NE monsoon should have set in

Sunday 7 November 1999. My brother Edward ('mission control') and his wife Philippa arrived. On Tuesday, after a tour of the island and shopping, we set off in the rain for a cruise in Thai waters. The first night was spent anchored off the sheer limestone cliffs of Ko Hong, which gave off remarkable echoes.

For the first time in almost two weeks we awoke to the sun shining into the boat and blue skies. It was a motor through the limestone pillars and then a very pleasant sail and beat against the tide into Chong Ko Ka. Dinner was eaten ashore in a rather basic restaurant with a primitive 'comfort room'.

Phi Phi Don proved to be a back-packer's paradise; part of the beach had been built over with indiscriminate shanty development, but we found a reasonable restaurant.

There was considerable activity on the water the next morning – high speed long boats and their unsilenced motor car engines taking out tourists. Fishing boats were coming in after a night of fishing. We sailed to Phi Phi Li a few miles south and picked up a mooring. The day was spent snorkelling and lazing in the sun. On our return we completed the circumnavigation of Phi Phi Li and its spectacular cliffs, latticed in places with bamboos to aid bird's-nest collecting for soup.

The next morning was spent snorkelling on the west coast of Phi Phi Don in Yong Kasem bay. That night we enjoyed an upmarket dinner at the Palm Beach Resort on the east coast, awaking the next day to light northeasterly airs. It was motoring all the way to Ko Rang Yai where the anchorage was in a deep cove. The restaurant was extremely rustic but the snorkelling was good.

Caplin *under full sail, Bantry Bay, 1983*

vater

Gibralta

Canary
Islands

Cape Verde
Islands

Panama

Caplin *'s skipper and mate, Grandfather and Aunt Marguerite*

maris
hquelon
ez

ti

The end of refugee dream, Ashmore Reef, Timor Sea

ater

Gibralta

Canary
Islands

e Verde
nds

Under repair. Half Moon Bay Marina, Auckland, New Zealand

Independent Freedom *anchored off 'The Beach', Thailand*

Sunset over the Zuhair Islands in the Red Sea

Independent Freedom, *author at the helm: across the Atlantic*

Mary Helen leaving the Canaries, November 2000; the author's mother, Caplin's mate's sister, at the helm

Captain Ian Tew, respledent in sarong

Independent Freedom and Mary Helen *reunited in the Caribbean*

Grandfather's Wake

Tuesday 16 November. Edward and Philippa had been onboard a week when we returned to the marina to bunker, store and obtain port clearance. When we sailed away in the afternoon, heading south for Malaysia, there was only just enough water in the channel out of the marina. It was a very pleasant sail for the first twenty-four hours, but on the approach to Langkawi the rain started, and it continued all night. *Independent Freedom* was anchored half a mile off the shore at 20.00; we entered the marina the next morning. The ferries passing the entrance caused a tremendous wash, making the berths most uncomfortable. The swimming pool was enticing in the sticky weather and an early morning swim was most enjoyable.

An enjoyable tour of the island was followed by a day spent in the luxury of the Sheraton pool. Hugh and Cathy Marriot (RCC) came to lunch and we all invaded their bungalow for dinner which was great fun.

MALAYSIAN EXCURSION

Saturday 20 November 1999. Malaysia, a Moslem country, proved very different from Buddhist Thailand. I visited the harbour master and Customs and Immigration to obtain the port clearance. It was drizzling when we left the marina; the engine was in use all day as we passed Langkawi to port. The border with Thailand was crossed shortly after noon and the ex-prison island of Tarutao was also left to port. Paul Adirex's book 'The Pirates of Tarutao' makes fascinating reading. Dinner was eaten in the cockpit where it was cooler than below, the rain pouring down on the awning. *Independent Freedom* was anchored between the islands of Ko Bucan and Ko Kuao.

It rained most of Sunday, the wind in the NE gusting up to force 7. Was this the monsoon at last? The night was spent anchored off Ko Muk. The next day was spent motoring close along the coast, anchoring for lunch in Laem Koh Kwang bay where the restaurant was extremely rustic. The tide was falling and we only just made it out of the bay in time! Dinner was at Phi Phi Don enhanced by a procession to launch the flower boats. We purchased one and launched it from the yacht, encouraging any evil spirits to float away. We passed quite a few flower boats the next day, motoring to Ko Racha Yai.

Fine at last, with blue sky and sun, and a sparkling sea for Edward's birthday. We had a jolly beat to Ko Rang Yai Island, picking up a mooring off the Greek-columned resort. Michel dived to put a line through the concrete block, as it was quite rough on a lee shore. The hotel speed boat took us ashore for an excellent lunch in the elegant resort. An architect with imagination had put the lounge on the first floor with a magnificent vista up the Gulf.

Time passes so quickly when one is having fun, but time was up for Edward and Philippa – England called. In the sixteen days they had been on board, by the time we got back to the marina in Phuket, we had sailed 438 miles and visited seventeen anchorages.

INDIAN OCEAN TO SUEZ

ANDAMAN SEA/BAY OF BENGAL: PASSAGE OF A LIFETIME

Camilla, my niece, joined us a few weeks later and after sightseeing and shopping, preparations were made to leave Thailand.

Tuesday 21 December 1999. *Independent Freedom* was shifted to the fuelling berth. While taking fuel, the black Phuket adventure boat was inexpertly manoeuvered in the fresh breeze and her long prow caught our foresail halyard, bending the mast and heeling the yacht. I was not best pleased, in fact I was incandescent with rage – for this to happen at the beginning of an ocean passage! There did not appear to be any damage apart from a bent shackle, but only time would tell.

While running down the east coast of Phuket the main boom kicking strap connection parted from the mast, which was a nuisance. It was essential to have a kicking strap down wind so a temporary arrangement was rigged. Just after noon we passed Laem Phra Chao and the lighthouse and museum which we had visited. Course was set for the Nicobar Islands and so commenced the passage of a lifetime.

The wind freshened as the distance from the land increased until by tea time it was ENE force 4, and early evening force 5. *Independent Freedom* was flying along under full sail at over 7 knots; the weather was fine and clear. The boom vangs, which held the sails steady in the moderate to rough seas, were rigged for the broad reach.

It was a bright moon-lit night as the yacht continued to fly, the occasional water coming onboard to keep the decks wet. The wind remained steady between E and ENE. and did not exceed force 6 – magic sailing! The next day was hot and sunny, and from noon until 04.00 on 23 December she had sailed 137 miles, an average speed of 8.6 knots – what a crossing of the Andaman sea!

At 06.00 course was altered to pass through the Revello channel between the Camorta and Katchall Islands. Michel needed some shelter to adjust the alternator, and we studied the shore of Camorta Island through binoculars. No people or boats were seen, only a few huts and green fields.

'11.00 Nicobar Islands past, gone, as Xmas songs ring out from *Independent Freedom*, looking out for Santa', and so began the crossing of the Bay of Bengal.

At noon the day's run was 189 miles, an average of 7.9 knots, including the reduced speed through the Revello channel. This was Camilla's first ocean passage, but she took it like a veteran, retaining a healthy appetite.

Once we were clear of the Nicobars, the wind increased to force 6/7 and the rough sea made the yacht too wild. Early in the morning on Christmas Eve the foresail was lowered and two reefs were put in the mainsail. Even under the much-reduced sail, *Independent Freedom* was still sailing at well over 6 knots. We had been carrying far too much sail! She was much more comfortable but was still rolling.

Camilla was only able to add to her suntan after lunch on Christmas Day, when the sun came out making the white horses sparkle. On Boxing Day, in the morning, the wind moderated to force 5/6, so the double-reefed foresail was hoisted, but the sea remained rough.

Two days later the sea moderated when Dondra head light was in sight, and we came into the lee of Sri Lanka. The foresail had been lowered to reduce speed for a daylight arrival at Galle. We saw yachts in the harbour just after dawn, and made for the entrance. At first I could not understand what the frantic waving at the end of the jetty meant and waved back as we were about to enter.

"Stop" shouted the man on the breakwater.

"This is *Windflower*; the Navy have a chain across the entrance to the port with mines or depth charges on it." said a voice over the VHF. 'You should come to the anchorage.'

I rapidly reversed the course! *Independent Freedom* was anchored next to the yacht *Windflower* who very kindly ran a line to a buoy to hold the bow into the considerable swell. *Independent Freedom* pitched and rolled but it was not too bad.

So ended the passage of a lifetime – 1186 miles at an average of 7.2 knots in fine weather, and a broad reach all the way.

The port, which yachts were not allowed to enter due to breakwater improvements, was under Sri Lankan naval control. The war in the north had taken a bad turn – the Government and the President of Sri Lanka had been injured in an assassination attempt.

I called the Lloyds Agent whom I had appointed to act for us, and told him we had arrived. Shortly afterwards the pilot called on the VHF for our details. At 10.00 a naval crew under a petty officer boarded *Independent Freedom* from a dirty fibreglass dinghy and rummaged the yacht. A rating in shorts asked for cigarettes and brandy which he did not get.

The Agent met me ashore at the very rickety dinghy pontoon inside the port, and so began a saga of clearing the yacht in. The immigration officer relieved me of 2,000 rupees as a loan for his sick mother! I returned to *Independent Freedom* at 18.00 when the port curfew started; clearance was still not complete.

Clearance was finally completed the next morning. In the afternoon a heavily laden avon entered the port, containing Camilla and all her luggage, myself and Michel and our luggage, together with three garbage bags. *Independent Freedom* was left riding to the main anchor and a kedge and *Windflower* promised to keep an eye on her. The naval lookouts on the breakwater waved us in to their steps, and ordered us to open the luggage. I refused and forcefully demanded to see their commanding officer. Michel gave them a garbage bag. The rating who had asked for cigarettes and brandy again asked for cigarettes, so I again insisted on seeing their commanding officer. With a flick of his wrist the rating waved us away. If the navy treat visiting yachtsmen in this way, I dread to think how they treat their own people.

The Agent drove us to a seaside resort hotel where we spent the next few days. The Millennium party was fun and we danced until dawn. We hired a mini van and the next ten days were spent touring Sri Lanka; the driver proved to be a very good guide. Camilla was then dropped off at the airport outside Colombo.

To Kadmat Island, Laccadives: carried ashore in the boat

Thursday 13 January 2000. I took my leave from the helpful Lloyd's Agent and, armed with the port clearance, went onboard *Independent Freedom* from *Windflower*'s dinghy, both our outboard motors having broken down. Many more yachts were in the anchorage and the port had laid out more buoys, one of which looked suspiciously close to our kedge. However, with the aid of *Windflower* who let go the line to the buoy and then pushed to keep the yacht clear of a trimaran, we managed to release the main anchor and kedge.

The wind was out of the W or NW and variable in strength so the engine was used at times. During the night there was a lot of lightning 'sometimes like a firework display', also thunder and rain. Not like the NE monsoon I knew! The wind boxed the compass for the next few days in varying strength, up to force 5, and there was rain in the squalls. The engine was used as little as possible to conserve fuel, for we had more than 2,000 miles to make good.

Early on Saturday morning (15 January) the unmistakable smell of India came wafting in on light NNE airs. At noon there was a plague of flies and a few butterflies. *Independent Freedom* was 22 miles off the Indian coast and Cape Comorin, the southern-most tip of India, bore NE by E, distance 30 miles. During the afternoon when a nearby bulk carrier altered course towards the yacht I called her up and instructed whoever was on the bridge to alter course to starboard, which he did!

That night it cleared and Polaris was seen for the first time, while in the south the southern cross was still visible. The wind continued variable and very light.

03.20, Tuesday 18 January. The yacht was sailing quietly on the moon-lit silvery sea, when a naval warship passed close ahead at 10 knots, her diesels making a filthy racket in the quiet night. At noon the south side of Androth Island in the Laccadives was about a mile to windward, with breakers at both ends. The swell went down closer in, so Michel refueled the port tank from the cans on deck. When we were 2 cables off the reef in 23 metres of water, an open fishing boat – the *Mohammed Rafeck* – circled us three times, waved cautiously and then made off. I could see people net fishing on the reef, also palm-thatched huts, some sea defences against the SW monsoon, thick palm trees and what looked like a blue satellite dish.

There was a lot of traffic on the VHF between 'control tower' and 'port control' and it eventually dawned on us that it was about 'a sailing yacht drifting off Androth'. It was time for *Independent Freedom* to go! Special permission was needed to visit the Laccadives, and I did not want to upset the Indians. Once the north side of the island could be seen, lo and behold a port under construction was sighted, with a large crane at the end of the breakwater and a container-type crane inshore. There was nothing about it on the chart or in the Pilot book.

The moon had just set, the pole star and southern cross were still visible, and the object of my large detour to the north, Kadmat Island, could be seen at 6 miles on the radar. A quarter of a century ago I had been here in very different circumstances. The SW monsoon was blowing, the tug I commanded was towing a 50,000-ton storage tanker, one engine had packed up and could not be repaired at sea, and I had just received a message to go and salve a freezer ship aground on the windward side of Kadmat Island. What to do? It was too deep to anchor in the lee of the island so the next ten days was spent steaming up and down. The only way to reach the *Pacifico Everett* was across the lagoon, but the entrance appeared closed by breakers. It was raining. Eventually I did enter the lagoon with a volunteer crew in the zed boat – it was a matter of waiting for a break in the surf and then full speed before the next roller broke. Getting out was slightly more difficult and on one occasion, lepers from the colony helped us.

The ship was right up on the reef, with great waves breaking over her. Her bottom was breached and she was finished. When I landed on the island to call on the Administrator, hordes of young people kept touching my bare arms. It turned out that for anyone under the age of 26 I was the first white man they had ever seen.

'What does it feel like to be Jesus Christ superstar?' asked one of my Filipino crew.

The local policemen were rowed out wearing full uniform, their boots highly polished, to inspect the tug. I was taken ashore with them, the rowers skillfully negotiating the way through the surf. The boat was carried up the beach with me still onboard so I would not get my feet wet. A convivial evening was spent with the Administrator over a bottle of Black Label whisky I had brought ashore.

When being rowed back to the still-steaming tug and tow, the rowers sang a song in praise of this white man who had come with a black monster. I wondered whether I had inadvertently entered H. G. Wells' time machine and returned to the last century. The saga ended when the Selco tug *Salvanquish* turned up and took over my tow. The Swedish surveyor onboard declared the *Pacifico Everett* a total loss, and with the islanders' help the crew were rescued. I took them on board my tug, the *Salvaliant*, to Cochin where the engine was repaired.

Independent Freedom rounded the north end of the island where the lepers had helped and I saw what appeared to be the masts of the wreck. However they were not in the position of the wreck marked on the chart; it was further south than I remembered. As I skirted the reef, a gentle swell was breaking, and it became apparent that the *Pacifico Everett* was no more and that the 'masts' were in fact two substantial beacons marking a pass into the lagoon. They were not marked on the chart nor mentioned in the pilot book.

I altered course westwards for Arabia, my head filled with memories another era, another lifetime.

ARABIAN SEA AND GULF OF ADEN

And so began a week of perfect sailing. A fair wind at first but light so the reaching staysail was hoisted between the masts. The days were hot and sunny and the nights bright with the moon in a clear sky. Gradually the wind increased, so the staysail was stowed; the days' runs had increased from 71 to 168 miles when we eventually had to reef the sails.

Socotra (in the southern end of the Gulf of Aden) was left 150 miles to port. There were reports of pirates in speed boats and just before we left Sri Lanka I had been told about an Australian yacht which had been pirated and a woman injured. There is also a warning in the latest Admiralty supplement to the 'Red Sea and Gulf of Aden Pilot'. 'Piracy and Armed Robbery' in the south of the Red Sea, W and SE of the Gulf of Aden against vessels of any size, especially those at speeds of less than 12 knots. It really is quite outrageous that this scourge of the seas has been allowed to return. Halfway through the last century it was eradicated by concerted and firm action.

Friday 28 January 2000. *Independent Freedom* was off the Yemeni coast, and the courtesy ensign was hoisted. There was traffic about and we felt we were clear of any pirate danger. The wind had eased to force 3/4 and it was very pleasant coasting. In the evening log, 'Rās Fartak and the hills beyond were bathed in the yellow sunset light, their outlines faint like an Impressionist painting'. 'Dolphins were playing, their trails twisting and squirming snake-like, glowing in the bioluminescence'.

Aden was passed on 1 February and the anchor was let go off the Djibouti yacht club, just after daybreak the next day – 2449 miles covered in 21 days, with only 3 days of motoring.

DJIBOUTI AND THE RED SEA: SAILING AT GUNPOINT

Not much had changed; the place was as grubby as fifteen

years before and no less expensive. A chic airconditioned shop with the perfumes of Paris looked incongruous in the main square, with its hawkers and beggars and crumbling buildings. The French military presence is much reduced, but there was a modern warship on the naval pier. Djibouti benefits from the loss of the Ethiopian ports to Eritrea, and a couple of container cranes were being off-loaded from a communist Chinese heavy lift vessel. Armed guards force anyone on foot to pass the presidential residence on the far side of the road. French food is available but at a price.

The hull of *Independent Freedom*, filthy with long weed, was cleaned by Mustapha and his mate. The water tanks were filled using cans borrowed from *Tom*, a French yacht that had been at Galle. *Havenga*, another French yacht, used his special fitting to fill our gas bottles from the large bottle I had purchased ashore. I then donated the large bottle to the yacht club! Bunkers were taken from the Total filling station by the club, although duty-free was available in the port. Duty-free cigarettes were purchased for use in the Suez canal, when I obtained the clearance.

Thursday 10 February 2000. A week after arriving in Djibouti, we moved out to the anchorage amongst the reefs off Ile Maskali and swam in the clear water. A very pleasant couple of days were spent preparing for the rigours of the beat up the Red Sea. I had visited the British Consul, who was away, but his secretary whom I knew from my salvage days was very helpful. The basic advice was 'don't stop'! Saudi Arabia discourages yachts, there was a war on between Eritrea and Ethiopia, Mig fighters had been reported over Massawa (Ethiopia), and the twenty-five-year war continues in Sudan. So we decided to make a passage direct to Suez, with a stop at Massawa unless a fair wind took us past!

Saturday 12 February. The waters of Djibouti were finally left when we sailed out of the anchorage. There was enough south in the wind to fetch Rās Bir, past the ruins of Obock, and to ease the sheets and reach along the desolate barren cliffs of north Djibouti. There was a good breeze from the SE and the speed was a satisfactory 7 knots. The traffic lanes outside the Straits of Bab el Mandeb were crossed at right angles, and course had to be altered to pass round the stern of a container ship flying light – the *Colombus Olivinos*.

I had a healthy respect for the prohibited zone round Perim Island on the east side of the strait, having been fired on by a machine gun when I passed too close in my tug *Salvanguard*. The wind had freshened but I was keen to clear the straits, and we were running fast goose-winged. At 18.30 it was gusting force 7, and Perim Island was on our quarter. The foresail was lowered and *Independent Freedom* continued fast under the full main. She was still well balanced and easy on the helm.

'20.00 sailing very fast indeed – should reef! 21.00 Rough following sea – rolling and yawing. 21.30 Wind increased, gusts force 8 – now surfing up to 9 knots. Put in three reefs. 22.00 2/8 cloud fine, rough following breaking seas, still sailing very fast up to 7.5 knots, alter course 335 so as not to hit Al Mukha.'

Sunday 13 February. Log entries: '01.00: cloudless, wind backing to south. Running very fast, breaking seas. 02.00: very rough, gusting 45 knots, big breakers. 03.00: inadvertent gybe broke boom lashing and bent rail. 03.18: very rough, gusting 46 knots.' It seemed to moderate a little for a time and then increased, and at 07.12 there was a gust of 47 knots. Abu Ail was close to starboard, the seas a white mass, the tops of the waves blown off, breaking and leaping up the rocks. The lighthouse buildings looked a bit dilapidated. Thirty years ago I was Second Officer on the *City of Poona* and we had stopped in answer to a flag signal and picked up a sick lighthouse keeper. Eighteen years ago I had salved the *Cape Greco* ex *City of Worcester* on which, coincidentally, I had also served as Second Officer. She had been aground in the bay on the opposite side of the channel to the lighthouse, and the accommodation had been burnt out.

The wind moderated, or at least there were no more gusts over 40 knots, to SSE force 7/8. However, the sea increased and at noon the breaking seas were coming onboard. For the first time since New York, two-and-a-half years ago, a breaking sea came in over the stern. A ship passed bound south, shipping it green over the bows.

At tea time the Zubayr Islands were in sight and the wind moderated. What a fantastic 24-hour run!

The wind continued fair, albeit light. The reefs were shaken out and Jabal Atair was passed the next morning although we did not see the lighthouse. At noon we passed the 'Pearly Gates' entrance, not to heaven but to Gizan! I had salved the I*sland Transporter* loaded with cement inside the Pearly Gates and had had to find a channel to extract her from the reefs. We had also found an abandoned ship aground on the reefs and salved her as well!

In the afternoon, although we were still running with a fair wind, the swell built up from the north which, combining with that from the south, made for an uncomfortable time.

At 18.00 the wind veered and went light. It continued round over the next few hours to NW and then NNW. The foresail was hoisted and the engine started, to make progress through the meeting place of the north and south winds. It was calm for most of the next 36 hours. On the evening of 16 February the wind filled in from the NNW and it was a dead beat for the next 700 miles! The fair wind had carried us well past Massawa.

The wind was pretty steady out of the NNW with occasional variations to N or WNW and for the next ten days did not blow harder than force 7 nor less than force 3 – mainly force 5/6. The main problem was the Red Sea; the seas were steep and short, so the yacht had to be sailed fairly free. It was starboard tack at night, port tack during the day and dinghy-style tacking on any wind shift. It was easy to go east and west. The problem was to make a northing. 'Ocean Passages of the World', sailing ship routes, recommends that sailing ships hold the Arabian coast, which is what we did. At night there was a bright moon, and the sun was out during the day, although it slowly became colder as we made our way northwards. In winds above force 5 we reefed; the yacht goes better when not pressed. Although *Independent Freedom* usually sailed about 90 miles a day, she was making good a steady 70 miles, which I was pretty pleased with, considering the seas.

Thursday 17 February. Sailing towards the Saudi coast, I was looking for Qadd Humais reef with its sand islets. At noon, when the yacht was in their position and nothing was to be seen, the adrenalin began to run! I found them about 3 miles ENE of their charted position. It was a beautiful day, sparkling blue water, white horses and a cobalt sky.

It was Michel's third 'birthday' on board the next day, when we passed the entrance to Jeddah. The tack out to sea was made when Shib al Katir light bore NE by E, distance 3 miles. It was a full moon that night, rising minutes after the sun set so it was visible all night.

On Sunday afternoon the entrance to Yanbu was passed and for half an hour the water was smooth in the lee of Shib al Suflani, but it was soon rough again once clear! In the evening the wind freshened to force 6/7 and it was very rough tacking between Shib as Sabah and the outer reef, and I was glad when we were clear shortly after midnight.

Monday 21 February. Noon found *Independent Freedom* tacking off the Saudi shore, south of Râs Bardi with its factory belching smoke. The sea was much calmer 2 or 3 miles offshore and it was very pleasant.

No boats were seen until, at 17.40, we were accosted by two armed soldiers in a Boston-type speed boat with a small cuddy. When they waved I waved back, but when close to one of them cocked his gun and pointed it at us, so I realized we were in trouble. They shouted and indicated we should proceed directly into the wind. When I pointed to the sails and indicated we had to tack, the one with the cocked gun aimed it at us. I luffed up into the wind the sails flapping and eventually they got the message. For the first time in my life, my mouth went completely dry and my tongue felt twice its usual size – fear! Michel, who was below, wrote in the log 'These boys mean danger. Hope we will be OK'.

I pulled myself together and began to think. I did not think they would actually fire at us, but they might fire and hole the yacht. I was not doing anything wrong but it is foolish to argue with armed men who do not speak your language, and they were soldiers not sailors. I knew from the chart there were no anchorages along the immediate coast. It would shortly be dark. It seemed to me that if I could delay reaching wherever they were taking us as long as possible, they might become discouraged in the cold and dark or run out of fuel. The one thing I wanted to avoid was being taken ashore, because once ashore I lost any control and was completely in their hands to face any charges that might be trumped up. I sailed as slowly as I dared, tacking when told to. It became rougher the further offshore we went. We threw overboard in a weighted bag anything that might possibly be construed offensive to the sensitive Saudi morals. The boat had no lights and it was becoming nice and cold.

We appeared to be heading for some bright lights on what we thought was a truck, but it was taking a satisfactorily long time.

Suddenly about two hours after dark the speedboat pulled up alongside and one of the soldiers said 'Name, name'.

Back in the seventeenth century my ancestor, the privateer Captain Thomas Tew, had made a considerable fortune pillaging in the Red Sea; how long were memories round here? I shone a torch on the name painted on the side. The soldier indicated in the torch light that I should write it on paper.

Michel, who was still below, passed up paper and pencil. The soldier steering tried to come close enough so I could hand over the note. Eventually he made it and they shouted 'Go, go!'

We went, reaching fast out to sea.

At 23.00, Beacon no. 11 on Shib Shu Aybath bore north, distance 6 cables. The sheets were hardened and we were back on the wind. I kept 12 or more miles off the Saudi coast from now on!

There were no more excitements apart from having to tack and avoid a collision with a coaster (despite illuminating his bridge with the searchlight). The further north we sailed the stronger the wind tended to blow, and it became colder.

Early on Thursday morning the wind backed and we were almost able to make the course for the straits of Gubal. It freshened and the sea became rough, but later died and freed even more. What a break!

On Friday morning it was blowing N, force 6/7, and *Independent Freedom* was close-reaching fast, the bright moonlight emphasizing the very rough sea. At 08.00 the sea moderated as the Sinai peninsula was approached. The great barren mountains, in the words of Adrian Hayter 'giving a sense of timelessness as if they had outlived their own souls', lay on the starboard side. The Pilot book warns of the strong winds and rough seas in the straits. Quite suddenly at 08.45 the wind dropped. We could not believe our luck and turned on the engine and motored hard. We went through the inner channel in a calm, the sun shining on those brown barren mountains.

At tea time the engine was turned off and at 17.30 two reefs were taken in each sail. The night was spent beating up the east shore of the Gulf of Suez amongst the oil fields with their platforms pipes and flares, the radar on to watch for anything without lights. The motor was used when the wind failed.

By morning it was blowing a gale and the third reef was taken in the main and foresail. It was very rough and cold. The traffic lanes were crossed and the west coast of the Gulf was closed. In shallow water, with a much reduced sea, we beat up to the lee of the reef off Rās Ruahmi and anchored in 4.5 metres. There was no wind shelter but it was reasonably calm. Two fishing boats joined us in the anchorage. Anchor watches were set and a worrying night was spent with the shallow-water alarm going off at intervals as the yacht yawed over a coral head. I might have preferred it dodging the oil paraphernalia and shipping but I am not sure!

On Sunday morning it was only blowing force 6 so the anchor was raised and we beat up the coast, reef-dodging in quite calm water. The wind moderated and it was motor-sailing to Suez bay.

I think my grandfather would have found it very difficult if not impossible to sail up the Red Sea in the gaff-rigged *Caplin* and he planned to return to England via South Africa.

SUEZ TO THE CANARIES

SUEZ TO ASHQUELON

We allowed ourselves to be 'picked up' by Prince of the Red Sea agents off Newport rock, and entered the Suez canal just ahead of a large loaded tanker. *Independent Freedom* was moored between buoys at the Suez canal yacht club, with the agent running the lines! We had sailed 1,535 miles (through the water) at an average speed of 4.1 knots to make good 1,250 miles and the engine had been used 25% of the time.

I was very pleased with *Independent Freedom*'s progress and it was in some euphoria that I phoned 'mission control', but it rapidly evaporated when I received some business news which required my immediate attention and a return to England for a spell. I arranged to go to Cairo the next day and commence transit of the canal on Thursday. I would fly to the UK from Israel.

Thursday 2 March 2000. Military exercises were to take place, so the pilot boarded at 04.30 and by averaging 6.4 knots Ismalia was reached at 11.30. Honorariums induced a new pilot to board and he was picked up by the pilot boat at 19.42 in Port Said.

The barometer was sky high and when it fell it would blow hard, so we motor-sailed the 125 miles to Ashquelon. An Israeli gunboat, with guns, circled us three times 10 miles off and, satisfied with our answers, made off at high speed. The marina staff welcomed us and, after interrogation by security, immigration cleared us in.

A total of 8,166 miles had been sailed since Darwin in 73 days at sea, at an average speed of 4.7 knots with the engine used for just under 20 days, and 105 days spent at anchor or in port.

Ashquelon took my mind back to my grandfather, somewhat indirectly via a piece written by my mother (*Caplin*'s Mate's elder sister). In 1929 she had accompanied him on a cruise to the Faroes in *Emanuel*, the 30-foot cutter in which he later sailed single-handed across the Atlantic. My grandfather was very seldom seasick; however, at the very beginning of the cruise, just out of Burnham, the unthinkable happened.

"Crew and Skipper had both been feeding the fishes, and I soon followed their example—a good beginning for a cruise! The situation was really rather humorous, though at the actual time it did not strike us as such. Hush! 'Tell it not in Gath, publish it not in the streets of Ashkelon,' but I had never seen Skipper seasick before and he was more upset than I."

I am happy to report that Ashquelon's streets remain innocent of my grandfather's fleeting weakness – we published it not.

Three months at Ashquelon was more than enough, although I had been to England and the mate to Bangkok. I enjoyed my trip to Jerusalem, Bethlehem and the Dead Sea and to see the these biblical names on the road signs was a sort of revelation: the places were real! I found, whatever the security reasons, the sight of girls and boys carrying guns unsettling, especially when asleep on buses.

ORDERED OFF OUR BOATS

The final prod to be away was the visit of the Prime Minister to the marina when we were ordered off our boats, to which I took exception. There were so many gun-toting people around it is a wonder there wasn't an accident and I was glad to go into town.

Friday 9 June 2000. We said our goodbyes to the friendly marina staff who had looked after us so well, and early in the morning left under sail. There was just enough wind in the marina to manoeuvre but unfortunately it was too early for anyone to be up and watching! Once clear of the breakwater, which in rough weather sheltered the marina but not the entrance from breaking seas, the mainsail was hoisted. It was easy close-hauled sailing all day into a head swell and it became hot.

In the evening the wind all but died and the engine was started. It stopped almost as soon as it was put into gear. There was oil in the bilges and the nightmare of the broken gear box at Moorea reared its head.

"I told you we should not have sailed on a Friday," reproached the mate.

A line left out on the foredeck had fallen over the side and wrapped itself round the propeller. Friday or not the mate donned diving gear and as darkness closed in cut free the rope.

The engine ran all night without further incident but the shackle on the mainsail clew parted at the end of the boom. When rehoisting, the new easi-sail slides caught on the lazy jacks, which is something we had not foreseen when having the new system fitted at Ashquelon. Easy Sail, who fitted the system, had been economical with the truth concerning the return of VAT, as with the drawbacks of the system. It is almost impossible to reef or unreef unless heading into the wind, which is a major drawback in bad weather. The sail is indeed much easier to hoist and lower but the fact that the new track and slides stand proud of the mast causes the problems.

It was mainly motoring, past Cyprus, until finally the Turkish coast came in sight, dark and brooding in the bright moonlight. It was a beautiful night when the anchor was let go outside Finike. The moon was setting and the surrounding mountains were outlined stark against the cloudless sky, a welcome change from the flat desert of the Israeli coast. The trip across the Mediterranean sea had taken almost four days for the 357 miles and typically more than half the time had been under power.

Magnificent ablutions

Later in the morning we motored into the well run marina and moored. A month was spent here and we found Finike unspoiled and friendly. There was a week-long music and cultural festival held just outside the marina, which attracted thousands of young people, and not even a whisper of any trouble, nor any loutish behaviour. The marina ablutions were magnificent, with marble floors and spotlessly clean, but the ones in the park outshone them with flowers and classical music playing. I made a few bus trips to enjoy the splendid scenery. A short business trip to Munich was a welcome break from the 40°C summer heat.

Wednesday 12 July. Early in the morning, the lines were slipped, the bicycle stowed on deck and *Independent Freedom* motored out of Finike past the mountainous rocky coast to Kekova, a distance of some 19 miles. The landlocked lagoon proved a most pleasant place to spend a week relaxing and swimming with the occasional dinner ashore.

Twenty miles further on, after a motor with the awning up through spectacular scenery, Kas was reached. The night was spent alongside the wharf of the uncompleted marina at the head of the sound, with the anchor down to keep the yacht off the wharf if the wind got up.

Kalkan Bay some 14 miles westwards was reached the next day and the night spent amongst galiots with their tourists. It was almost 50 miles to Fethiye along more spectacular coastal scenery, the mountains falling steep to into the sea. A United States warship was anchored in the Bay.

The next week was spent in the bay which included Fethiye and Gocek with the numerous anchorages near Gocek all in sheltered waters. We anchored alongside *Pala*, first met at Noumea, New Caledonia, in Sarsala Koyu, and had a jolly evening with the mate's canapés instead of supper.

The apparently permanent fine weather remained with us to Marmaris where the many hurrah boats, speed boats, yachts and other assorted water-borne craft brought us back to civilization and a most unfriendly marina. I suppose with five or six charter companies operating out of it they did not need visitors. It would have been better to have cleared out at Fethiye and save US$100 agents fee!

Monday 31 July. We extracted the yacht with difficulty from the berth, with none of the promised help from the marina, only to be chased at the entrance by a speed boat asking if we had paid the bill. I was not best pleased especially as I had informed the over-manned office that we were leaving. It was late afternoon so I decided to spend the night anchored in Kumulubuk Bay some 8 miles from Marmaris.

It was a red dawn when the anchor was aweigh and *Independent Freedom* sailed out of the bay and along the coast. The engine was used a couple of times, when the wind died, but by 09.00 one reef had been taken in the mainsail and at noon three reefs in the mainsail and two in the foresail. In Rhodes channel there were lots of ferries.

I had heard a gale warning on the VHF but I could not discover where, so assumed it was our area. The wind had headed so it was a dead beat in an increasing sea and at 13.45 it was blowing force 7 from the west, the direction we wished to go. There seemed no point in slugging it out so at 15.30 Urak Koulandris light was rounded and we beat into the bay behind the light and anchored. The bay was sheltered from all directions except east. There were three small fishing boats moored close to the shore, one small yacht and some sort of minicamp ashore on N Seskli Island. The kedge was laid and if anyone queried why we were there without a Greek flag or having cleared in I would claim port of refuge. During the evening it was gusting force 8 so were glad to be safely at anchor.

I was awoken at 04.00 by someone knocking hard against the hull and my immediate thought was it was the customs!. It turned out to be some men in a zed boat demanding a torch. Before I could utter a suitable reply I saw the reason why and called to the mate for the searchlight. A very large luxury motor yacht, almost a mini passenger ship, her foredeck nearly under water and obviously sinking, was making her way into the bay. The mate shone the searchlight onto the moored fishing boats and yacht. She grounded just ahead of *Independent Freedom* having just missed one of the fishing boats. The yacht appeared to be on top of the anchor. Just after 05.00 the mate heaved up the anchor which was opposite the *Ontario*'s gangway and just clear of the hull. We reanchored clear astern of the settling casualty and awaited events. The crew of the grounded yacht started to take clothing and suitcases ashore and by daylight the whole of the starboard deck was under water. When the lifeboat and a fishing boat turned up it was time to leave!

There was a gale warning, NW force 7/8, but it was moderating further west. The reefs were left in and were needed once clear of the land. I decided to take the southern route south of Crete because it gave a fair wind initially and good would be made in the lee of the island in sheltered waters.

The sky was blue and the sea dotted with white horses as *Independent Freedom* flew SSW, the wind slowly increasing to gale force. It was rough but passing between N. Khalki Island and Rhodes gave time for an early lunch in comfort. It was very rough during the afternoon and the yacht was surfing on the waves and shipping water but it was sunny and hot. N. Karpathos Island was reached but there was no shelter off the port but once round the point a beautiful bay opened up and the anchorage was swell-free. Seventy-five miles had been covered at a very satisfactory average speed of 6.5 knots. It had been an exhilarating sail to our second port of refuge!

It blew hard from the NW the next day when we made an attempt to carry on. It was very rough and unpleasant once clear of N. Karpathos across the channel to N. Kasos so I turned back to the anchorage.

Friday 4 August. Although there was no gale warning on , the third reef was taken in the foresail while still in the lee of N Karpathos. It was a close reach across to N Kasos, which was topped by cloud, in fine and sunny weather. One reef was shaken out of the foresail and it was magnificent sailing, albeit a little wet, across to Crete, the wind WNW force 6 and quite rough.

It was still daylight as the lee was reached and the sea went down. The wind headed as the sun set, a fiery red, with the hills of Crete to starboard. Severe squalls blew off the land as Koufonis Island was left to port and later the wind became very flukey. One minute it was calm and – bang – it was blowing force 8, which made for an interesting time. The mainsail was lowered for a few hours.

The next day was pleasant, sunny and hot and we had a grand sail in sheltered waters. That night the wind died and the motor was used. Early in the morning the wind came in from the NW and by 03.00 it was blowing force 5/6. Two reefs were taken in both the sails and as the sun rose over western Crete it looked as though it was going to be a bit of a slog to Malta, hard on the wind. It was quite rough and the yacht was shipping water.

In the evening the wind moderated but it was much colder. The mate had a near miss with a ship which was apparently not keeping a lookout early in the morning. During the day the wind increased again and about noon the main boom kicking strap fitting on deck broke with a loud bang. So much for the special bolt I had had made of metal supposedly one-third again as strong as stainless steel!

Tuesday 8 August. The yacht was still hard on the wind not quite making the course, but sailing under full sail. It was a lovely day and the wind moderated further in the afternoon; all in all very pleasant. Gales were forecast the next day for south of Crete so I was glad we had pushed on. The wind died further and the engine was used to keep going, Malta being sighted on Friday afternoon.

Permission was granted by Valetta port control for us to enter Marsamxett harbour, and what a magnificent entrance it is too. The very stones of the fortifications exuded Malta's turbulent history. We moored at the customs jetty while I went to clear in. The marina office was just closing, but they allocated a temporary berth, warning me the marina was full, and I would have to move in three days time to a different berth.

The mate worked on the engine but the Volvo agent did not have any injectors which were needed. The engine was giving trouble, being very temperamental in starting. I found Malta fascinating especially as the bucket-and-spade brigade kept to the beaches, leaving the sights uncluttered with people, so a joy to visit.

The day we made up our minds to leave, the bunker barge, which is normally moored near the entrance to the marina, decided to take the day off for repairs or a refill. No one knew when it would return. I therefore arranged for a road tanker to deliver fuel. Unfortunately its hose was not long enough to reach the berth so we had to moor alongside the road.

It was very pleasant motoring up the coast to Melliela Bay in hot sunshine. The mate let go the anchor but unfortunately managed to let all the cable run out, breaking the rotten lashing holding the end in the chain locker. I rushed below to press the MOB button on the GPS and the kedge was laid. Luckily the water was clear, and warm, and part of the cable lay on sand so it was easy to see. It was in 11 metres of water so the mate dived to retrieve it. It was a joy to swim off the yacht and be out of the marina.

Mgarr, the port for Gozo, was reached just before noon, passing the blue lagoon on the way. It is very small. There is nowhere to anchor so permission must be obtained and a berth allocated before entering. The marina official on duty was incredibly stupid, not helped by the letters on the pontoons being different on the outward end to those on the inward end. Adding to the drama the new large ferry to Malta was leaving. It is a very pretty little harbour with a fine church standing on the hill overlooking it. I couldn't resist the investment of a couple of pounds to ride the new ferry to Malta and back! She is quite well thought out and was built in Malta dockyard. We dined ashore in the pleasant restaurant next door to the ferry terminal.

Saturday, 19 August. Today dawned fine and clear – we had not seen rain for months! The weather forecast was good so I paid the marina and cleared out from immigration and customs who were conveniently housed next door in the new office block.

There was no wind so we motored close round the south and east coast of Gozo with its steep cliffs, caves and coves. Once clear of the land a light southerly air enabled the motor to be turned off but when it was required in the evening it would not start, despite the mate's work on it. Eventually it started and we motored all night. There was a very heavy dew and it was almost like rain dropping off the mainsail.

Pantelleria was passed in the afternoon with its terraced hills, many of which do not appear to be in use. Tourism has taken over; I noticed hard-bottomed zed boats inshore.

There was heavy traffic during the night with a lot of fishing boats as well, when the fog came down off Cape Bon. I was exceedingly glad of the radar. The visibility cleared at noon when a fair wind got up and the yacht ran goosewinged along the Tunisian coast. The lure of a new country proved too much, so course was altered for Tabarka, the last port before Algeria. The many fishing floats were missed in the darkness. Port was entered at 08.30 the 450-year-old Genoese citadel dominating the harbour.

We moored alongside the road opposite the fishing port just outside the Capitainerie and were well looked after. Bunkering was rather an effort, carrying five-gallon cans of diesel about a mile, but the assistant to the harbour master carried the heavy ones! There were lots of restaurants around the harbour and the bank was only 3 minutes' walk. The beach, crowded with Tunisian holidaymakers, was only 100 yards from the yacht.

Everyone seemed to be enjoying themselves and there was a happy atmosphere with live music in the evening. I made a bus trip to Tunis and back to view the countryside which was much greener than I thought. The only sour element was the theft of our bicycle, much to the consternation of the harbour master and police.

Friday 25 August. Risking a Friday departure I cleared out and we motored all day. It was very hot, and flat calm or light head winds until Sunday, when the wind got up from the east in the evening, giving us a fair wind, up to force 7, for two days. On Tuesday night there was much lightning over the Sierra Nevada and heavy traffic along the Spanish coast with numerous fishing boats. During the day we motored along what appeared to be a continuous concrete jungle, past the man-made port of Malaga: much yacht traffic, dinghies and paragliding. Just before midnight thick fog came down and so we anchored off Duquesa.

Oil in the bilges

Thursday 31 August 2000. The anchor was aweigh at 06.30 and motoring continued, dodging the fishing nets, until disaster just after Gibraltar was sighted. The bilges were found to be full of engine oil and the pressure was rapidly falling. My heart sank – and the engine is nearly new, I thought. The mate refilled the sump with the reserve oil and I restarted the engine. It was flat calm so could not sail. I called Shephards marina on the VHF but without success. I called our agent on the mobile but could not get through (I later discovered that with a mobile phone you had to use the Spanish code) so called 'mission control' in England and told him to arrange a berth on arrival. The mate reckoned we just had enough oil to reach Gibraltar.

Europa Point was rounded and I finally got through to Shephards Marina who said the marina was full. I pointed out this was an emergency and they were the Volvo agent. Eventually Marina Bay arranged with customs for us to go straight to one of their berths, which we did on the last drop of oil! There will be no more Friday departures for us. A few days later *Independent Freedom* was ignominiously towed round to Shephards for repairs, the spectacular backdrop of the Rock hidden by some extremely ugly buildings.

In two-and-a-half months from Ashquelon, 24 days were spent at sea, of which half had been under power, to pass through the Mediterranean sea, and no rain!

GIBRALTAR TO THE CANARIES

Five weeks was too long in Gibraltar but Shephards were busy and there was no point in hassling; the spares had to be ordered from Sweden and so on. *Independent Freedom* was on dry land for ten days for a wash and brush-up and a new coat of anti-fouling; it was a year since she had last been out of the water in Singapore. Gibraltar has its own rhythm, an hour and a half for lunch, a leisurely start in the morning, and early knock off in the afternoon. Weekend work was simply unheard-of! It was better to go with it than fight.

I made use of the cheap bus service and spent a couple of very pleasant Sunday afternoons on the terrace of the Galetea hotel on the east side of the rock. I watched the power boat race from the top of the rock (pity the café is so awful). The Trafalgar cemetery inspired me to buy two books on Nelson. The acoustics in St Michael's cave near the top of the Rock are quite magnificent and I went to a wonderful concert of Beethoven's Choral Symphony with a huge Spanish choir. The RAF Central Band two weeks later were fantastic. National Day was colourful with everyone wearing red and white. English politicians would have been green with envy at the size of the crowd listening to the speeches, and cheering, too.

Clifton Shipping let me use their offices with fax, telephones, secretaries and computers which meant I completed a project I was doing. I first met the owners, Martyn and Solen, when taking over a Russian naval tug on behalf of Singapore owners five years ago!

There was a nice weather window with easterlies in the Straits of Gibraltar and we were keen to get away before the westerlies set in again. The final repair was to the wind generator (the electrician had been away) but we were not leaving on Friday, although we did take bunkers!

Saturday 7 October 2000. The sails were hoisted and reefed in the lee of the breakwater, watched by port control from their tower. The top of the Rock was shrouded with a cap of cloud and as the distance increased so did the wind. By noon it was free of Europa Point although the sea was still smooth in the Bay. Pta Carnero was passed 3 cables off and we had a magnificent sail, goosewinged, close along the Spanish coast, rock hopping, inshore of the current and tide. *Independent Freedom* showed a clean pair of heels to two yachts further out in the Straits and by Tariffa Point at 14.30 they were almost hull-down astern. Once clear of the Point, the wind had increased to NE force 7. I headed out into the Gibraltar Straits and lee-bowed the current, shooting across the sparkling white-horse-covered traffic-filled Straits, to the African coast. It was sunny and warm despite the wind. By 16.40 Tangiers was abeam and at 17.40 the substantial Spanish lighthouse on Cape Spartel was half a mile away. It had been a very satisfactory exit from the Mediterranean into the Atlantic.

It was very pleasant running southwestwards in the lee of the Moroccan coast, the sea almost smooth. As the night drew in the wind dropped and early in the morning headed. It had become quite cold and damp. At noon it was calm and the engine had to be used for a couple of hours. At 17.30 I called up the QEII bound north out to sea and told her we had last seen her in New Zealand! There was bright phosphorescence that night but little wind and the engine was much in use.

On Monday at noon we retarded the clocks to GMT and the wind started to fill, first from the WSW, and as it increased it veered until at 20.00 it was blowing NW force 5/6. The yacht was sailing at over 7 knots but when the wind veered further to north east, which was right astern, the foresail was dropped. A school of dolphins played around the boat, visible in the moonlight.

The first reef was taken in early on Tuesday morning and, just after 09.00, the third. The yacht was running very fast in an increasing sea and swell before a force 7 NE wind. The day's run was 170 miles, an average of 6.5 knots for the 26 hours. Early on Wednesday morning there were gusts of force 8 and a wave came on board during the mate's watch but she was really very comfortable. The wind moderated during the day and two reefs were shaken out but the day's speed was better at 6.7 knots.

There was quite a heavy swell running as Roque del Este, an unlit rock off the north coast of Lanzarote, was sighted. It was dark when Estrecho del Rio, the narrow strait between Lanzarote and Ile Graciosa, was entered, a bit too close to Ile Graciosa, the breakers ghostly white in the moonlight. The swell quickly went down and we had a gentle sail through the strait to Baiha del Salado where the anchor was let go at 20.24. The steep cliffs of Lanzarote less than a mile away were very black against the sky.

A very pleasant few days were spent in this unspoiled anchorage, the only yacht; eighteen of them were in the next bay!

Tuesday 17th October. The anchor was aweigh while it was still dark and we beat out of the straits and then had a fair wind and fast sail down the coast to Puerto Calereo. There as we entered the marina was *Mary Helen* with my mother, my grandfather's elder daughter, standing on deck to welcome us. She is 88 and her yacht is 63 years old, designed by my father as a gaff cutter 26 feet overall. She was launched in 1937, a year before *Caplin*. My parents had just married and opened a 'yacht fund' in lieu of wedding presents.

My mother, together with my elder brother, who has just retired, are sailing across the Atlantic in a few days' time – a fitting meeting as *Independent Freedom* has now crossed, or will shortly, the outward track of *Caplin* as we continue our voyage to complete our circumnavigation in the Bahamas.

My grandfather and aunt were unable to complete their circumnavigation due to the War; in a sense, we are completing it for them and we join them again, my aunt's diary providing the guide, for their first ocean crossing and our last.

For my mother, who had already missed a transatlantic passage with my grandfather when he decided to go single-handed in 1934 and who, but for her marriage, would have been mate on *Caplin* instead of my aunt, this was the Atlantic crossing she had been denied all those years ago.

THE ATLANTIC CROSSING

ALTHOUGH *CAPLIN* SAILED this leg at the start of her voyage, I have saved my aunt's account of it to set alongside *Independent Freedom*'s transatlantic passage, the final leg of our circumnavigation.

CAPLIN: BANTRY BAY TO MADEIRA

Monday 2 May 1938. We sailed for Bermuda. We rose early and had a good wash before filling our tanks with water. We had three extra oil drums of water lashed on the counter, one ten-gallon and two five. Paddy (O'Keefe) did everything for us. Took us around the shops and had a joint of beef cooked for us at his house. An old lady, the character of the town, gave me a little medallion and wished me good luck. We leave with about 2d in cash on board, 1d of which I shall throw overboard when we sail which the Irish say is good luck. Paddy's men brought all our provisions and water on board for us. I have loved the little bit of Ireland I have seen, the people are so kind and friendly and the scenery great. There are few cars about compared with England but lots of donkeys and horses. We had a telegram from Dick wishing us 'fair winds'. Everything has been so easy so far I am getting cold feet and wondering if it isn't all too good to be true.

Paddy and Mike and another man came out and helped us get ready for sea. We hoisted our main sail, stay sail and jibs at 14.15 and got under way. We ran down Bantry Bay before a fresh wind; reefed main sail and spinnaker, got out of bay in two-and-a-half hours. Very good. Out to sea there was a big sea running and what skipper calls a freeze breeze and I call a gale. Wasn't long before I was definitely feeling rather squeamish so lay down for a bit. At 21.45 I took the helm and Skipper went below for a sleep until 24.00. I then turned in and Skipper took a four-and-a-half hour watch. Skipper slept until 07.00. (During the night one of our five-gallon cans was lost overboard, can't think how it happened as neither of us saw it go and it was lashed as securely as the others.)

Tuesday 3 May. The port runner had chaffed badly, two strands gone and a third nearly. Still a big sea running, waves like mountains and both of us feeling queer. I managed to try a piece of bread and butter and half a piece of bacon. I soon turned in again, Skipper too. We made *Caplin* take the night watch, both of us sleeping below. In the morning felt a bit better but inside still weak.

Wednesday 4 May. Managed a fair breakfast of scrambled eggs. Wind freshening, a big sea piling up. Soon blowing strong, about force 6. Seven rolls in main sail, looks like pocket handkerchief. Sea getting bigger all the time. Skipper went forward to get the main sail down and I stayed at the helm. Skipper put a life line on and gave me detailed instructions what to do if he fell overboard. He didn't. *Caplin* running very well under head sails but mon dieux how she rolls. Soon began to feel very seedy again so turned in. Skipper cleared up cabin and got various stations on the radio. Skipper cooked some sausages for supper; I managed two but this awful roll is too much and I turned in again with a hot bottle. I fear my sister Helen might be calling us a sissy ship.

Thursday 5 May. Skipper woke me at 05.30 and I turned out feeling much better; actually managed to wash my face and brush my hair. The galley powder is proving very good with salt water – can get quite a lather and my nails are beautifully clean. We set the balloon stay sail which increased our speed, Skipper now at the helm. I got the breakfast below. Unfortunately the cooking too much for me and I felt seedy again so I took a rug and went up to steer. Soon felt better. Skipper's trousers have huge tears at both knees. In another day we ought to be in a warmer climate and they will come in useful as shorts. Ship practically steering herself. Both spinnaker booms out, running dead before the wind, still a fair sea. After supper 20.30 Skipper turned in and I took the watch till 23.30. Cloudy sky, moon appears very bright at intervals. Glad to turn in.

A TOAST TO CAPTAIN WALLER

Friday 6 May 1938. Turned out at 07.00. Found Skipper had rigged up Waller Steering and had been turned in himself for a couple of hours. Sea piling up again, reduced speed. A curlew-like looking bird flew around he ship. Discovered a queer dead fish on the counter, must have been washed over by a wave and couldn't get off again, put it in a bottle with methylated spirits (two long, eight shorter tentacles – more tentacles on the shorter ones, pale greeny-gray, splat out black ink on the deck). Ship steering herself all morning but plenty to do – keep trying to wash but haven't had time yet. Stormy Petrel flew around the ship and another new bird which we could not identify. Skipper cooked supper, very good. Haven't touched helm for hours, steering SW. Turned in early.

Saturday 7 May. Breakfast at 07.00, bacon and tomatoes. A super wash all over and Skipper cleaned the frying pan! Put up the trysail to try and stop this awful roll, not much good. Still wearing two jerseys and socks. Don't know where this terrific heat is that Skipper keeps saying is here. Saw two more birds. After lunch, Skipper on deck, sighted a ship. Terrific excitement, I flew for the glasses, she seemed to be a large frigate. Thought at first she was coming towards us so hoisted the Ensign and our number but she soon steamed out of sight. Doubt if she saw us at all. At 18.00 opened a Winsers and Ferands bottle of sherry and drank Captain Waller's health.

Sunday 8 May. Wind much lighter, set the main sail and balloon stay sail and spinnaker, sunny and much warmer, decided to go to the Azores and not make the trip to Bermuda without a break so altered course to S by W instead of WSW.

Monday 9 May. Wind freshened during the night. Skipper got topsail down and reefed main sail. I turned out at 06.00. Very dull day, slight drizzle, looks as if it might clear. One week at sea and not much sign of this tropical sun Skipper talks about; however, I am still hoping.

Tuesday 10 May. Lovely sunny day, really warmer now, have discarded my jacket but still two jerseys. Put up a mizzen stay sail – looks a bit odd but Skipper says other yachts have it but I bet no other yacht has had some of the queer rigs we have had. We tried our Webley Scott 3.2 automatic revolver this evening. It's a jolly little toy but I am rather frightened of it. We towed a tin astern for a target. Skipper showed me how it worked and I plucked up courage to fire. Unfortunately at the critical moment of firing I shut my eyes tight so missed. Skipper took the log to pieces as it wasn't working very well but it isn't any better. I took a watch from 21.00 till 24.00. It really was a glorious night, fairly warm and *Caplin* sailing along quite fast with her topsail and the moon shining brightly in the starboard rigging. I had the headphones on in the cockpit and listened in to some rather jolly music from Radio Toulouse. I had been on watch for about an hour and a half and was more or less lost in thought building castles in the air when I suddenly heard a huge splash and saw a big black thing leap out of the water right alongside the ship. I nearly jumped out of my skin, I was so startled. I dashed below to call Skipper who was fast asleep and he came on deck. It was only a shoal of porpoises and Skipper wasn't a bit enthusiastic at being hauled out to see them. No novelty to him. They were really rather fun and followed the ship for about three-quarters of an hour and seemed to be having races with the ship and each other.

Thursday 12 May. The wind for the last few days has been such that we've more or less been sailing on the direct line for Madeira so we've definitely decided to go there and not the Azores. Skipper called down that there was a Portuguese man-of-war passing so I dashed up to see but he said it had gone out of sight astern. I scanned the horizon but could see nothing and couldn't understand how it had gone so quickly. He said it was about six inches long and three high and after a second of blank amazement I realized he meant a fish not a ship.

LAND AHOY!

Friday 13 May 1938. We might sight Madeira today so I've cleaned up the silver and brasswork. Our shopping list is miles long already. More wind and slipping along nicely at 5 knots. Heard a strange noise up on deck whilst I was below clearing up breakfast, sounded like groaning so I dashed up to see if Skipper was alright. He was. He was singing! 11.50 WE THINK WE SEE LAND. It must be 80 miles away but Madeira is very high and the atmosphere is very clear. Anyway, it's very exciting and we drink a glass of beer. Full marks for the Navigator. It really is exciting, Caplin's first foreign port and my third. We have a tot of rum at 18.00. Skipper suggests we finish the bottle in celebration but we think we might not see the island so refrain. About 19.00 we see the lighthouse on the western point of the island. It must be very high up for us to see it so far away.

MADEIRA: WARSHIPS AND A BAD LEAK

Saturday 14 May 1938. Skipper calls me at daybreak and the land seems quite close though we have some way to go yet to Funchal. We start our engine to round the southern point, wind heading us and light. We have developed a bad leak and water is pouring in through the stern tube bearing. Skipper pumping pretty frequently.

Three French men of war, a cruiser and two destroyers come in to Madeira at the same time as us. They look very smart with men lined around the decks. There is a terrific row, the French saluting the Portuguese Government with guns and the Government replying. We are going ahead dead slow, Skipper very worried, trying to give me directions at the helm and pumping at the same time. I simply cannot keep my attention on the steering, what with the excitement of the French Navy and looking at the shore and all the boatmen getting in the way and jumping a mile every time a gun goes off, I steer a very erratic course. We dip to a Portuguese man-of-war, who replies. We anchor close to a lovely Yugoslavian training ship, a three-masted barquentine.

I hoist the 'yellow flag' and the boatman takes me off to

see the doctor. The doctor was friendly and takes the Bill of
Health to the Consul where we can collect it when we leave.
Skipper can't leave the ship; has to pump nearly all the time.
We have a hired boatman and his friend for 5/– a day. Juan
Costa and Manuel. They are very friendly, speak English and
wait on the ship. We are both much too harassed to think of
going ashore or doing anything except fixing the leak so Juan
takes me ashore to a yard where they build yachts and I get
one of the owners and foremen to come off and see the
trouble. We had to walk quite a long way through the streets
and I felt 'eyes' on my trousers but I hadn't time to change.

The foreman looks at the leak and there is much shaking
of heads and talking and gesticulating and finally the owner,
who speaks English, says it can either be cemented up and we
shan't be able to use the engine or the yacht can be hauled out
at his yard but they will have to make a cradle specially for us.
The latter proceeding will cost £20 so we decide to cement.
Luiz says he will send a man after lunch.

We have lunch, but too tired and worried to eat much.
After lunch Skipper turns in and I get a bit of rest but have to
pump about 100 strokes every quarter of an hour. About
14.30 the man comes and starts to stop the leak by pressing
packing into the joint but it only makes the water run up and
come out just as fast in another place; he seems pretty hopeless
and says it can't be done from inside. The owner (Mr Luiz)
says we shall have to haul her out after all, but he does have an
old cradle which can be made to do so it won't be so
expensive. They can't be ready till Monday and we have
visions of never being able to leave the ship, night or day, and
we shall have to pump. There seems to be no way of stopping
the water. Finally Skipper suggests we get a boy to dive and
see if anything can be done from the outside. Manuel goes
ashore for some plaster and he dives and puts some around the
outside bearing. We nearly whoop with joy as it seems to do
the trick. Only a little water is coming in now. It is a relief and
we have a cup of tea and feel better.

One of Luiz's ships came in loaded with sugarcane and
he gave me some; it's funny looking stuff like bamboo. Juan
comes back at 18.30 and we leave him in charge and go
ashore for a stroll and dinner at Theo's. Very pleasant English-

speaking waiter; we eat on the balcony and it's just like a storybook, banana trees opposite and a tree with lovely red flowers. The streets are full of French and Yugoslavian sailors and Portuguese soldiers. We are too tired to look at the sights much and after our excellent dinner we go down to the pier early where our boatmen are waiting to take us off. We turn in early about 21.30 and have a really good night's sleep.

Sunday 15 May. The rest has done us good and we both feel much more cheerful. Mr Luiz comes about 11.50 in his launch and takes us to see a 60-ft yacht his firm is building. She is a lovely strong-looking yacht, built of Madeira pine and eucalyptus. As we leave the pier an excursion steamer comes in from Porto Santo. There are a lot of cows forward, considerably less crowded than the passengers herded together aft.

Monday 16 May. Juan and Manuel come early about 07.30 and wash down the ship. Luiz comes off to say he will be back about 14.30 to say when we can be hauled up. After tea Luiz takes us in his launch to see the cradle which they have made. It looks a good solid one.

HAULED OUT

Tuesday 17 May 1938. We met Mr Luiz at 12.00 and he took us in his launch to the yacht and towed *Caplin* over near the yard. About one dozen men came on board and the cradle was towed out and two men swam about fixing things. Skipper and I had no lunch so we ate chocolate. The cradle was sunk under the yacht and then the men on board pulled it into position with ropes either side. The first time they didn't get the ropes tied across the yacht quickly enough so the cradle floated out one side. The second attempt fixed it and lines were passed from the shore and she was pulled up. The whole thing was done quickly and easily and very efficiently in spite of much shouting and gesticulating.

The damage was less than we thought. The brackets holding the shaft had broken and the increased vibration had shaken out the packing. We now had a high tea while the men got on with the job. The engine has been taken out and put in the cabin with resulting chaos. The workmen all very friendly; a customs officer has to stay night and day in the yard, more a matter of form than anything else and no trouble about taking suitcases to the hotel. Mr Luiz took us to the Savoy hotel. He has something to do with a shipping agency and got cheap terms for us. It's a lovely big hotel, ballroom and swimming pool etc. Height of luxury and I am dying for a bath.

Wednesday 18 May. Went down to see the yacht after breakfast. Skipper decided to have the yacht coppered.

Friday 20 May. Went down to look at the yacht and Skipper gave Mr Luiz a copy of 'Rough Passage', his book about his single-handed Atlantic crossing in his previous yacht Emanuel in 1934. Mr Luiz took us to see over a wine factory; it was very interesting. The work is all done on much the same lines as 300 years ago. Had a siesta after lunch and then met Mr Luiz at his office and he took us to see over a big sugar factory. It was very up-to-date and the machinery was lovely, very beautifully kept. There were about 500 men working in the factory and the smell of the sugar was pretty grim and so was the heat of the boilers. We have seen lots of soldiers in the streets taking flowers and greenery for a fiesta tomorrow. It is a treat to see soldiers carrying bouquets of flowers instead of rifles.

Saturday 21 May. Went down to the yacht, getting on nicely with the work. After dinner met Mr Luiz and he took us to see a Chapel fiesta, a sort of fête for the fishermen. The Chapel was beautifully decorated with flowers. It was destroyed by the sea some years ago and the Cabristante firm built a new one. It was very interesting seeing all the local people, mostly fishermen and workmen from the yard, thousands of children. The Cabrastantes gave all their men a glass of wine.

Friday 27 May. The yacht will be finished today so we hope to get off tomorrow. Took a lot more photos. after lunch, rowed round to the Pontinya to look at four French sea planes which had come in. They were huge. I have never seen one so close before. I was nearly dead when we got back; had no idea it was so far.

MOST ALARMING LAUNCH

Saturday 28 May 1938. Caplin looked lovely with her new copper, or rather muntz metal. She was launched about 10.30: a tug just pulled the cradle down into the water – most alarming! Mr Luiz came with us and we motored round for about an hour and then anchored off the pier and had lunch. We were rolling badly so decided to move into the harbour; I went up to the hotel while Skipper attended to the water. We invited various of our friends and they came down to the yacht about 18.00. Most of them brought bottles so we had quite a merry party. The foreman came to see us in a speed boat and took some of us out for trips in it. Our guests all left about 19.00. We have a letter for the yacht Latisa (in Bermuda) on board, a letter for someone in Trinidad and an introduction to someone in Australia. Looks like we are in for a long trip! About 20.00 we weighed anchor and motored out of the harbour. We said goodbye to our boatmen Juan and Manuel and hoisted our main sail with four rolls – quite a fresh wind blowing. I was sorry to see the lights of Funchal getting fainter and fainter as the night wore on. We have had such a lovely time in Madeira but it is rather exciting to think that our next land will be about 500 miles off the American coast.

INDEPENDENT FREEDOM: CANARY ISLANDS TO CAPE VERDE ISLANDS

It was fun sightseeing with Mum and Donald in a hire car, which was full when Donald's wife Lucy and son Edward arrived for half term. The results of the huge six-year eruption some 270 years ago were particularly interesting.

MARY HELEN

When *Mary Helen* departed, the mate and I followed her out in the dinghy to take photos. She looked small as she dipped and rolled in the swell, the tan-coloured gaff mainsail very distinctive, my mother old but full of spirit at the helm and Donald white-haired on the reeling foredeck with black volcanic Lanzarote as a backdrop.

Meanwhile, *Independent Freedom* was about to gain an addition to the crew. A friend of the mate's had fallen out with her skipper but wanted to complete her circumnavigation by crossing the Atlantic. She was due in a few days time from England.

Saturday 4 November 2000. *Independent Freedom* left Puerto Calero at first light, her three crew having attended a cocktail party thrown by the marina owners the night before. The wind was light but filled in from the north when the yacht came clear of the lee of the land. Our additional crew, Karen, was keen to start the engine, saying she felt safer with it on! Evidently, on the boat she had left they motored most of the time carrying a large quantity of fuel. She quickly learned that whenever possible we sailed.

At noon *Independent Freedom* was clear of the southern end of Lanzarote and running fast at 7 knots with full sail set, the wind gusting up to force 7. There was a heavy northerly swell and she was rolling. The white horses on the waves sparkled in the bright sunlight – glorious sailing.

The wind dropped at night and it was a less boisterous sail past the north coast of Grand Canaria Island. It was quite cold and the air was very clear. In the morning the wind increased again running down the coast of Tenerife under mainsail only. It was rough and the wind increased to near gale force in the acceleration zone along the south coast. *Independent Freedom* was surfing at times, which was exhilarating in the bright sunshine.

Once past Cape Roca lighthouse the wind failed, blanketed by the huge volcano on Tenerife. We motored the rest of the way to San Sebastian on the island of Gomera.

Mary Helen was still in port waiting for a weather window to make an early voyage across the Atlantic. It was important not to arrive in the Caribbean before the beginning of December to miss any late hurricanes. In a hire car we enjoyed sightseeing the lush forest high up in the mountains while below it was barren, and in places spectacular views. Santiago was a little sleepy port, very different from the Santiago we had visited in Cuba.

The mate and I were beginning to think it had been a mistake to have Karen onboard. After four years sailing she was simply not 'boat-minded' and still called the galley a kitchen. When I threw away her vodka bottles (one empty, one still half full) I was within an inch of telling her to go. I wish I had been tougher and done so. When two people have been sailing together for a long time, as Michel and I have been, it can be difficult for a third person to fit in. The two know each others' idiosyncrasies and often there is no need to talk about what has to be done. Passengers can be rewarding companions in fair-weather cruising but on the trip which was to follow there was no place for anyone other than trusty crew.

DEPARTURE AND DISASTER

Wednesday 8 November 2000. The weather had not been particularly good for some time, and *Mary Helen* had had a rough passage from Lanzarote, but today dawned fine and clear. The forecast for the south Canaries was wind NE force 4–6 and moderating although the sea was rough. Mum and Donald had been onboard *Independent Freedom* for dinner the previous night and Donald and I had agreed to meet at the harbour master's office at 09.00 when the weather map was posted. There was a low, 994 mb, in the Atlantic, heading SE for the Canaries, which indicated we should stay in port. However, the harbour master was very helpful and showed us the computer forecast for the next few days. The low would alter course to the NE giving fine weather for the next three to four days with NE trade winds down to the Cape Verde Islands. This looked like the weather window we needed and we returned to *Mary Helen* for a final consultation with my mother. The decision was 'go' and my mother (who had been bitterly disappointed at her father's refusal to take her on his own Atlantic crossing in *Emanuel* in 1934) said "My dream is coming true".

At 10.30 the harbour master brought the port clearance to *Independent Freedom*, the lines were let go and we followed

Mary Helen out to sea, ready to cross the Atlantic.

At noon *Independent Freedom* was rolling heavily in the swell and *Mary Helen* even more so. Santiago was abeam. Shortly afterwards I lowered the mainsail to slow down when the first disaster occurred. The luff of the mainsail tore. I simply could not believe my eyes for the sail was only 18 months old and made of special cloth. Later I reefed the foresail and the second disaster happened for the luff tore. It seemed quite impossible for both sails to have torn at the same time (and the sailmaker was subsequently sufficiently shocked that he paid for the repairs).

I called up *Mary Helen* on the VHF.

"Donald, both the sails have torn. I am going to the Cape Verde Islands for repairs and then will head straight for Antigua."

"OK we will head for 20°48'N 25°00'W and head for St Lucia" he replied.

"Right, well see you on the other side, and love to Mum, Bon Voyage."

The mate taped and glued the tear in the foresail and the double-reefed sail was set; the mainsail remained lowered. There was a very unpleasant confused rough sea, much too much sea for the wind blowing, and a heavy northeasterly swell. The yacht was rolling and pitching uncomfortably, but was not as uncomfortable as *Mary Helen* would be and I felt for them. What a terrible start to our transatlantic crossing, the last ocean for the mate and I. I felt very uneasy, the first time ever I had felt like this at the beginning of a voyage.

There was little wind during the night and the motor was on to make progress and stop the foresail slatting. After daylight the mate and I tried to set the reaching staysail but the wind was too far aft for it to set. We inspected the mainsail tear and decided to sew it, glue the ends of the tear and tape it.

It was still rough and the motion most unpleasant. The mate quite magnificently spent the whole morning tied to the mast in the bosun's chair making the repair, collecting many bruises at the same time.

Just after noon we carefully hoisted the double-reefed mainsail, with bated breath, but the repair held. The sails were goosewinged and the yacht went much better in the breeze from the NE. The wind died in the night and the motor was used, which kept Karen happy! Unfortunately I did not trust her on watch especially after she told me she was bored and her idea of keeping watch was to watch a video with the radar on guard.

There was great excitement the next morning when three whales were sighted and they kept close to the yacht for half an hour. Despite our excellent book on sea life, purchased from Foyles in London prior to the start of our voyage, we could not identify them for certain. They are magnificent creatures.

Saturday 11 November. In the morning the engine was turned off and the reefs shaken out of the mainsail. The repair held. The sea was smooth with a low northerly swell. The bright almost light golden moon set in the west while in the east the dawn colours were almost the same, a very special beginning to the day. We tried to get the reaching staysail to set but without much success. At noon only 90 miles had been made good despite using the engine for over six hours. All day there had been much activity in the sky with the clouds continually changing and a halo round the sun. There were rain squalls in the evening but they only produced about 10 knots of wind.

During the night the wind failed and the motor was switched on. It was a lovely night, the bright full moon giving almost enough light to read by. The sky had cleared of cloud and it was much warmer. There was a northwesterly swell presumably generated by a storm to the north but the sea was smooth. The tropic of cancer was crossed so we were back in the tropics, the first time since beating up the Red Sea some nine months ago.

At noon *Independent Freedom* was sailing slowly, the sails goosewinged and the reaching staysail set between them. There was a confused lumpy sea and the yacht was rolling. The mate was working on the engine trying to stop a leak in the new salt water pump which had been fitted in Gibraltar.

Early the next morning the staysail was lowered as the wind increased and for the next two days the yacht averaged 5 knots. It was much hotter. We tried to teach Karen the delights of silent sailing but she was not really interested in the boat or our voyage. She seemed to have a different agenda and the atmosphere onboard was not good. I had a discussion with the mate and suggested she should go in the Cape Verde Islands. It turned out that she had no money despite having told us the opposite. I decided to leave things as they were until Antigua, a decision I subsequently regretted.

CAPE VERDE: REPAIRS

Thursday 16 November 2000. Lights were sighted on Wednesday night and at 02.00 the anchor was let go in Porto Grande on the island of Sao Vicente off the town of Mindelo, Cape Verde Islands. The smell confirmed we were back in the third world! Eight hundred and four miles had been made good at an average speed of 4.4 knots with the engine used for 17.5 percent of the time.

The stop was only for repairs to the sails, bearing in mind that *Mary Helen* was still out in the Atlantic! At 08.00 the anchor was lifted and we reanchored stern to *Eirene*, the German yacht service centre, where they ran a continuous taxi boat service ashore. The hole in the taxi boat summed up everything and the mate and I had agreed I would buy repair material and we would repair the sail ourselves. I cleared in at the Policia Maritima in an ugly concrete building, in contrast to the Portuguese colonial buildings, and then immigration inside the port. A severe drug warning notice was posted on the wall leaving no doubt what would happen to anyone caught with them. The town is not very big and with the help of a guide I purchased everything I wanted. 'Mission control' was faxed and when I was back onboard he phoned on the mobile! Modern communications never cease to amaze me.

There had been enough bad luck on board without sailing on a Friday so the mate made further repairs to the sails while I went ashore to clear out. While ashore there was a severe squall and a French catamaran dragged across the chain of *Independent Freedom*, putting the yacht in great danger. The Frenchman onboard just laughed at the mate, who was forced to produce our plastic pistol before he made any attempt to clear the chain. I was enjoying lunch in the hotel while this drama was going on!

During the afternoon final shopping was done and then

we moved the yacht out to the anchorage, which was much more comfortable, ready to sail next day.

CAPLIN: MADEIRA TO BERMUDA

Sunday 29 May 1938. We had taken it in turns to keep watch through the night so have made quite good progress. A few birds about; feeling very seedy. Hope it won't last, no interest in food.

Monday 30 May. Feeling no better. *Caplin* sailing herself with double spinnakers. I turned in about 16.00 and Skipper woke me to take the helm. The wind has freshened so he took the spinnaker down but not before it got a horrid tear. I turned in again about 19.30.

Tuesday 31 May. Still feeling rotten. Lie down after lunch but Skipper calls me on deck. Find he has been experimenting with all kinds of queer rigs and has broken the spinnaker boom. Turn in early. Can manage no supper.

Wednesday 1 June. Breakfast at 07.30. Eat a little porridge and some loquats but still feeling pretty mouldy. *Caplin* behaving beautifully. Steered herself all night; I think she knows how rotten I feel. She did just over 5 knots through the night. We have done 411 miles at noon today. Skipper got a time signal yesterday and today.

Thursday 2 June. Turned out at 05.00. Wind gone light and Skipper wanted to set main sail and top sail. Glorious sunny day and I got into my shorts for the first time. Skipper had siesta after lunch and I read with a finger on the helm. Another of those queer fish with tendrils got washed on deck, smaller than the one we have kept. Turned in at 20.45 for three hours and then took the watch from midnight to 04.00.

Friday 3 June. After breakfast I put on my swimsuit; it was lovely and warm and sunny. I mended the spinnaker, putting a big patch of grey material in. The sail was a secondhand one and not very good so I don't think it will last long. Skipper mended the spinnaker boom but mizzen set shading the sun off my back; felt I wanted to alter course a point to W so I could get my back brown but felt it wouldn't go down well with Skipper. Put the clock back an hour. I read on deck: Gerbault's 'In Quest of the Sun'.

Routine continued for a few more days and then the wind fell very light.

BECALMED

Monday 6 June 1938. Boiling hot day again. Had a lesson in navigation today. Took a sight then spent practically the whole of the morning working it out and having it explained. It's a good thing navigation of the ship does not depend on me but I dare say I shall learn in time. Almost too hot on deck after lunch. Boiled a bit of bacon for supper. Quite good but too salty. Practically no wind. Had a night in.

Tuesday 7 June. Threw our last four grapefruit overboard. On to the last of our bread, too. One and a half loaves left but rather mouldy. Saw a lovely white bird after breakfast. It flew around and around the ship having a good look at us and flying very high. We looked it up in the book and decided it must be a Tropic bird or a Bosun bird. More lessons in navigation; felt very clever when my latitude came out at exactly the same as Skipper's and I took my own sight. Practically becalmed, very hot. Skipper below after lunch, self on deck. No wind, just steerage way. A slight air at 19.00. Have another night in.

Wednesday 8 June. Still hardly any air; day passed without incident. Skipper woke me at 04.45 – had been squally during the night, top sail and spinnaker lowered. Hoisted the stay sail.

Thursday 9 June. Breakfast at 08.00, porridge, scrambled eggs, eating ship's biscuits in lieu of bread; not bad. Absolute flat calm, sea looks oily it's so smooth; first time that we haven't even had steerage way.

Friday 10 June. Skipper called me at 07.00 to watch while he had a bathe. He said the water felt quite warm. Becalmed again; getting rather tired of our slow progress. Very slight air in the afternoon; steerage way, not much more.

Saturday 11 June. Put the clock back an hour so it makes a long morning. Skipper had a bathe, still no wind. Have read dozens of books. Had rather a scare that the wireless had gone wrong, it seemed so dead; pictured our not being able to find Bermuda. We depend on the radio for time signals, the chronometer not being too reliable. It worked later; just bad reception, I think. We are over the halfway line today. Still another 1300 miles to go. However, in spite of the calm we must have a few hopes left as we got out the Bermudan charts. At 16.00 at last a slight breeze. We did 4.5 knots for the next two hours. We both feel a lot better and are finding it less of a strain to smile. If only it will last, the wind I mean.

To Bermuda with sharks

Sunday 12 June 1938. Woke to find practically no wind again, but wind again in afternoon blowing quite fresh and continued through the night. Monday: Still a wind. Have done 111 miles in the last 24 hours. Longest run for a week. Perhaps we will keep our appointment in Bermuda after all. Wind still fresh – lovely. Skipper took 20.00–24.00 and 04.00–08.00 and I took the middle watch.

Tuesday 14 June. Best run for centuries, 121 miles at noon. Last of bananas eaten. Still a good wind. Glorious moonlit nights, light enough for daylight. I play patience on the cockpit floor to make my watch go quicker. Four hours seems a lifetime. It is a joy to be warm though. Leaving Ireland it was difficult to keep warm at night. Wednesday: 118°F at noon. Listened to a whole lot of American stations trying to identify them. Caplin steering herself practically all day; had a night in. Thursday: 99 miles at noon, 831 to go. Had a bathe after tea – water was lovely and warm once one was in. Felt a bit odd swimming about in so much water. Wind very light again.

Friday 17 June. About 11.00 I spotted a ship on the horizon.

She was astern of us and heading about W by S. She gradually got closer and closer but didn't think she would come close enough to wave unless she altered course; terrific excitement when she DID alter course and came straight towards us; I was much too excited to do anything but watch her but Skipper managed to take a sight before she was very close in. She slowed right down as she came up and called out 'is everything alright, can we do anything for you', to which we replied 'yes'. She then asked if we wanted to be reported and we said we did. All the crew were aft and three or four on the bridge kept their eyes glued to glasses watching us. We did the same. She then slowly drew ahead, much waving on both sides but she eventually couldn't make up her mind to leave us as she circled the whole way around us again. I held up the lifebuoy so she could see our name. She finally wished us 'bon voyage' and she blew on her siren and dipped her Ensign. We dipped our Ensign and blew our foghorn which caused a laugh among the crew. She then steamed ahead full speed; more waving and then she finally disappeared over the horizon. Hardly any wind and very hot and we both felt rather exhausted from the excitement. The ship was the *Josiah Macey*, Panama. I wonder if the news will get back to mum?

Our distance at noon 65 miles (766 to go). Masses of seaweed floating about. I wonder if we are going to get caught in the Sargasso Sea? I took second watch; practically flat calm all the time and no better in Skipper's.

Saturday 18 June. Flat calm but then slight air; tried to sail again but it was hardly more than enough to give us steerage way. The boom swung over and knocked Skipper's head; much swearing so I hope the damage was not great. The chief calamity was his hat went overboard. We tried to manoeuvre the ship around to it while I stood by the boathook but the wind was so light it couldn't get close enough so I dived in to collect it. I had a bit of difficulty climbing aboard again but managed it by the bobstay and shrouds. With a bit of practice I think I could get in that way fairly easily. Fifty-two miles at noon, poor run, 714 to go.

After tea Skipper had another bathe. I kept the ship on her course and towed him astern. *Caplin* was moving along quite well and Skipper was being towed fairly fast. As he was climbing back to the ship I saw a huge fish come up astern and sniff at his lifeline. I am certain it was a shark; how awful if it had sniffed at skipper's legs! When I think that I swam round the ship twice this morning with no life line and I might have met a shark face to face!

Sunday 19 June. Nice fresh wind blowing, going along so well, not worthwhile stopping for a bathe for which I am secretly glad owing to my shark scare yesterday. Only 674 miles to go. We have been three weeks at sea. Monday 20: log going very badly; every now and then makes an awful noise. Bearings worn. Also it keeps catching this seaweed which is floating about everywhere.

Tuesday 21 June. The American Bermuda Yacht Race starts today. We are about the same distance the opposite way; if we get a good wind and they get a head wind we might arrive at the same time. Friday: wind continues. Run at noon 113 (277). Skipper's hat blew overboard. Fresh wind blowing so I did not repeat my offer to dive in and get it. Went back to look for it without success and I'm afraid it's lost and gone forever. Saw the smoke of a ship; seem to be in a crowded area.

Saturday 25 June. Cleaned all the brass handles on the drawers in preparation for land. Hope I am not being too optimistic. Run at noon 102 (175 to go). I took the first watch. *Caplin* very good and steering herself so I wrote letters below. After about 2 hours the wind freshened and it began to rain. I called Skipper and we got the spinnaker down. It simply poured and the decks leaked like sieves; I shone the torch below from the cockpit and saw my letters in a sea of water. We put blankets over the books in the cabin. It was only a rain squall and the wind dropped completely so we left *Caplin* to look after herself and both turned in. Sunday 26: more rain squalls and we seemed to take most of the morning taking the spinnaker down and putting it up again. Run at noon 81 (116).

Monday 27 June. Nearly there! Terrific excitement all day. Expect to see land about 18.00. Feel very restless all day watching. Saw a man-of-war ahead so felt we must be getting warm. Soon afterwards, did see land, so we had a tot to celebrate. It soon got dark but we made out St David's lighthouse. We decided to heave-to outside and turn in for a night's sleep but there were three Men of War messing about; a mock battle or something so we had to keep watch.

Tuesday 28th June 1938. We found that we had drifted further out than we intended so it was well after daylight by the time we got back to St David's lighthouse. We had a nice breeze blowing and *Caplin* seemed flying along, eager for harbour. Parts of the channel are quite narrow but there were not many ships, but a dockyard ship passed us and waved; probably knew Skipper. We had a terrific rain squall and the wind blew quite hard so we reefed our main sail. Some of the buoys were different from those marked on the chart and the rain was so thick we couldn't see so we sailed around and around the buoy till it cleared. We then had a lovely sail and as we approached Hamilton we could see all the racing yachts there and wondered if Kenneth Pattison would see us. We didn't use our engine but sailed right up to out anchorage, Kenneth following us and Skipper's friend Major Kitchener and his daughter in another boat.

The Health officer came on board, and Kenneth and Major Kitchener. The yacht was rather upside down both below and on deck. It certainly seemed strange to be anchored in a nice little harbour with land all around! We have sailed 4,000 miles and are two days late for our appointment with Kenneth. Major Kitchener brought us some fresh bread and chocolate biscuits. It was grand eating fresh food.

In the evening we hurried back from visiting Mrs Kitchener and got ready for the cocktail party at the RBYC, after which the prizes for the races were presented. The *Van Bremer*, Kenneth's yacht, had a prize for the only foreign entry. I met masses of people. I was the only girl invited so I felt highly honoured. We got back to the yacht for supper. We hadn't had a moment to turn round and do any serious cleaning up and we were too tired to do much that evening so we turned in early.

We spent four months in Bermuda, waiting for the

hurricane season to pass, before setting sail for the Caribbean and Panama.

INDEPENDENT FREEDOM : CAPE VERDE TO ANTIGUA – A DIFFICULT VOYAGE

Saturday 18 November 2000. It was overcast and squally in the harbour when the mate weighed anchor. The single-reefed foresail was hoisted and *Independent Freedom* sailed out of Porto Grande and into the Canal de Sao Vicente. It was rough until the island of Santo Antao was reached. The wind increased to force 7 and it was fast sailing along the coast with the desolate barren mountains rising sheer out of the sea; not a place to be shipwrecked. Pta de Peca was left three-quarters of a mile to starboard, the last land for almost 2,000 miles.

'May we all be lucky and God look after us,' the mate wrote in the Log, unprompted by me though it rather summed up my feelings as well. I was still distinctly uneasy and the incident with the French catamaran had not helped. However, the forecast from 'Gary's' net, such as it was (for the French weather people were on strike) indicated moderate trade winds. The reports from the yachts at sea suggested winds up to 30 knots which was not so moderate!

I decided to head NW towards the way point Donald had given me and then follow the track towards St. Lucia. It would be fun to meet *Mary Helen* in the Atlantic. The wind died down and was all over the place in the lee of Santo Antao. The sea was most confused and pyramidal, this being a junction between that rolling round the north of the island and the sea from the south. The three-reefed mainsail was hoisted and the engine switched on to save the sails from slatting.

A couple of hours later *Independent Freedom* was sailing fast, the wind ENE force 5 and increasing. It was rough and there was a heavy swell running. By 20.00 it was blowing a 'yachtsman's gale', force 7, and the crests of the swell were breaking. The yacht was sailing very fast; so much for the moderate trades!

The mate and I worked watch and watch about – I did not trust Karen enough with the rough weather. It was a wild night and a careful watch was needed. The autohelm worked perfectly.

No engine, no power

At 06.00 the next morning the engine was running to charge the batteries when I noticed a funny smell, like bakelite burning. The engine was switched off and the smell forgotten in the wild sailing. It was time to reef and we took in two reefs in the foresail, making three reefs in both sails.

The yacht was much easier although still sailing very fast. The mate investigated the 'funny smell' and after running the engine for short while announced,

"The alternator is burning out and we cannot use the engine."

My heart sank and I began to sympathize with those sailors who believed that one could have a 'Jonah' on board. I kept my thoughts to myself and said,

"We've got sails, albeit damaged, the trades are blowing and we carry on. We will use minimal power, off fridge, off autohelm, no lights at night, torch only and off water pump." The monitor wind vane self-steering had not been used since it had been fitted in Fort Lauderdale, apart from the test run. I set it up and after adjustments it worked very well which meant we would not have to hand-steer all the way across the Atlantic. At noon *Independent Freedom* was sailing fast, a broad reach with the wind ESE force 6/7. It was overcast, the sea was rough and the monitor was steering well. 164 miles had been covered in the last 24 hours at an average speed of 6.8 knots which was very satisfactory. The repair on the mainsail was holding and that on the foresail was covered by the third reef.

It continued to blow for the next six days and remained overcast until Tuesday morning when the sun came out. What a difference the sun makes!

Monitor steering broken

Wednesday 22 November 2000. I was in bed when I awoke to a shout from the mate at 04.15. I rushed up on deck to find that the monitor was broken and the yacht was being hand steered. The mate had been quick enough to prevent a gybe which would have been disastrous. Luckily the paddle had a line attached and we were able to recover it. The shaft had broken. I felt very low and told the mate we were experiencing a run of bad luck and we must be very careful in everything we did. The only way to combat it was to be ultra careful and hope and pray nothing major happened like being dismasted or a gas explosion. It was bad enough having to hand steer.

After breakfast we discussed trying to repair the monitor. It was fine, the sun was out and *Independent Freedom* was sailing fast in the rough sea and heavy swell with three reefs in both sails. I had put shock cord on either side of the wheel to dampen the ardour of the helmsperson to oversteer. It was very noticeable how little helm either the autohelm or the monitor used.

In the middle of the morning the mate donned bathers and climbed over the stern outside the rails and onto the ledge under the platform washed by the sea. The connection piece was disconnected and I heaved it onboard. The mate climbed back dripping wet. I do not know why I had not luffed up and hove to, which would have been much more seamanlike and safer.

At noon 617 miles had been made good at an average speed of 6.4 knots. New holes were drilled into the shaft and the mate refitted it during the afternoon. This time I luffed up and hove to! In the evening the wind increased to force 7 and although it was wild and exciting sailing we lowered the mainsail to save the monitor. With the main down and only the three-reefed foresail set there was little chance of a gybe and so Karen kept a watch. I was up on deck quite a lot checking and tweaking the monitor. I wondered how *Mary Helen* was getting on in the rough weather, being so much smaller and consequently having a much more violent motion. My mother at 88 was hardly in the first flush of youth, even though her spirit might be.

A lull just after daylight tricked me into shaking out one reef from the foresail. However the wind increased and it blew hard all day. It was very rough with breaking crests but it was fine and sunny and the yacht was sailing well and fast.

At midnight the mate had been hand steering for two hours and said that two huge waves had been very frightening but they had not broken and *Independent Freedom* had just lifted her stern and surfed down the front. I reset the monitor and remained on deck for a while to check it, and see what the approaching squalls brought. The squalls, which brought a little more wind and some rain, lasted for eighteen hours. The last one was heavy, producing gusts of 40 knots.

Saturday 25 November. Gary's net suggested a moderating in the wind, as did the reports of other yachts. We had started listening to 'Herb' as well who also suggested better weather. During the morning another reef was taken out of the foresail. The repairs were still holding. At noon we had been at sea a week and sailed just over 1,000 miles. The wind lightened further and the three-reefed mainsail was hoisted, goosewinged with the foresail. What I had taken for a fish following close astern turned out to be a piece of net caught, we thought, on the propeller. Yet another problem to be sorted out.

Monitor shaft broken again

The mainsail was lowered before dark to reduce the risk of a gybe and enable Karen to keep a watch. At 22.00 the mate called me; the foresail was aback on its vang and the monitor shaft had broken again. The paddle was recovered and it was hand steering all night. However it did not feel quite so bad; we were on the 'down hill' run, the half way mark having been passed! On the other hand I kept wondering when the next disaster was going to occur.

The next morning, Sunday 26, there was a heavy confused swell, the swell from the north caused by another storm in the Atlantic which no doubt would go on to lash England yet again. The mate once more went over the stern and confirmed the net was caught on the propeller. The paddle fitting was recovered but there was not enough left of the shaft. Eventually the mate cut off the emergency steering tiller which was the right size and made a shaft. Late in the afternoon the monitor was again steering with a much stronger stainless steel shaft, which we hoped would hold especially now the weather seemed to be moderating. There was a minor panic when the adjusting rod on the monitor came loose; I thought it had broken.

We tried hoisting the mainsail in the morning but although the wind was only ENE force 4/5 the very confused swell put too much strain on the monitor so we lowered it. The speed was down, but better that than a broken monitor. The yacht was rolling heavily.

Gary's net was unreadable but I was able to pick up the forecast from Portsmouth in the USA and listen to Herb. There were no warnings and the weather appeared fine for the next few days.

Monday 27 November 2000. During the afternoon the mate went overboard and disconnected the paddle and its attachment and found the shaft almost torn through. It would have parted in a short time; our bad luck was still with us. The mate shortened the shaft and cut new holes, going over the stern to refit it just before dark.

The weather was fine for the next three days although the heavy confused swell remained. It was quite comfortable with only the reefed foresail set, averaging about 120 miles per day or 5 knots, and really very enjoyable except for our continuing atmosphere of ill luck. It was like a great black cloud hanging over the yacht just waiting for something else to go wrong. There seemed no way to dispel it, even if it was only a perception, until land was reached.

Friday 1 December. With under 400 miles to go to Antigua we hoisted the double-reefed mainsail. It was fine and clear with the swell and sea down and the monitor was steering well. In the afternoon we goosewinged the foresail and I watched the self-steering like a hawk but it worked beautifully. It was fine all night; much more like the trade wind sailing I'd expected.

In the morning the wind increased and we took the third reef in the mainsail but shook it out again in the evening. On Sunday more reefs were taken out 'for the home stretch.'

"*Independent Freedom* has been talking to me: we must get rid of Karen on arrival. She has brought a gremlin onboard," the mate told me. I explained about the belief in 'Jonahs' and said that, for whatever reason, we must be ultra careful in everything we did and avoid making mistakes. Maybe my background anxiety over my mother on board *Mary Helen* was affecting everyone's mood, maybe it was nothing more than trying to fit an incompatible outsider into a tight-knit team, but I would tell Karen, as politely as possible, to go on arrival.

Mounting tension

Monday 4 December 2000. At 01.00 the lights of Antigua were sighted. We were almost across and the tension mounted. There was a confused sea and swell and at 04.00 the mainsail was lowered; lots of things seemed to be going wrong. The invisible Cade Reef was passed and I luffed up to the north for the harbour entrance.

As soon as it was light the mainsail was hoisted and all the reefs shaken out. It would have been a most enjoyable beat but my nerves were on edge waiting for the final disaster to happen. The mate pumped up the new dinghy ready to launch when a gas bottle fell over the side. I was not very clever manoeuvering the yacht but the mate finally recovered it from the quickly launched dinghy. The entrance beacon was made and I close-tacked up the channel, the water grey and muddy, continuously watching the echo sounder. The swell had started to heap up and it was breaking on a shoal to starboard and on the beach to port. Half way in the sails were lowered and the new Mercury outboard engine secured on the dinghy. It was secured for 'towing on the hip.' The mate then dived and removed the net which had been towed for more than a thousand miles.

Independent Freedom had drifted out of the channel and I was glad to have the sails rehoisted and be under command. The wind increased and it was quite an exciting beat into Jolly harbour and fetch up to the marina at the southern end. I had informed the marina on the VHF that the engine was not working and I would be sailing in, requesting an immediate berth . I asked them to inform Customs and request permission to go straight to the berth, which was granted. Off the marina I rounded up and the sails were quickly dropped. The mate jumped into the dinghy and started the engine which in the smooth water gave manoeuvering speed to the yacht. No marina personnel were on hand to help but it did not matter and *Independent Freedom* was berthed alongside without incident. The mate and I felt most relieved we had sailed across the Atlantic.

Our 'Jonah', perceived or not, left in the afternoon and the feeling onboard was completely different, back to normal. From Cape Verde Islands 2143 miles had been sailed in 16 days at an average speed of 5.6 knots. Repairs to the engine and the sails were put in hand immediately, followed by a voyage spring clean.

Caplin: Bermuda to Antigua

(Written records of this leg of *Caplin*'s voyage were subsequently lost in a fire, and this account was recalled by the Mate sixty years later.)

We waited in Bermuda until the hurricane season was over. We had fine sailing until about a week out of Bermuda, when we caught the tail end of a late hurricane. For two or three days we were hurled about in mountainous seas. The sky was very dark and threatening. When we looked out, these huge mountains of water were towering all around, thirty, forty feet above us, the tops curling over in the screaming wind. One thing you don't imagine until you've been in such a storm is how deafening it is. The wind howled at us through the rigging and over the crests of the waves; the waves hissed and roared, the boat creaked and anything loose slapped and banged. We were surrounded by cascading water. Anything not nailed down or stowed away flew about as the boat was hurled in all directions.

For the duration of the storm we were unable to eat; the primus stoves were mounted on gimbals but this wild motion was far beyond their control. We did manage to brew cocoa from time to time, and heat up some soup. On deck it was impossible to communicate; words were torn from our mouths and lost. Below, where we spent most of our time, we just jammed ourselves into our bunks, dead tired, though rest was impossible. We had a sea anchor out but it was just an endurance test, for *Caplin* as well as for us. Had she sprung a plank we would have been lost. I remember lying on my bunk and watching the mirror above my head swinging wildly. When it broke loose and crashed straight down onto my forehead I didn't even move.

When at last the hurricane passed and the seas eased down we were able to resume our course and sail normally. We eventually made landfall in English Harbour, Antigua. When we were tied up, the Skipper, who was never one to let his emotions show, leaned down and patted the deck and said "Well done, *Caplin*".

INDEPENDENT FREEDOM AND *MARY HELEN*: ANTIGUA

Three days after our arrival in Jolly harbour my mother and Donald walked down the jetty. *Mary Helen* had arrived in English Harbour a day after our arrival, crossing the Atlantic in a fraction under 27 days. My mother was floating on a cloud!

Mum and Donald came onboard, she looking tanned and well although, not surprising at 88 rising 89, she looked a little frail and needs a stick for walking. I could not but admire her courage and spirit. Donald at 60 was fit and healthy but it is 30 years since I last sailed with him and the resilience and quick movements of youth are gone. He was, nevertheless, the youngest of their party – *Mary Helen* is 3 years older than him!

We sat in the large cockpit of *Independent Freedom* under the awning, for it was hot in the sun, and reminisced.

"All blights are forgiven" said my mother. "We've done it, crossed the Atlantic" she beamed, still floating somewhere up in the clouds. Donald and I compared our tracks across the ocean and on 29 November the yachts were within 10 miles of each other. What a pity we had not met. They were not without their problems, notably not being able to use the mainsail.

When they had gone I reflected on our voyage around the world with the mate.

"We nearly lost the yacht at Rabihorcado Cay, Cuba" I said.

"Ah, but it was so exciting," exclaimed Michel "the adrenalin was running, giving me tremendous strength to wind in the anchor. The rain was so heavy I could not see you at the wheel, nor the reef just feet from the stern; the thunder and sizzling hissing lightening added to the drama. And you were wearing your rubber boots!" the mate laughed "I have never been so alive, and we won through."

No sign of fear here, I thought, and that sums up Michel: fearless.

"What about going on deck forward in heavy weather?" I asked.

"Exciting and stimulating but not like Rabihorcado."

The mate has changed out of all recognition in the last three-and-a-quarter years, and matured as a person. The quick flash of temper is still there or the sulks when all has not gone right, but like a tropical squall the moods are intense but quickly past.

The voyage would never have been completed without the mate, whose skill at fixing things is so important. I am not good at such things. We have had more than our fair share of things going wrong and Michel always found a solution. A hot meal was produced each day at sea whatever the weather and the ability to cook in bad weather is a boon without price.

I don't suppose I am the easiest person to get along with although I do try and remain cheerful most of the time. I am too quick tempered and don't like saying anything more than once.

Although Rabihorcado was the most dangerous incident of the voyage it was short-lived, and I did not have time to be frightened, unlike my grandfather on the voyage down to New Zealand in bad weather. He had plenty of time to reflect and be fearful of *Caplin* sinking. I have been apprehensive in bad weather and I was certainly frightened by the soldiers off the Saudi coast in the Red Sea, but again it was short-lived. As we were being escorted, the mate wrote in the log 'We have been taken to shore by two soldiers in a boat. They have a gun and look like we have been arrested. These boys mean danger. Hope we will be OK.'

The best sail was from Thailand to Sri Lanka with Camilla on board. It was fast and exhilarating, but not so rough that my niece could not improve her tan. The most challenging part of the voyage was beating against the wind up the Red Sea although, as my grandfather found, the New Zealand coast is no picnic. The mate does not enjoy sailing against the wind and slept a lot!

I think my grandfather would have been proud of his grandson achieving what the Second World War denied him, a circumnavigation of the world. There is a sense of completeness at having met up with *Mary Helen* in the Caribbean; her skipper, Commander Graham's elder daughter and my mother, has achieved what she felt he had denied her, an Atlantic crossing, and in her own boat; this, too, would have been a source of pride to him.

In order to cross our outward track we have fewer than 2,000 miles to go now, sailing in one of the world's best cruising areas, a tropical paradise. To add to the sense of completeness, my Aunt Marguerite, *Caplin*'s Mate, will be flying out to join us when *Independent Freedom* and *Mary Helen* arrive in the Bahamas.